SEARCHING FOR HOME

by Martha Nelson Vogt and Christina Vogt

Best Wishes,

Martha "Pat" Nelson Vogt

Christina Vogt

Triumph Press

Dedicated to
Anna and Dwight Nelson
and Edna and Loren Forrest
Our loving parents and grandparents . . .

And for Debbie, Jack, Matthew, and Michael

And for all those whose stories appear on these pages

ISBN #0-931515-00-9

© Copyright 1995

Martha Nelson Vogt and Christina Vogt
Triumph Press
Box 93
Hillsboro, KS 67063

1st printing, September, 1979
2nd printing, September, 1980
3rd printing, April, 1983
4th printing, March, 1986
5th printing, July, 1995

Homes For Children
═══ WANTED ═══

A Company of Homeless Children from the East Will Arrive at

McPherson, Friday, September 15.

These children are of various ages and of both sexes, having been thrown friendless upon the world. They come under the auspices of the Children's Aid Society, of New York. They are well disciplined, having come from various orphanages. The citizens of this community are asked to assist the agent in finding good homes for them. Persons taking these children must be recommended by the local committee. They must treat the children in every way as members of the family, sending them to school, church, Sabbath school and properly clothe them until they are 18 years old. Protestant children placed in Protestant homes and Catholic children in Catholic homes. The following well known citizens have agreed to act as a local committee to aid the agents in securing homes:

Dr. Heaston	H. A. Rowland	C. W. Bachelor
F. A. Vaniman	W. J. Krehbiel	K. Sorensen

Applications must be made to and endorsed by the local committee.

An address will be given by the agents. Come and see the children and hear the address. Distribution will take place at

Opera House, Friday, September 15

at 10:00 a. m. and 2:00 p. m.

Miss A. L. HILL and MISS C. B. COMSTOCK, Agents, 105 East 22nd Street, New York City.   W. W. BUGBEE, Eldorado, Kansas, State Agent.

Handbills promoted the orphan trains. This one is for McPherson, KS, in 1911.

Home is a destination—the ultimate destination. "Going home" has a meaning more poignant than perhaps any other phrase in our language . . .

This is the story of three families of children who came West on the orphan trains, and their search for home. Beyond that, it is, in broad terms, definitive of the search that each of us makes for security and a sense of belonging.

The Prologue

Home is more than an address. It is more than a building, a dot on the map, or even a certain combination of people. Home is that "center" for each of us, the focus from which we draw strength and courage. And everyone knows "there's no place like home."

This is the true story of three families of children searching for a home. They came West on the orphan trains, uprooted from birthplace, familiar landmarks, oft-traveled roads, and the security of any relatives. None of them knew—though all of them doggedly hoped it—that they would ever find home. Would they someday *belong* somewhere? As you will see, many of those hopes were rewarded. These pages record a genuine human drama, for the characters in the book are real people. They have, at great personal cost, recounted their own life stories, and approved the result. Real names and towns have been used, (though in a few instances, names of minor characters have been changed).

The events and dialogue have been reconstructed as accurately as possible. Every effort has been made to authenticate characterizations, actions, and intentions of the individuals and the settings in which they lived.

But this is more than a history, more than a compilation of biographical facts. By detailing these families' brave and stubborn struggles to belong, SEARCHING FOR HOME reflects the yearning each of us has—for comfort, security, and most important, love.

Charles Loring Brace, Secretary of the Children"'s Aid Society, believed that "the longer a child is in an asylum, the less likely he will do well in outside life." Even as he helped organize orphanages and lodging-houses to rescue deserted and orphaned children from the ravaging circumstances of street life in New York City, Reverend Brace knew that this was only a temporary solution. Thus it was, in 1854, a year after its founding, the Children's Aid Society began sending groups of children "out West" to find adoptive homes.

Reverend Brace believed that "the best of all asylums for the outcast child is the farmer's home." He said, "In every American community — especially a Western one, there are many spare places at the table of life. On the farms of America there is always room for one more pair of hands to help with the chores, and with the prevalence of Christian charity, the addition of another child to a farm home is a blessing."

So ready or not, farm people in the midwestern states were to become the sponsors, the employers, and the foster parents of this homeless throng.

The placing-out system went hand in hand with the Society's many other efforts to salvage orphaned, destitute, and deserted children. In the next seven decades, over 100,000 children were transported via "the orphan trains" from New York to new homes in the Midwest. This was the greatest mass movement of children since the Children's Crusades of the thirteenth century, and it holds a unique place in American history.

"Orphan trains" were a creative solution to a critical problem of the times. In the context of those times the best solution, considering the child's dependent status, was to remove him from street or asylum into a home and family.

How each child fared in the new enrivonment depended on many factors — the agent, the child, the placing, the new home, attitudes of the adoptive families, even the child's early home life and his sense of self-worth.

The orphan train movement, with its tantalizing images of waifs being whisked away to a new life, holds thousands of stories entwined in its history. Here are some of them.

❦ THE AGENT

From 1854, when the Children's Aid Society began the orphan train movement, it employed "western" or "placing" agents to escort the children and help them find homes. Most agents were men, as befitted the times and the hazards of travel. But in 1902 an unusual young woman applied for the position.

She was a teacher, with a certificate from the Mansfield (Pa.) Normal School in hand. Her brown hair was done up in a bun to add maturity to her twenty-four years, and her high-necked white blouse and dark skirt flattered her sturdy, five-foot, ten-inch frame. Round glasses encircled her soft brown eyes.

"I want to work with the children," she told Robert Brace, who had succeeded his father as a leader of the Children's Aid Society. "I have a calling to this work."

She looked authoritative, yet kind. Her words revealed a strong personality and high ideals. But could she handle the problems involved in transporting bands of children across the country? "Without a doubt." Discipline? "They'll obey me. The secret is love, coupled with firmness."

And so, for more than a quarter of a century, until the Society stopped sending orphan children West, Miss Anna Laura Hill served as an escort. She placed children in foster homes and maintained contact with them until they grew up. The job involved as much traveling as a salesman's. Miss Hill kept her residence in Elmira, New York, returning there for her annual one-month vacation. Most of the rest of the time she was on the road.

After the first few years, Miss Hill was joined by a counterpart, Clarabelle Comstock, who also served as a placing agent. The two women sometimes traveled together, and they became close friends. Miss Hill never married, and she remained an obscure figure who worked out her life removed from public attention. But she is warmly remembered by the orphans, now in their sixties and seventies, whose fearful early experiences were eased by her gentle touch.

After the orphan trains stopped operating in 1929, as social conditions and philosophies of social work changed, Miss Hill retired to Elmira in 1932. But she kept in touch with "her children," knitting socks for boys at war overseas, sending wedding dresses to girls who could not afford to buy their own, and writing thousands of encouraging letters through the years. For countless children, she was the bridge that sustained them in their transition from one kind of life to another. She never failed to respond to notes and letters telling of a graduation, an engagement, a new job, or other highlight in their lives. They never forgot her.

As she grew older, Anna Hill lived modestly in a small apartment in Elmira. But she had much to look back on, reminiscing with Clarabelle Comstock on the young lives they'd touched.

It is from recollections of Miss Hill by three families of children she took West between 1911 and 1924 that this book developed.

❧ THE CHILDREN

Ida and Bill Elder — 1911

Ida Elder was sure she was the ugliest of all the children on the "orphan train." Her dark hair, shorn for sanitary reasons at the orphanage, was shorter than a boy's. Her teeth were stained and decayed; she didn't know why.

But she was sure of one thing — no matter how many people came to the adoption meeting, nobody would pick her. Nobody.

Why should they? she asked herself. There were ten kids to choose from, and every one of them was better looking than she. The other girls had come from orphanages that didn't require short haircuts; they all had long, lustrous hair. One girl, Lottie, even had beautiful red curls, which she tossed proudly with each turn of her head. And the boys were sturdy kids — somebody would want them. Even her brother, Bill, three years older than

Ida longed for a pretty hairdo, like she used to wear.

her own eight years, was certain to find someone who would offer him a home.

Ida sighed and turned in her seat, seeking comfort in the face of their supervisor, Miss Anna Laura Hill, who was seated three rows back. Miss Hill was such an optimist. But then, Miss Hill was a lady. You could tell she'd been raised right, from the way she spoke with that dignified eastern accent. And all the way out here, for two days and a night on this train, Miss Hill had treated all the children as though they were special — not just homeless kids, poor orphans, but people!

Miss Hill had kind brown eyes behind round, black-rimmed spectacles. She was a big woman, motherly, and gentle with the children. But she knew when to step in and settle things down, as when Bill would start his ornery tricks. There was a limit beyond which the children could not go. Sometimes she would distract their antics by telling stories about her own childhood in Pennsylvania, and she could make everybody laugh.

Ida smiled at Miss Hill, then turned and leaned back against the horsehair seat cushion. She drummed her fingers idly, trying to imagine whether her own mother might have looked like Miss Hill. Ida couldn't remember her mother — she'd been just three years old when her mother died in childbirth and their world fell apart.

Now Ida began envisioning a fantasy in which she would stand before the crowd of strangers tomorrow: her hair would be long and curly, her teeth white and pretty, and her dress would be a new red taffeta. People would gasp at her loveliness, and many hands would go up when Miss Hill called out her name.

Cliff and Bernice Switzer — 1920

"Wait for us, Ma!" Cliff cried. "Oh, please wait for us!" He could see her climbing a steep hill, alone, a young woman whose face looked old. Finally his screams seemed to reach her, for she turned and looked toward them — six small children clustered together. Cliff, the oldest, tried to grasp all the others to him as a creeping flood of black water lapped and ebbed at their feet.

"No! No! I can't!" she called back. Then she turned and began scrambling upward again, until she crested the hill and was gone from view. As Cliff watched, the water rose menacingly and seemed to engulf them all.

He awoke in panic, drenched in sweat, wondering where he was. Peering into the dimness of the unlit railroad car, he could make out the forms of thirty sleeping children, draped and cuddled together on the train seats. He felt a jolt as the train passed over rough roadbed, and he remembered that he and most of his family were on an "orphan train" headed West to find homes. His dream was only a dream and they hadn't drowned.

Cliff (left) recalled earlier, happier days back home, caring for Howard, Bernice, Harold and Nellie.

But were they really much better off? He wondered. Cliff felt a great concern for his younger brother, Harold; his little sister, Bernice; and the baby, David. They were all on this train with him. Another brother and sister had been left with grandparents in New York, but these four had been turned over to a charitable organization and eventually put on this train. At the end of the line, he knew, they would all be placed in foster homes.

Cliff pulled up the extra coat, given to him by Miss Hill, their sponsor. He clutched it to his thin shoulders to shut out the chilliness of this strange night. But he could not shut out the coldness that he felt in his heart. He hated his mother for abandoning them. He told himself he would always hate her. So what if Dad had abandoned them! Mom could have kept the family together if she'd really wanted to. But she didn't.

The only time this terrible coldness of spirit seemed to leave him was when he was with Harold, David, and Bernice. The day before, as their journey began, he had sat with them in the coach car. Feeling all of his eleven years of responsibility, he'd told them solemnly, "We're going to stay together, no matter what. I'll always know where you are."

Meanwhile, Bernice was silently dealing with her own heartbreak. She wept alone and yearned for her mother. Somehow she grasped that only those most loved had the power to hurt her most deeply. Her father, who had walked out on them, had come back to see Bernice while she was in the hospital, but she was unable to overcome her hurt. Would she ever have a father again? Would she ever want a father — if all it meant was sadness?

Anna (right), wished she were a carefree little girl again, playing at home with Margaret.

Anna Fuchs — 1924

Anna could hear the steam engine backing toward their train. It was too dark to see, but the whistles and bumps told her the switch was being made. Two long whistles pierced the night air and the train moved forward. The journey had begun at last.

Although she was ill with the flu, she summoned the strength to sit up and watch the exit from the station. She hoped she would feel better tomorrow.

Anna wiggled her legs. Her heart seemed to beat in rhythm with the clicking wheels. She glanced at her little sisters, Margaret, nine, and Helen, seven, who were busy playing with toys handed out by Miss Hill. Miss Hill was to be their supervisor on this trip "to the West." It could be a trip with hopeful possibilities, yet Anna's thoughts turned sober as she wondered what would happen at the journey's end. What would this new place be like? Where would she and her sisters live? With whom?

If only her parents had been along — but, of course, that was the point of the whole trip: the girls were orphans. Their father had died two years earlier of tuberculosis, and when their mother died a few months ago, the girls became wards of charity.

Anna realized she was the least adoptable of all the nine children in Miss Hill's care. Not only was she the eldest, just three days away from her eleventh birthday, but she had physical deformities as well. A crippled leg, caused by a congential hip defect, forced her to walk with a limp. The first two fingers of her right hand were missing and only a webbed stump remained where those fingers should have been. Anna seldom thought of her afflictions, yet she knew that adoptive parents would hesitate to take a child who was "different."

But I'd rather go on the orphan train — no matter what happens — than stay at the orphanage, she told herself. She sat back in her seat and waited.

1

The Promise of Rosettes

Ida's daydreams were interrupted as Miss Hill slid into the seat beside her. She admired Miss Hill tremendously, but grew shy whenever anyone tried to engage her in conversation. Ida smiled, carefully keeping her lips over her discolored teeth.

From a colorful carpetbag at her feet Miss Hill drew a book. "Would you like to look at this, Ida?"

The girl was surprised that Miss Hill remembered her name. There had been twenty children from several orphanages in this group. Half of them got off in Missouri, leaving ten children on board after the last stop in Kansas City.

Ida accepted courteously. Although she'd been deprived of a mother's early training, her father had stressed social graces as well as learning. He had exercised fatherly supervision even while she and Bill had lived with one set of relatives after another before they were finally sent to the orphanage.

"We'll be getting off at our stop before long now." Miss Hill's brisk tones conveyed enthusiasm as she attempted to draw some comment from this serious-looking, shabbily-dressed girl. She patted Ida's head tenderly, noting that except for the bangs, which were so dark they almost matched those black eyes, she seemed to have almost no hair. Ida's ears stuck out, and without the graceful concealment of hair she had a disheveled appearance.

"You'll be happy to be on firm ground again, won't you? I know I will," Miss Hill laughed.

Ida smiled, and this time she forgot to hide her teeth — Miss Hill was so kind to her! She answered softly, unable to overcome her shyness and remorse, "Yes'm, I'll be glad when we stop this jiggling back and forth."

She looked down at the book Miss Hill had laid on her lap. It had a pretty picture on the front. Before she could open it to the first page, Miss Hill spoke. "I heard you were an excellent reader, but I don't know what kind of stories you like. Is one about animals suitable?"

"Oh, yes. I like animals. I didn't see many in New York, though."

"I expect you'll see plenty here in Kansas — some you have never even heard of before, like buffalo and jackrabbits."

A commotion in the aisle behind her drew Miss Hill's attention. "I'll be back," she told Ida, moving swiftly toward the racket. There was a flurry of fists as two boys rolled on the floor. The six boys weren't always as amiable as the girls, and fistfights and other battles often broke out. Ida turned to catch a glimpse of her brother Bill, standing on his seat and yelling encouragement to the warriors.

She turned back, encountering the confident gaze of Lottie among the spectators. Lottie — the prettiest girl on the train. Red-headed and poised, Lottie was as unlike an abandoned orphan as one could imagine. Whatever had happened to Lottie, she had come through it with her dignity intact. "I wish I could be like you," Ida whispered under her breath. She sighed and turned her attention to the book.

The story was about a duckling. Ida was so immersed in the tale when she got to the last page that she didn't notice Bill standing beside her.

"Whatcha readin' now, Kid?" Bill snatched the book from her hands just as she was reading the ending.

"Give it back, Billy! I'm not through reading it!" Ida pleaded, irritated by the interruption.

"Kid stuff," he pronounced, tossing the book back into her lap. He dashed off in search of some new mischief.

Miss Hill noticed that Bill, armed with a peashooter, was about to launch an attack on the hat of a portly male passenger who was not a part of their group. Beckoning, she called, "Bill, I wonder if you could help me. I need some information — for the

2

report I'll be making about you and Ida."

Bill jumped up quickly. "You see," Miss Hill explained, "we always tell the audience out here something about each child's background. In looking through my files, I found that your records and Ida's are missing. If you'll tell me a few things about yourselves, I can make my report." With pencil poised, she awaited his reply.

"Sure, Miss Hill," he said, leaning comfortably against the seat nearest her.

"Now, I know that your birth certificates have been placed in your traveling cases — "

"Yeah — along with a change of underwear," Bill remarked.

" — so I can obtain some information from the certificates later. I understand your father is living, but he wanted you to come West to find new homes."

"Dad didn't want to give us up." Bill's facade of assurance began to falter. "But he couldn't make a home for us — said he'd never be married again." His face sobered.

Miss Hill, noticing his discomfort, quickly diverted his attention. "Tell me about your mother."

"She died five years ago. The baby died, too. I remember that my aunt came over, and then my mother died. We lived with Aunt Min and Uncle Jim over a bar in Paterson, New Jersey, for awhile. Then I went to a boarding house with my dad. Finally Dad put us in the Prison House on Ashes — "

"The Prison House! Come now, Billy!"

"Yeah, that's what we kids called it. It was really the Protestant Half-Orphans Asylum, over on Manhattan Avenue, but us kids decided the initials on the front spelled Prison House — "

"On ashes," Miss Hill finished, shaking her head and smiling. "Your father's occupation?"

"Painter. He worked for Adams Express Company, painting signs for the sides of trucks and wagons. Sometimes I helped him chalk the string and pull it. But after mother died, he went into railroad work. Then he couldn't take care of us, so . . . "

"So that was when he put you in the Home?"

"I remember when he took us. He was crying, and he had Ida in his arms, and he held me by the hand, and we stood across the street from that big red building, and he said, 'You're going to live there.' Then he took us over and left us."

"But you saw him after that?"

"He came to see us sometimes, and he brought us books.

He's smart, Miss Hill. Real smart." Suddenly the brash assurance crumbled, and Bill slumped against the seat to hide his tears. Miss Hill, quick to recognize the bravado that failed to cover his hurt and helplessness, put her arm around his shoulder for comfort.

Bill recoiled and pulled away from her, wiping his face with his sleeve. Ashamed of his tears, he blurted, "Heck, I bet my dad read books you've never even heard of. Once he read me a whole book about Ulysses Grant and days and nights on a battlefield."

"I'll put in my report that you're a good reader and enjoy books. Many of the children haven't had much schooling." Miss Hill smiled, "You and Ida are lucky your father cared about such things. Now, what about your health? Have you or Ida been sick much?"

"Just mumps. Ida had the mumps at the orphanage. I got to see her, though. Climbed over the board fence between the girls' and boys' sides of the playground and yelled up to her window. The caretaker saw me from another window and shook her fist and yelled, but I just sneaked out of there."

Miss Hill jotted a note to herself about the mischievous, inventive spirit that lived behind the sober face and black eyes of young Bill Elder.

"Very well, Bill. Thank you. This will be enough to help people know you and Ida."

Bill lingered. Finally he forced out the words, "Do you think someone might take us both?" It was practically a whisper.

This was a question Miss Hill was surprised was not asked more often by siblings on the orphan trains. Family members almost always hoped to be placed together, yet they seldom voiced their hope. Instead it lived as a silent yearning in their expressions as they vacantly watched passing scenery. It sometimes manifested itself in restless troublemaking, fights, and sudden bursts of tears.

"I certainly hope so," she answered. "But don't worry about that now, Bill. You see, I've taken hundreds of children out here to find new homes, and when I visit them afterwards, they tell me how happy they are."

Bill nodded and moved away. Miss Hill closed her report book.

The train chugged into a wooded valley which cradled the little town of Marion, Kansas. A tall, spare man with glasses boarded the train and came into the car, seeking Miss Hill.

4

"Doctor Jones! I was hoping you'd take time off to come along."

"Couldn't miss it," Jones said, settling himself and glancing about at the children. "Everything seems to be in order — the local committee tells me the handbills have been posted all around town for over a week, and the paper has carried an item about the mee ing, too."

"Good," Miss Hill responded. "We'll be there soon."

⋆⋅☽☾⋅⋆

"Sterling Kansas Next Stop! Sterling!" The conductor bellowed as he threw open the door, bringing sounds of clattering wheels on steel with him. His voice was a monotone. This stop was no different to him than the last one, or the next.

Bill Elder worked to keep his face as expressionless as the conductor's voice. He was thankful that none of the other kids could see how hard his heart was pounding. He peered with interest at the landscape moving more and more slowly beyond the train windows. Was this what Miss Hill had called "the prairie," he wondered?

Once more the conductor bawled, "Sterling. All out for Sterling!" and the train lurched to a clanking halt.

"Well, here we are!" Miss Hill called out, and the children began milling around in their usual noisy way, dawdling, gathering their traveling cases, struggling into coats and hats. Bill snatched the cap off the head of the boy beside him and tossed it so high up on the luggage rack that the boy had to stand on the seat, grumbling angrily, to reach it.

"Ida Elder," Miss Hill called, "would you please come with me?" She waved to Ida while giving general directions to the others: "Please go with Miss Jewell — she will take you all to the hotel." Bumping each seat with his valise, Bill followed the others, giving Ida a quick wave before disappearing around a corner of the depot.

Ida watched him go, then stepped down from the train and looked about. Oh my, this country was flat! You could see for miles. She had never been exposed to open spaces before, and suddenly felt an awesome paralysis. She felt she was sticking up on the horizon — defenseless, as if anything might reach out and strike her down.

"Come, Ida, we're going to the Mercantile!" Miss Hill's en-

5

thusiasm soothed Ida's anxiety as they began a fast-paced trek along the town's main road.

"Yes'm," Ida answered, trotting to keep up with the tall woman in the black coat. She held her breath against the frigid air as long as she could, then shielded her face and mouth with her mittened hands. It was very cold, yet no snow fell. Although it was mid-afternoon, there was no sun. The low sky was a deep blue-gray, and fluffy gray clouds scudded fast from north to south as if in a hurry to escape something. Even the air had the feel of impending change. The world around them seemed to be holding its breath; like a deer sensing a hunter nearby, the midwest atmosphere seemed to tingle at the presence of these strange children. Ida's footsteps made small dents in the frozen sand as they crossed the main street.

A bell tinkled as Miss Hill threw open the Mercantile door, and a middle-aged woman looked up from the counter. The Mercantile was a medley of fragrances and sights that Ida was unaccustomed to, but found exhilarating. There was the fresh, exciting fragrance of new fabrics and a tangy odor from a keg of pickles; fat bolognas hung from the meat counter, and to the right was another counter crowded with rows of colorful, candy-filled jars. "Oh," breathed Ida, moving near a glowing, potbellied stove and rubbing her hands. As the warmth of the store surrounded her and the stove glowed its welcome, Ida's fears began to subside.

Miss Hill came to the point. "Mrs. Cantwell, I'm traveling again, so I don't have sewing materials with me. I need hair ribbons for this little girl, and I'd like to borrow a needle and thread to fix them with."

"Of course. Right over here." Mrs. Cantwell pointed toward a glass case with a rainbow of ribbons. Ida peered at them in wonder. There were wide, bright blue and cheery yellow grosgrain, silky green, and another that reminded her of the last time she saw her father.

"With her dark hair and olive skin," Mrs. Cantwell assessed, "I think a bright pink would be nice." She held out the ribbon spool for inspection.

"What do you think, Ida?" Miss Hill turned to the girl.
"Oh, yes," Ida nodded. "Miss Hill," she hesitated shyly,

6

"that's the exact kind of ribbon my father brought me at the orphanage. He trimmed the ends into V's with his pocketknife. He turned a chair upside down to cut it on."

"Fine," Miss Hill decided. "We'll take this. Now, let's fix

Ida and Bill Elder before being taken to the orphanage.

it this way," and she took the ribbon and wrapped it around and around on her hand until she had made a thick loop. Then she gathered it in the center, tied it with another ribbon, and fluffed out each loop until the whole thing looked just like a rosette.

She held it beside Ida's ear, nodded and smiled. Ida waited breathlessly as Miss Hill constructed a second rosette just like the first.

"Now, the needle and thread, please," Miss Hill requested. Mrs. Cantwell produced these items and Miss Hill quickly sewed the rosettes onto another ribbon of pink.

7

"You see," she explained as she sewed, "they kept her hair cut short at the orphanage. They had so many to take care of they made the girls wear their hair as short as the boys!"

"Don't worry about a thing, dear," Mrs. Cantwell said sympathetically, as Ida bit her lip in embarrassment. "It's going to be beautiful," Mrs. Cantwell continued, "And you certainly are handy with a stitch, Miss Hill."

Miss Hill smiled as she gently fitted the creation onto Ida's head and attached an elastic band in the back to hold it all in place.

"Look in the mirror," Mrs. Cantwell coaxed Ida, tilting the counter mirror so that Ida could see her reflection. "Just look at that! It's lovely!"

Ida stood on tiptoe and hestitantly peered into the mirror, carefully keeping her lips over her teeth. There was a pink rosette beside each ear. Why, yes! The rosettes were as big as her fists! And a wide ribbon connected the rosettes and crossed the top of her head. The black velvet with elastic in the back didn't seem to show, as she tilted her head to see. It matched her hair.

The overall effect was a startling change. Ida's short, dark hair now became a foil for the ribbon, which was a headdress of impressive style and color. The pink livened her pale complexion and accented her dark eyes. "It's beautiful," she smiled.

"Look how it makes her eyes show up," Mrs. Cantwell exclaimed. "It really brings out her pretty features! I have to hand it to you, Miss Hill."

Ida studied her reflection, looking this way and that, as Miss Hill paid the bill.

"Goodbye, dear. Good luck!" Mrs. Cantwell called as the door closed.

Ida fairly danced along beside Miss Hill as they headed toward the hotel. Her ears were icy; her hair, lifted by the wind, stood on end; and she could hear the rosettes crackling and fluttering at her ears. But she didn't care. It couldn't blow off, because it was fastened tight.

"This is even better than the rag braids we used to make for ourselves at the orphanage," she confided to Miss Hill. As they came to the hotel, Ida couldn't resist glancing again at her reflection in the window glass. She definitely looked girlish. Quite, quite nice.

2

An Opera House Welcome

The prairieland spread out like a giant's cream-colored bed-spread, smooth and level except for the gentle rumple of occasional hills. Rows of cornfield stubble and overturned sod were dusted with snow, giving a pleasing patterned effect to the quilt. Bare-limbed, squatty hedgeapple trees, planted to protect the crops from the wind's relentless force, marched around the sections of land, with the squares divided into smaller plots and dotted with farmsteads.

The wind, which in summer coursed over wheat and corn, scorching it with hot breath, now blew cold and strong across the flatland. Farmers who had planted winter wheat were working to protect it by spreading straw over the delicate young crop. Windy times were ideal for spreading straw; the wind scattered anything loose or not securely fastened, pushing it carelessly over the clods and under fences.

White buildings far in the distance signaled the town of Sterling. Two miles south ran the Arkansas River, a life-giving source that abruptly intersected the square-mile sections and rambled from northwest to southeast between Colorado and Oklahoma. The river was the nourishment that had attracted the town's founders, a colony of Quakers, to settle on the immense, barren grassland forty years earlier when the Civil War's end brought about Western expansion. The Quakers established this community like many other small western towns, around a nucleus of church and school. They hauled sand from the river's wide, sloping banks to cover their dirt streets. Later, other groups such as the River Brethern also settled near Sterling. This religious sect practiced baptism by immersing their converts in the river.

Through the years, Sterling had flourished. It served a farming community within a thirty-mile radius, and was connected to the rest of the world by the high iron of the Santa Fe Railroad and a network of narrow dirt roads. A college had been established and businesses built. The state bank on the corner was notable for its brick exterior and a paved walk. The Opera House brought featured performers from afar and also provided a place for local entertainment.

Dominating the main street was the rectangular bulk of a huge white building, with a sign in black letters on its side, "Jennings Hotel." In addition to its regular clientele of local working people, the hotel's spacious rooms provided shelter for many travelers on their journeys. . .

"New York City's a bum place. Nothing but a hellhole to raise kids in. That's what my dad used to say."

Five of the boys sprawled on the faded hotel room carpet paused in their game of marbles to stare admiringly at the speaker, Bill Elder, who dared to spike his conversation with swear words.

"Brooklyn was pretty bad, too," another boy put in.

"New York was worse," Bill argued. "I remember living in a crowded old tenement where people just dumped their thundermugs down the dumbwaiter to the basement. Stunk terrible! The streets were full of mud and muck, too."

Frank, at sixteen the eldest in the group, was especially impressed with Bill. "Hey, Bill," he encouraged his scrappy friend, "tell 'em what you used to do to the peddlers."

"Well, we used to hang around the Flatiron Building and steal Sweet Mickeys from the peddlers around there."

"What're those?" little George wanted to know.

"Sweet potatoes, dummy," Bill answered. "An Irish potato is a Mickey, see, so a sweet potato is a Sweet Mickey. We'd steal 'em and take 'em back in an alley, dig a hole, build a fire, and bury them in the coals. We'd warm our hands and wait till the taters were ready to eat. Tasted swell on a cold day."

"Wish I coulda had some fun like that, but I was in the or-

10

phanage from the time I was a baby," Joe said wistfully.

"How did you get away from your orphanage to do all that stuff, Bill?" asked George.

"Wasn't there yet," Bill retorted. "My dad had someone taking care of Sis and me. But I'd skip school, and a bunch of us boys would go after the peddlers. One of us would run up and kick the leg from the cart and everything would go rolling. We'd grab what we wanted, then scatter."

He paused to survey the effect on his listeners. Seeing that they were impressed, he continued: "Those peddlers were Italian. They had a call that sounded like 'Peachie, peachie, Delaware peachie! Appo, appo, appo!' "

"Hey," Frank said, "I remember hearing something like that!"

"We used to throw rocks at the frying pans on the junk peddlers wagons. They were Jewish, and they'd call like this: 'Any rags, any bottles, any bones? We pay cash OLD CLOTHES!'" he shouted.

"Gosh, Bill," Joe said, his eyes wide with respect, "you musta had a lot of fun."

"Oh, I did! Till I got to the orphanage. Then it was me against the caretakers. First we had an old sailor with tattoos all over. He was okay. I liked to hear him cuss. Then we got an old witch. I hated her!"

He glanced around, licked his lips, and went on. "She had long, straggly hair, baggy socks, and a screechy voice, and she was always knocking somebody across the playroom floor. One day I found a pin and crawled under the table where everyone was sitting. I jabbed the pin into every kid's leg, and then I came to Old Baggy Socks. Boy, did I let her have it!"

"Wow! What'd she do?" Frank asked.

"Walloped me, of course," Bill replied, and with a twinkle in his black eyes added, "But I was glad I done it."

Miss Hill suddenly appeared in the doorway, interrupting the discourse with a tactful "Good morning, boys. Ready for breakfast?" The boys jumped to their feet, quickly stuffing the marbles into their pockets. Bill's eyes were round with surprise. He wondered if she had been listening to his tales, but she made no comment.

"The girls are already in the dining room with my assistant. Follow me, and we'll go meet them. After you've eaten,

11

I'd like you to come back here, pack up, and be ready to go to the meeting."

As she led them down the stairs and toward the dining room, they passed through the lobby. There Bill noticed a small handbill on the wall. "Wanted: — Homes for Children," he read to himself.

"Look at that," he whispered to Frank. "Bet that's about us."

The dining room was cozy with the fragrances of sizzling bacon, fresh rolls, and coffee. The large windows trimmed with gingham curtains revealed swirling snowflakes outside, making the room seem snug and warm. A row of men in work clothes drooped like heavy-headed sunflowers over their coffee mugs at the counter. Miss Jewell had her little encampment set up in a corner where three tables were reserved for the group. Bill spotted Ida, sipping cocoa and waving at him.. Her hairbow was as eye-catching as a peacock's plume. He went up to her. "Hey, Kid. Where'd you get that hair ribbon?"

"Do you like it, Billy?" She smiled shyly. "Miss Hill took me to a store yesterday and got it for me. Now my short hair won't show so much."

"You look like the first horse in the parade," he teased her gently. "It's real nice," he added with a grin before he took a seat at another table with his buddies.

After they had eaten, Miss Hill led the way back to their rooms. Bill sneaked through the lobby and removed the handbill. He shoved it into the pocket of his knickers and caught up with the others on the stairs.

"Lookahere!" he called when the boys were alone in their room. "This is about us." He read the message aloud.

A company of homeless children from the East will arrive in Sterling, Kan., on Friday, Dec. 1 , 1911. These children are of both sexes and various ages, having been thrown friendless upon the world. They come under the auspices of the Children's Aid Society of New York. They are well-disciplined, having come from the various orphanages. The citizens of this community are asked to assist the agent in finding good homes for them. Persons taking children must be recommended by the local committee. They must treat the children in every way as a member of the family, sending them to school, church, Sabbath School, and properly clothing them until they are seventeen years of age.

A committee of well-known citizens have agreed to act as the local committee to aid the agent in securing homes. Applications must be made to, and endorsed by, the committee. An address will be made by the agent. Come and see the children and hear the address. Distribution will take place at the Opera House, Dec. 15, 1:30 p.m., Miss A. L. Hill, Agent for the Children's Aid Society.

Bill finished reading. "Hey, Frank," he jeered, "are you friendless? Do you want a home?"

"How 'bout you, Bill?" Frank answered. "Are you well-disciplined?"

"They musta put these up all over," Bill said. "I s'pose there'll be a whole crowd of people there gawking at us. Reminds me of the slave auctions I read about. I wonder if they'll pry our mouths open and look at our teeth?"

An awkward silence descended on the group, and no one made a reply. Bill looked around. Their faces showed their hurt. Bill crumpled the paper and shoved it back in his pocket. "Don't matter none," he said. But still no one answered him. The boys milled about aimlessly, and Bill went to the window to gaze out at the gathering storm.

Eventually Miss Hill and her assistant came back with the girls. Miss Hill wore her heavy black fur coat, and all the others were dressed warmly, too. "Bundle up, boys." she cautioned them, "we're walking to the Opera House. It's not far." They all followed the women down the worn staircase and out the front door, pulling up their coat collars as they felt the wind.

Yesterday's ominous clouds, and the morning's snow flurries had now strengthened into a storm. The wind blew hard little pellets of snow with such force that it stung their faces. The horses tied at hitching posts along the way laid back their ears, whinnying and stamping restlessly. Bill found it hard to keep his sense of direction, but he followed along.

At last they reached a doorway. Miss Hill held open the door against the wind. "Hurry inside, children," she called. "Go right up those steps, take off your wraps, and hang them on those hooks. Then be seated in the chairs there." She pointed to a neat row of chairs placed in a semi-circle in a clear space. "Sit by your brother or sister."

The children did as they were told, hanging their coats, hats, and scarves on the wooden pegs and organizing themselves in family units. Bill and Ida were on the far end.

13

Ida scooted her chair closer to Bill's. She touched her rosettes and smoothed her dress. "Where do you think we are, Billy?" she whispered.

"This is a stage, Kid" Bill replied. "And that curtain's the only thing between us and a whole bunch of strangers. Don't you hear that rumble? That's people talking. People who came to see us. Take us home, maybe."

Ida listened carefully. "I hear laughing — and people saying hello. They sound pretty nice," she ventured hopefully.

Bill shifted in his creaky chair; the handbill crunched in his pocket. No, he thought, he could not tell Ida what he knew. She would just have to wait. He hoped that when the curtain opened the "right" people would be there.

"You scared, Billy?"

"No," he answered, his voice strong. "Just watch the crowd, Ida. When the curtain goes up, see if you can pick out a friendly face. Then try to smile."

"I'll smile with my mouth shut," Ida replied fiercely. "Oh, Billy, I hope I look pretty!"

"Kid, you look fine."

The curtain was of canvas and ropes at either end could roll it open from the bottom up. Small rectangles of advertising covered its faded yellow front. Ads for the local bank, grocery, funeral home, and other shops gave the audience something to look at while they waited.

Bill glanced down the row of children, all perched like birds on the edge of their chairs.

Slowly, slowly the curtain began to roll upward. Bill scrunched down in his seat so that he could be the first to see what was behind it. Sure enough, the place was full of people. The seats were crowded with men, women, and children, and people stood along the walls while even more flowed in through the front door. Bill looked up and noticed a tall glass dome in the ceiling. A skylight. But now it let in only the storm's bleakness. He saw snow accumulating around the latticework.

The odors of wet coats, pipe smoke, and farm animals wafted on the air. The crowd murmured; people squirmed in their seats, looking this way and that. Bill sensed an electric excitement in the audience, similar to what he'd felt when he'd attended the Orphans Fair at the Hippodrome in New York. This was a per-

14

formance too, he thought, only now he and the others were the "main attraction." He remembered a little toy he'd gotten at the fair. It was a glass donkey filled with candy. When its head was unscrewed, the candy poured out. Donkeys. The West. Bill gulped and concentrated on watching the crowd.

Toward the back he saw a woman in a fancy hat with feathers. Up front an old man in a checkered coat with frayed sleeves stared at him. Over there was a pastor with a turned-back collar.

Miss Hill came out on the stage, and the audience greeted her with applause. "It's very nice to be back with you all again," she said. "Miss Jewell and I have found this whole area to be very friendly, both to us and to our little charges. Right off, I'd like to introduce you to the local adoption committee. They've been very helpful in arranging this meeting, and they'll aid families in finding the right child." She named the druggist, a pastor, a doctor, a lawyer, and a businessman. She also asked Dr. C. C. Jones of Marion to stand, and she thanked him for his work as a local representative who checked on the adopted children in the area.

Next, for the benefit of those who had not previously been acquainted with its operation, Miss Hill outlined the benevolent work of the Children's Aid Society. She recalled fondly the dreams of the West that led the founder, Reverend Brace, to launch the exodus of children from the teeming metropolis in the East. She concluded her talk by quoting Brace, "The central figure in the world's charity is Christ."

Miss Hill smiled and nodded to both sides of the auditorium. "As you can see, these children are a fine group." She beckoned to the semi-circle of serious young faces. "I'd like to introduce you to each child, and give you some information about them — their nationality, diseases they've had, their education. The meeting will probably take several hours — we don't want to rush things — but that will give the storm time to pass," she added. "The Ladies Group has some refreshments prepared for later on."

She began with the two sisters, who were nearest her. Gently she told the story of their lives.

As the program went on, Bill noticed a nice-looking, well-dressed woman who hurried in late to the meeting. She wore a heavy green hat and a brown coat. Behind her came a tall, bearded man with snow on his coat and a Russian cap with flaps over his ears. Bill observed people waving to them, beckoning them toward two empty seats up front. He decided they must be important.

15

After each child was introduced there was a pause and a flurry of interest and chatter in the audience. People came forward to ask questions, to get a closer look at the child, to confer with the committee. All of this took time, and the afternoon wore on slowly. The children squirmed in their seats and made occasional visits to the restroom and, later on, to the refreshment table. The younger ones twisted in their seats and tried to keep quiet. Little Joe fell asleep, his head leaning against the back of his chair, a lock of dark hair falling across his innocent face.

At last Miss Hill came to Ida and Bill. She asked them to stand as she told the audience their names. She went on to mention their mother's death, their father's efforts to keep the children, their two years in an orphanage culminated by their father's decision to give them up in hopes they'd find "a mother's love and a father's guidance."

"Now," she said, "if there's anyone here who wishes to be considered for the adoption of these children, please come forward."

Bill scanned the audience, his eyes wide. He looked over at Ida, but she had her eyes squeezed tight. "Oh, Billy," she whispered, "I can't stand it. What if nobody wants me? What if we can't be together?" She started to weep and quickly put her hand over her mouth, but tears oozed from under the scrunched-shut lashes.

"Now, Kid," Bill consoled her. "There's nothing to it. Somebody will want us."

Ida opened her eyes just in time to see a fearful sight. "Oh, look at that woman in the green hat. She's coming! I hope she doesn't get me. Oh, Billy, I don't want *anybody* to get me. I want to go back . . . to the orphanage."

"Hush, Ida," Bill replied, "don't ever say that. Dad wanted us to come out here. Look at that woman. She's not scary. It's just that you aren't used to the way people look here. They look different here than back in New York."

"It's her hat," Ida decided, trying to compose herself. "It's just her hat." She reached up to touch her own headpiece for reassurance.

"Must be some kinda sunbonnet for winter," Bill "It looks like a bonnet, but it's heavier and tighter-fitting. You can't see her face very well. A lot of the women are wearing them, but hers is the fanciest. I bet she's rich!" Bill bit his lip, put his arm around Ida, and heaved a sigh.

The woman and the bearded man had disappeared beside the stage. Soon Ida and Bill were called to a corner backstage by the man who Miss Hill had said was Mr. Duff, the druggist. He led them over to the couple. Bill heard the woman tell Mr. Duff, "We really wanted a boy to help on the farm, but if he has a sister, we'll take the girl, too. She's a pretty little thing." The woman turned toward Ida and smiled down at her. Ida's mouth dropped open — someone thought she was pretty! She said to Bill, "She's nice! Sort of like Miss Hill, isn't she, Billy?"

Bill thought the couple looked good, too, once he had a chance to see both of them up close. The woman's coat was very grand; the collar had been unbuttoned and it lay back in a long, flattering lapel. The man, tall and light-complexioned, made a striking partner for her. They were a handsome couple.

Mr. Duff turned to the children. "Ida and Bill Elder, I'd like you to meet Mr. and Mrs. Bishop. They would like you to come and live with them." He paused, then spoke gently, "Would you children like to have these people for your parents?"

Ida looked at Bill, who sent a silent message in his eyes. Gripping her hand as she leaned against him, Bill felt Ida relax a bit. "Yes," they answered together.

Riding home in the Bishops' buggy, Bill and Ida snuggled together under a heavy black fur robe, their little cases at their feet. Miss Hill had placed them there as she kissed the children goodbye. Two matched bays pulling the buggy plunged smartly through the new snow as frost snorted from their nostrils. The storm had cleared. Now, a weak ray of sunshine drilled through the clouds as they broke up and moved on. Between the occasional drifting snowflakes, Bill could see a farm in the distance. Then they turned in at the lane, and Mrs. Bishop leaned around in her seat. "Well, here we are," she said, smiling. "Welcome home, children."

3

Young Winter Wheat

The buggy rolled to a stop near the back door of the farmhouse. Mr. Bishop tied the reins and leaped out, then lifted his wife down. They turned to the children, nestled in the back. The wind drove hard across the flat land, and they had to call loudly over its persistent wail. "Carry the girl, Ward!" the woman shouted, holding onto her flapping bonnet. "The snow's too deep for her shoes."

"Bill, just step high and come to the door," Mr. Bishop called as he gingerly carried Ida and her travel case. Mrs. Bishop swung open the door and then closed it behind them. Everything was suddenly still; an uncomfortable quiet engulfed them all. Mrs. Bishop broke the awkward silence. "Why don't you children look around a bit?" She spoke shyly, unsure what to do, now that these children were hers.

Hesitantly Bill and Ida put down their little cases and removed their coats. They were in a long, narrow room, like a closed porch, that ran the width of the house. Racks for coats hung on the wall. On the left was an open stairway leading downward, and a large case full of eggs sat beside it. Bill thought he'd never seen so many eggs in one place before.

"Come into the kitchen," Mrs. Bishop said. "Let's have something to eat." She took off her coat and Ida noticed that the green corduroy dress that fit her slim figure matched the green of

18

her bonnet. Then she swept the bonnet from her head and hung it on a hook. At last, Ida could see her face clearly. She was fine-featured. There were a few gray streaks in her black hair, and she smiled pleasantly.

Bishop went out to put the team away as his wife beckoned the children toward a large table in the kitchen. "Sit here," she said. The children quietly slipped into the oak chairs at the round, polished table, and Mrs. Bishop put a pot of milk on the wood-burning stove. Ida caught a glimpse of the still-scarlet coals when the woman opened a little door and tossed in a few sticks of wood from a box alongside. The cozy feeling of a flickering flame warmed Ida and made her feel more secure.

Bishop returned, stamping snow, and joined them at the table. "Well, here we are — the four of us," Mrs. Bishop said brightly. "We always wanted children, and now we have two!"

"Right," Bishop replied.

"I'll fix up the extra bedrooms upstairs, and we'll get you all settled." Again silence. The stove crackled.

Finally Ida spoke. "What should we call you, Ma'am?"

The woman looked surprised, then pleased. "You could call us Mom and Pop Bishop," she suggested. "Your father is living back East. I heard that you call him Dad. Isn't that right?"

"Yes," Bill replied with pride.

"Well, then, we'll be Mom and Pop."

Mr. Bishop began explaining to Bill why he needed help with the farm work. "We've got a quarter-section. Flossie's folks gave it to us. But we've never had any young ones to help out. And I can sure use some help with milking and other chores. Before and after school, of course," he added hastily.

"What's a quarter-section?" Bill was curious. He liked to know as much about things as he could. Bishop eyed Bill, perceiving him to be highly intelligent and inquisitive.

"Why, a section's a square of land, one mile each way," Mr. Bishop responded. "And a quarter-section is a fourth of that. An acre's another way to measure land. There's 640 acres in a section."

Bill nodded. "I'll remember," he said determinedly.

Mrs. Bishop set out a cup of steaming milk before each of them and a plate of cookies between the children. "Help yourselves," she smiled warmly.

Mr. Bishop continued his explanation of the farm's operation, and the children listened intently, for they had both been

19

told that helping out was expected and they were willing workers.

"The corn's harvested, and the wheat's planted. I finished covering it with straw today. So barn chores will be most of your work till spring. We milk four cows. I'll teach you how."

"Wheat? Under the snow?" Bill questioned.

Ward Bishop answered with a short story about the Russian immigrants who had settled in central Kansas forty years earlier, bringing with them the seeds for winter wheat from the steppes of the Ukraine. The young wheat, planted after harvest in the fall, sprouted and came up before going dormant. Wintering over under a protective cover of straw and snow, it clustered and grew thick and hardy, gaining a head start on the spring growing season. Bill nodded thoughtfully.

Mrs. Bishop was eager to get everything arranged, and she enlisted the children's help in getting beds made up. They arose and followed her through the house to gather the necessary items.

Bill and Ida had never even seen a farm home before — tenements, apartments, and the orphanage were the extent of their experience. Their eyes were large, their steps hesitant; they were taking all in with careful observation.

The farmhouse was a place of large rooms, cold wood floors, kerosene lamps, dark furniture, photographs on the walls, and windows that all looked out on the same view — flat farmland.

Peeking from the curtained upstairs windows, they saw behind the house a large barn and a long, low chicken house. Inside a circular fence, a windmill towered over a water tank, its blades spinning furiously as cows gathered around to drink. In the expanse of land and unfamiliar sights they sensed there was much to learn about living here.

They helped make up beds with colorful patchwork quilts. Mrs. Bishop showed them how she would heat bricks to put in each of their beds and keep their feet warm, because, as she explained, "there will be many cold nights to come."

After supper, the children prepared for bed. Mrs. Bishop left Bill to himself, but came to Ida's room. She helped Ida remove her hairbow, smiling warmly at the sweet, round, innocent face that gazed up at her. Then she opened the little travel case. "I see there's a Bible in your bag," she observed.

"Yes," Ida said. "We all have Bibles. The Society gave them to us."

"We go to church every Sunday. You can carry yours."

20

Then, glancing at the open case, she saw it contained almost nothing — just a set of underwear.

"My dear!" she exclaimed, "don't you have a proper nightgown?"

"No," Ida answered simply. She busied herself arranging the hairbow on the dresser.

"Tomorrow we'll go shopping. Bill needs some things, too." She tucked the child into bed. "Goodnight, Ida."

"Goodnight, Mom," Ida answered slowly. "And thank you."

Ida was alone, unable to see or talk to Bill. She felt defenseless, a little girl longing for a home and a life that was no more. She grew afraid. Then she crept out of bed, snatched the hairbow, and laid it carefully beside her pillow. Smiling, she fell asleep.

❧ ⟶⊙⟵ ❧

On Saturday the family went into town. It was even busier than the day before, and Bill learned that Saturday was "farmers day." Stores stayed open later, and farmers bought their supplies for the next week. Or, if they lived farther away, for two or more weeks. While Mr. Bishop went to buy feed and supplies, Mrs. Bishop outfitted the children. Bill got several pair of new bib overalls and work shirts, and Ida got a nightie and two new dresses, one a middy with a dropped waistline. Both got boots.

And lunch buckets. It gave Mrs. Bishop a thrill to purchase two lard tins so the children would be able to start off to school with regular lunch pails, "just like everyone else." She would empty them of the lard and on Monday morning pack them with nourishing food.

On the way home Bishop turned the buggy in a different direction. "I want you to see your school," he announced.

"You might think you're in the sticks," Mrs. Bishop said with a laugh, turning in the seat to speak to Bill and Ida, "but Kansas education is progressive. We're unifying the country school districts. You'll be going to Union 5 — one of the three best in this area. Here it is." She pointed to a two-story brick building surrounded by a large playground.

"Will we both go there?" Ida wondered aloud.

"Yes. And you don't even have to walk. It's only three-quarters of a mile from home, but you can ride. A team of horses and a wagon — they call it the 'kid hack' — will pick you up at the end of our lane."

That night Ida and Bill finally had a chance to talk privately. "Well, Kid. What do you think?"

"It's real nice here, Billy. But someday I'd like to go back to New York. How about you?"

"Don't know yet. We got to try it here, Kid. That's what Dad wanted," he said with a note of finality.

Sunday morning, the children dressed in their best clothes and went with Mrs. Bishop to the Baptist Church. Pop Bishop stayed home. At the service the children had a chance to survey the people more closely.

"None of them seem to be poor, like folks we knew in New York," Bill observed.

"No," Ida whispered back.

"But I feel more at home with those poor people in New York," Bill returned.

"Maybe we'll meet some friends at school tomorrow," Ida answered.

❦

"Better hurry! The hack's coming down the road."

Ida and Bill scurried downstairs. Ida adjusted the fancy hairbow and pulled at the waistline of the middy dress. Bill appeared in new bib overalls, a white shirt, and a necktie. The weather had turned mild for their first day of school. They slipped into their coats, gathered their pails and hurried down the lane.

Mrs. Bishop smiled after them. "Imagine," she said to herself, "I'm forty years old, and suddenly the mother of two school-age children." She watched as they crawled aboard the wagon.

As the kid hack rattled along the road, Ida leaned against Bill and sought his protection. "Will we like it, Billy?"

"School? Sure. Unless the teacher's dumb. Don't be afraid though, see — because when you're new, you have to act brave. Otherwise, kids think you're sissy."

"Don't start any fights, Billy," Ida cautioned. "Mom Bishop wouldn't like it." The "Mom Bishop" part wasn't easy to say yet, but she was practicing it. "What grade do you think we'll be in?"

"I expect they'll drill us to see what we know about geography and times tables and stuff, then they'll decide."

They sat uncomfortably on the hack as the other children surveyed them silently, but at the next stop an outgoing boy hopped on and spoke. "Hi. You the new kids? I'm Johnny Snook. We're neighbors."

22

Ida and Bill smiled in reply. "I'm Bill Elder. This is my sis, Ida."

"I'll show you around," Johnny offered.

Ida stuck close to Bill as they followed Johnny across the wide stoop through the front door of the school. "Here's where to put your coat," Johnny said, showing them the cloakroom and tossing his lunch pail on a shelf above. Bill and Ida put theirs on the shelf, too.

"See," Johnny went on, "there's a couple classrooms on this floor, but upstairs is the main classroom, the bathroom, and our assembly hall. Furnace is down in the basement." As a school, it looked first-class, Bill had to admit.

They climbed the stairs, Johnny in the lead, as Ida whispered to Bill. "What if somebody picks on us?"

"Kid, I'm tough," Bill answered. "I can take anything. Proved that in the orphan's home. And I'll look out for you."

The teacher was a tall, blonde woman with a wide grin. "Hello, children. I'm Mrs. Carlson," she said, showing them to empty desks.

After some checking of their knowledge, they were assigned to separate classes in the same room. Ida kept her mouth closed, looked silently at the others, but did not speak. Bill spoke up several times, each followed by a mysterious giggle from the children, even though his answers were correct.

At morning recess, Ida hung back and Bill stayed beside her. They leaned against the building, away from the wind, as they watched others playing ball.

At noon recess they ate their lunches, then went out again. "Come on, Ida and Bill," Mrs. Carlson called, "you come and play ball, too. I'm sure you know how."

Ida was finally lured into the game, and before long she forgot herself in the excitement. But when the ball rolled away from her, she squealed, "Oooh, look! The ball went into the street!"

At this, the other children began to jeer and mock this short-haired newcomer and her brother who talked so strange. All morning they'd noticed that Bill dropped his 'h's' from words like *where, white,* and *wheat.* Now the girl had proved she was a silly goose. "That's a *road*, dummy!" one of the farm children shouted crudely. "Boy, are you stupid!" "Doncha know a road when you see one?" another sneered. "You don't even talk right!"

Bill doubled his fists and raced toward the biggest boy, who had made the first insulting remark. But Johnny Snook stepped between them. "Hold on there, Bill." He turned to the crowd of unfriendly faces. "You shut up!" he roared at the classmates. "A road is a street, and a street is a road. Do you think you know everything? Well, you don't. You're a bunch of country hicks, and mean, too!" The fray dissolved. Ida exhaled a breath it seemed she'd been holding all day.

She knew she needed Bill's protection, and she sensed she'd need even more than Bill. Johnny Snook was her new hero.

That evening after school they started learning to do their chores. Ida gathered eggs, pumped water, and brought in firewood; Bill got his first lesson in milking a cow.

At last the chores were done. As Bill paused out back with Ida to watch the sun setting across the field, they noticed a horse and rider approaching. The horse's hooves arched high over the snowy ground. As the form approached, they recognized Johnny Snook.

He slid easily off the bare back of the tall horse and grinned.

"Hi, Johnny!" their voices rang out.

"Thought I'd come by and give you a proper welcome. I'm glad to have you two here. My brothers are older, and I didn't have any close pals till you came along." Ida colored a bit; Bill's chest lifted with pride.

Johnny Snook became their inseparable friend. He showed them secrets of this new country, and his stamp of approval was vital to their acceptance.

When spring came, he and Bill hid Easter eggs for Ida, scattering them all over the farm. But the wide open spaces and "nothing to do" bothered Bill and Ida. As Bill was diligent in reminding everyone, they'd seen and done things. They'd watched parades from the top of their orphanage and attended special shows and circuses. They'd been to Madison Square Garden to the horse show and seen Christy Mathewson play for the Giants.

One day Mr. Bishop invited everyone into the wagon — they were going to the county fair. "You been complaining that country life is too tame," he jibed Bill. "But you've never seen anything like this!"

"What is it?" Bill begged to know.

"A flying machine. A farmer over at Kingman, his name is Clyde Cessna, he built a monoplane called the Comet. Flies it at fairs and celebrations. If the weather's right, he'll take it up today."

The Bishops, Bill, and Ida, along with the crowd of more than 2,000, waited for two hours as the frail-looking plane, with bicycles tires, flat wings, and polished wood propeller, awaited proper air currents. When the wind was favorable, Cessna started the single propeller and lifted away, circling a three-mile patch of sky, then landing safely a fourth-mile from where he started.

"Now ain't that something to write home about!" exclaimed a farmer who'd been among the spectators. And that gave Bill an idea. He would write his dad.

But when the answer came back, there was just a short note for Bill and a longer message to the Bishops.

Dear Sir and Madam,

Willie's letter of the 21st reached me on the 26th. The fact that you permitted him to write shows you fair minded. I shall write him one letter, then he must lose sight of me. For I want him to grow up and remain in the west. I want him and Ida to look upon you as father and mother. This they will do if I fade from their memory. The step I have taken has cost me a hard struggle, but I took into consideration the future of the children and the course I've taken is the best. I want them to grow up with a circle of acquaintances. New York is a hell hole, to those who know it, although very few are willing to admit it. The girl needs a mother's care, the boy the companionship of a father, which both were denied at the Half Orphan Asylum where I had them.

I know you and your wife must be o.k. else you would never have taken two children. If you wish them to have your name, have your wish. Their birth certificates were placed in their respective traveling cases. I remain,

Most Respectfully, William E. Elder

Once a year Miss Hill came by to see the children, renting a livery rig and driving out without notice. Only once were the Bishops embarrassed when she dropped in. Ida had been out in the mud and Mrs. Bishop chided her, "Oh, I wish you were cleaned up, dear."

"I'll go put on a fresh dress," she offered. Then she added, "but could I show Miss Hill our pet calf first?"

Ida led Miss Hill to the shed and said, "This is Susie. We raised her ourselves." Snapping a halter to its fat face, she led the small, furry calf in a circle. "Look at that!" Miss Hill exclaimed.

25

"You're quite a cowgirl. Now didn't I tell you when you were coming out on the train you'd see lots of animals?"

Ida giggled happily.

The visits went on until 1914, when Miss Hill's arrival prompted a private conference with the Bishops. Bill and Ida, waiting in another room, were curious. "Let me look through the keyhole," Bill said. When the door suddenly opened, he stumbled to his feet.

"Miss Hill has something to tell you," Mrs. Bishop said.

"The Bishops want to adopt you. And I think it's a good idea," Miss Hill explained.

"But our dad — " Bill began. "Even though he said for us to forget him, he's still our dad."

"Children," Miss Hill broke in, "your father has died in a railroading accident. You have no family now but the Bishops."

⟨⟩

Ida and Bill had harbored thoughts of going back to New York someday. With their dad gone, they resigned themselves to living in Kansas. And when the paperwork had all been taken care of, they were legally adopted.

Ida and Bill Bishop with their pet calf on the Bishop farm, at about nine and twelve years of age.

As the months wore into years and the children grew, theirs was basically a happy life, with each doing his or her part for the good of the family and the farm. The children excelled in their school work. Bill was one of three eigth graders in the county honored for their academic records. Ida's bond of love grew, especially for Mrs. Bishop.

4

In Search of a Family

Cliff trailed slowly behind his mother, his bare feet shuffling along the plain wood floor, a stack of eight mismatched bowls gripped in his thin hands. His mother carried a pot of steaming soup to the center of the bare table. Cliff set the bowls beside it, glancing around at his brothers and sisters at play. They hesitated and looked to Cliff. Usually, when their dad was home for supper, he ate first and the little ones had to eat afterward. But this time their father hadn't waved them away from the table yet, and Cliff took this as a good sign. He nodded to the others, huddled in the main room of the humble apartment, and they hurried to their chairs swiftly so they would not be turned away. Harold lifted the baby Frieda into the old highchair.

Mrs. Switzer joined the others at the table and ladled the soup, handing the bowls to each, beginning with her husband.

"More bread, Cliff," his mother said, when she could see the meager loaf wasn't going far enough. Cliff rose and stepped into the kitchen. He opened the old cabinet — the one he and his father had found cast out in the alley — and as he removed a loaf, he heard his parents' voices rising. Another argument was building. His stomach began knotting as he unwrapped a flour sack from a fresh loaf of bread. Cliff wished this were another of his bad dreams, but he knew all too well how real it was. It happened so often that he had no reason to expect anything else, yet he never

27

gave up hope that someday they could be a "normal" family. He carried the loaf to his mother.

"Why don't you fix something more than soup?" Switzer erupted. "Something that will fill a person?" A frown creased his dark, handsome face.

"With what?" the woman demanded. "You drink up all the extra money we ever have. It's a wonder I can afford a soup bone and a few potatoes. Your bottle bill is always bigger than our grocery bill." Angrily she began cutting thin slices from the loaf.

"Oh, so I can't provide for my family?" Anger flushed the man's face. He stopped eating and glared at her.

"I guess that's right." She met his cruel stare. "I'm no magician.   I used to fix good meals — at least you thought I was a good cook when we were first married." She fell silent, contemplating a painful memory. "But that was an eternity ago — ten years, and seven children, one of them dead."

"That's a lot of appreciation for me working twelve hours a day in that miserable mill," her husband shouted, ignoring her last comment. Then he turned to look at the children. "Is that the way you kids think of your dad, too?" Their eyes were large with fright; they made no replies. Bernice put down her spoon and lowered her head. David began to sob quietly. Only Cliff met his father's accusing stare. He was old enough to know that his dad's temper was dangerous. He said nothing, but his brown eyes never wavered from those of his father.

"And while I'm out working," the man shouted, turning his attention back to the woman who hunched in fear in her chair, "you're out gallivanting around. Don't you give me that hush-up look! The kids know it!"

"You're no saint, mister." Her eyes blazed with hurt and humiliation. "I saw that girl sitting in your lap at the bar the other night when I went down there looking for you."

"You had no business coming snooping after me," he flared back and started to rise. "You shut your mouth or I'll — "

Suddenly the bread knife flew through the air, whizzed past his head, and fell against the far wall. Switzer looked to where it had fallen harmlessly, his mind raging with anger and fear. "That's it!" he shouted. "I've had enough!" He clenched his fists and, breathing heavily, turned and hurried up the stairs. Then Cliff could hear him rummaging through things.

"Eat your supper, children, pay no attention," the woman said.

Cliff tried to eat but his stomach churned so much he was afraid he would vomit. It was always like this — raging, arguing, confusion, upheaval — never happy like other families. He slipped out of his chair and went to stand outside on the back porch facing the dirty alley. He could still hear his father upstairs, changing clothes or maybe packing his things. He'd done that before.

His father was suddenly behind him at the door, in a brown suit and black derby hat, carrying a small bag. Cliff was right — he'd been packing.

"Well, goodbye, son. I don't know when I'll see you again." Cliff thought to himself that there was no hope now that things would change for the better. He watched wordlessly as his father walked out the door, down the alley, and out of their lives.

<hr/>

The sun sizzled down on Cliff as he maneuvered through the berry patch. His faded overalls hung loosely on his skinny frame. With heaving strokes he lifted dead brush with a pitchfork and tossed it onto a pile. His sunburned face was etched with sweaty streaks of dirt. He stopped to catch his breath and wipe his forehead with a rag from his back pocket. He glanced longingly across the pasture to distant trees along the creek. "Boy, would a swim feel good now," he said aloud, longing for relief from the heat. But he couldn't leave his duties without plenty of trouble crashing around him, even if the heat justified the needed break.

Cliff lifted the pitchfork again, not wanting to dwell on such futility. He had more important worries. When he finished the berries, he still had the cows to tend and the barn to clean. Then, after supper, when the others were in the parlor playing checkers, he would have to wash the dishes. His acquired custodians saved all their dishes until evening, then he had to do them all at once, pumping water from the cistern, heating it on the coal stove, slopping suds to his elbows, and finally drying each dish on a well-washed feed sack.

Work was his constant companion. Even when he'd been at home, he had often cooked the meager meals, thinned the milk with water to make it go around, and kept his brothers and sisters fed. He hadn't minded that so much because they were his family; but these folks were strangers. And that was part of the problem.

"You can sure tell I'm an outsider," he muttered as he threw another forkful onto the pile. "They're always saying, 'You have to earn your keep.' They work the daylights out of me, and they even begrudge me what I eat." He felt his body tense with

29

suppressed anger. "She's mean, too! Danged mean! Gets my ear and twists and pulls it. Like that time I was cleaning the barn and had such a headache. I thought if I laid down a minute, maybe my headache'd quit. But boy! There she was in a minute! Jerked me out of that straw and pulled my ear all the way to the house."

Cliff kept his complaints to himself. He had to. He wasn't used to an easy life, anyway — it had always been a struggle. But there was a difference between helping out to "earn your keep" and being treated like a pest and a bother. From his first day at this place, he'd known he wasn't wanted, but he'd tried to tolerate the situation with good grace. Now his patience and strength were waning.

"Where are my brothers and sisters? That's what's really worrying me," he thought. "I remember seeing Ma give Frieda to Grandma Moss there on the street corner. Frieda must still be with them. But where are the others?" He had promised to keep track of them. After five weeks of work and worry on this farm, he felt he had to take some action. But what could he do? There had to be some way to get back home.

He slumped down on the baking earth, searching for a solution. Engrossed in his thoughts, he pulled up a weed and chewed on it. The lazy drone of locusts made his spirit seem heavier.

He forced himself to think of a solution. Once he'd heard if you prayed you could maybe get help. He didn't know much about religion — he'd never gone to Sunday school or been inside a church. In fact, he seldom set foot in a public school, what with one thing and another. But at Nellie's funeral he'd heard someone speak of praying.

"Might as well try praying," he decided. But where? He'd heard somewhere that you had to kneel. And he was sure the words had to be said out loud for it to be right. But there wasn't anyplace he could go where they couldn't hear him — they always kept track of his whereabouts. At night he even shared a bed upstairs with another boy, their granson. It was almost as if they expected he might try to run away. That had crossed his mind. But it was too far back home, and he had no money. He'd probably end up in even more trouble if he tried something like that.

Now — where to pray? He thought of the barn. The fields. No, there was always someone around. He cast about for a likely spot, safe from eavesdroppers. What about the toilet? It was a long way from the house and it was the one place where he could be alone. "Yep, that's where I'll do my praying," he decided, jumping to his feet and spitting out the weed. He tackled the rest of his work with fervor, now that he had a plan.

Right after the noon meal he headed toward the old outhouse, following the worn path to the honeysuckle-covered gray board shack.

A lonesome darkness shrouded him as he hooked the latch and knelt down on the bare wood. He tried to ignore the swirling flies and suffocating odor. He folded his hands and tried to concentrate. How was it that preacher had talked at Nellie's funeral?

"Almighty God," he began, then paused. "This here's Cliff Switzer, from Corning, New York. I never talked to you before, but you know my little sister, Nellie. She's an angel up there, they say."

He put it straight to the Lord. "I don't know what's happening to my family. Please take me away from here and send me back to them." He spoke as loud as he dared. "Get me out of here. I've tried to get along with these people, but I can't. All I am is an extra mouth to feed — somebody to pick on. I catch it for everything. I've got to get away from here and find my family."

He stopped, shifted on his knees, and waited. His mind began to wander over the wretched events of the past months. He was pretty sure Howard, the next-oldest, was with Grandma and Grandpa Switzer. He was their favorite and always spent summers with them at their farm. But Harold, Bernice, and David — they could be anywhere. Even roaming the streets, lost and hungry. Tears began welling, but heck, he was eleven years old, a man almost, and men didn't cry. He wiped his eyes with a thin arm.

Cliff could never forget his folks' last fight. It wasn't long after that his Ma had told the children she didn't figure she could raise them — "didn't have time," she'd said. So she took a job in a cafe and the kids took care of themselves. Cliff tried to carry responsibility for them all, and Bernice, "the little mother" of the brood, watched over the two littlest ones, David and Frieda.

Cliff recalled the day his mother came home from work and bluntly told him he was being sent to live with relatives of her brother's wife's parents. He had come here. Since she'd given Frieda away the day before he left, he suspected the others might have been farmed out, too.

It wasn't much of a family, he had to admit — always poor as ragpickers, living in miserable places, moving with clocklike regularity. They were sometimes evicted for not paying their rent. They had never once had a decent Christmas. Oh, Dad had always managed to put up a little tree, but there were never any presents — not like the neighbor kids had. Just an orange and maybe a few pieces of ribbon candy. Somehow these circumstances had forged a deep bond among the children, and they clung together and tried to find happiness in the smallest things.

Cliff began his petition again. "I'm the oldest, you see, so I have to take care of the others. I don't want to lose track."

A rude shout from the house jolted him. "Clifford Switzer, get in here! There's work to do!" He got up uncertainly, not sure he'd made his case clear to the Almighty. How did you know if your prayer was heard? he wondered. Well, he'd try again tomorrow.

Day after day he continued to pray in the outhouse, putting his heart and soul into it. This praying business was hard on a fellow, he found, because tears came to his eyes whenever he prayed. He cried and prayed, and prayed and cried. He hoped the others didn't notice his eyes when they were red and swollen.

At nights Cliff lay awake thinking of his family. He often wished his mother knew how much his father had cared for her. Like that one night when she ran off while his dad was working at the glass factory. When his dad came home in the morning, he found the fire had gone out and the children huddled in one bed in the bone-cold house. He built up the fire, all the time raging over and over, "Oh, curse her! But I love her! Curse her! But I love her!"

But when the two were together, his father never seemed to tell her things like that. And she never let him know how it hurt her when she saw that woman on his lap at the saloon.

Looking back, it seemed to Cliff that he had always been hungry. And the hand-me-downs! His dad had one sister with two daughters, and their family was doing well. When those girls outgrew their clothes, the aunt passed them on. "Here, Ivan," she would say, appearing at their door with a big box, "Your children can make use of these things." His dad didn't like it, but the children wore the things because they had nothing else. Dresses were made over to fit his sisters. Cliff recalled with humiliation that he and his brothers had often worn the girls' shoes.

Sometimes he would look around at other families — the children happy at home, the parents considerate and caring — and wish theirs could be like that. But it never was. But even so, he missed his family. Anything was better than being all alone like this and not knowing where everyone else was.

One evening, after many of Cliff's visits to the outhouse, the grownups announced to Cliff, "Get your things together. We're taking you back to Corning."

It seemed to come out of the blue. Cliff was amazed. "Well, the Lord has answered my prayers at last," he thought. Joyful, he packed his few belongings in a paper sack and was ready to go within minutes.

But they took him only part way — as far as Painted Post — then gave him a nickel for the streetcar ride from there into Corning. He got off and made his way to the place where he'd last seen his family — the tiny, dingy apartment with the front door facing the alley. He found it empty.

"They've moved," said the old black woman who owned the apartment house. "Your mother is a cook at a cafe on Water Street."

"Are my brothers and sisters with her?" Cliff asked.

"Don't know. Tell her she still owes me *rent.*" The door slammed in his face.

Cliff knew the town, having worked briefly as a telegram delivery boy when one of his many illnesses — a breaking-out on his face — had kept him from school. He headed up Water Street, sack in hand, in the dark.

As he went around to the back door of the cafe he saw lights in a shack out back. He knocked. Harold flung open the door and shouted, "Hey, look who's here!" Bernice and David ran to see as Cliff stepped in, grinning. He searched their faces. Bernice looked pale, but she was thrilled to see him. Her brown eyes shone beneath her dark bangs. David smiled and sucked his thumb, and Harold looked like the same old "bean pole."

"Boy, am I glad to see you!" Cliff said, tousling Bernice's hair and giving David a hug. He socked Harold's arm affectionately. "Where are Frieda and Howard? How's everybody doing?"

After learning that Frieda and Howard were with their grandparents, as he'd suspected, Cliff went to the back door of the cafe and slipped inside. It was a sleezy, greasy-spoon place he'd been in before. An oniony odor wafted on the breeze of a small fan that stirred the heated air. His mother stood at the big stove with her back to him. When she turned and saw him, he could tell that her expression had grown even more grim. She wore an old housedress with a big white cook's apron spattered with food stains. Her eyeglasses were pinched on her nose as usual, secured by a chain that fastened with a large hairpin into her upswept hair.

It was hard to believe she was only twenty-seven years old, Cliff thought. She looked so old! Her wide brown eyes were empty of emotion as she surveyed him. At last she said, "Well, I'm glad you're back. Now you can go with the others."

"Where's that?" Cliff asked, fear welling in his chest.

"To the orphanage."

"Ma," he began his plea, "you don't have to send us away. I already seen the kids out back, and it looks like we're getting along okay right here. Now that I'm back, I can help. You don't need to send us to no orphanage!"

Cliff was a sturdy boy. Though slight in build, he had tremendous endurance and fortitude. He was sure if he could talk her out of this crazy plan to send them away, things would straighten out. He would give anything he had to keep them together.

"Have you heard from Dad?" he asked, trying to change the subject. Maybe his father would intervene.

"Your father deserted us, you know that," she answered in a flat tone. "No one knows where he is. Some say he left the country. And I don't have the time or energy, let alone the money, to raise this family alone. You're going, and so are the others." She turned and began stirring the soup pot. He knew there would be no more discussion.

The next two days hurried by as Cliff resumed his role of father-protector. Over and over Cliff tried to reassure them, "I'll take care of you. And we'll all stay together."

But Cliff was helpless against circumstance. Bernice took ill with stomach pains, and when she failed to respond to home remedies, her mother carted her off to the doctor. She came back alone with the news that Bernice had been hospitalized. The trouble was not diagnosed and no one could visit her.

The next day, a welfare agent came to see the children and took Cliff and Harold downtown with her in her little car. She ushered them into a fine clothing store. "These boys need suits," she told the clerk. After wearing hand-me-downs for years, Cliff was astounded to hear a stranger tell him, "Just pick out any suit you like. The bill will be taken care of."

The clerk displayed several good-looking suits for Cliff and Harold's inspection, and Cliff felt giddy with excitement. His first real suit! He took his time deciding, then selected a brown corduroy with knee pants. Harold chose a similar style in blue.

Back in the car, Cliff and Harold were lavish with their thanks. The woman explained it was part of her job to outfit children before they left for the orphanages. She told them they would be leaving on the evening train.

"But what about Bernice?" Cliff prodded. "I thought we'd all be going together."

"Since Bernice is ill, she and David will join you two later."

Later that day the boys, dressed in their new suits, went with their mother to a photography shop. She said she wanted to have a picture made of them before they left. Then she took them to the train. They waited so long that both had dozed off by the time it finally came. A big man got off and came over to her as she sat with them on a bench. "You Mrs. Switzer?" he asked.

"Yes."

"Are these the boys?"

"Yes."

"Well, we ain't got much time. Better get 'em on."

Cliff and Harold stumbled toward the train, ready to climb on. Trailing after them, their mother said, "Ain't you even gonna kiss me goodbye?"

Tired and angry, Cliff answered in total defeat, "Heck, I don't care if I kiss you goodbye or not, 'cause you're givin' your kids away."

"Oh, Clifford," she whispered, drawing back.

Harold leaned forward and mechanically kissed his mother. Then Cliff stepped forward and threw his arms around her neck. He kissed her hard on the cheek.

They climbed on the train as the woman turned and walked away in the dark. As the train groaned out of the station, Cliff looked back through the window and saw her in the shadows, her face in her hands — sobbing.

35

5

To Touch an Angel

Bernice's eyes fluttered, and she looked around the room. It was white. Everything was white — the walls, the curtains, the bedspread. She was in a hospital.

Gradually she gained consciousness. A nurse at her side stroked her brow. "I'm thirsty," she whispered, and she was given a sip of water.

"You've been a pretty sick little girl," the nurse said gently. "But you're doing fine now."

"What happened?"

"The doctors will tell you about that later," the nurse soothed, patting Bernice's hand. "Just relax and be still."

Bernice closed her eyes again. Once her memory began to return, she felt a deep ache inside, for she couldn't blot out the unhappiness she remembered.

When the nurse left on an errand, Bernice was surprised to hear another voice in the room. She had thought she was alone.

"I'm glad you finally woke up. It's boring. There's nobody to talk to."

"Who are you?"

"I'm Mitzi. I'm your roomate. I'm 14 years old and I had an operation like you did. But yours was worse. You were real sick for a long time."

As Bernice turned to look at Mitzi a sharp pain raced through her body. "Ooh," she groaned. But she had turned enough to see the bed beside the window, and in it a smiling girl watching her.

"What did we have?"

"Appendicitis. Don't you remember having a terrible pain in your stomach?"

"Yes, I remember. Ma took me to a doctor."

"Well, I guess your appendix burst, because they said you have per-ten-i-tis. That means a bad infection in your stomach. I heard them say you were in dangerous condition. You must have been here a month, because I've been here two weeks."

"Has my mother come to see me?"

"Yes. I've seen her. Nobody else came, though."

Bernice was afraid to ask more about her mother — whether she had come often, or what she'd said.

Mitzi went on, "Now that you're awake, I wish you'd take some of my flowers. My family brought me these bouquets, but they just fill up the windowsill. Would you like some for your bed-side table?"

"Oh," Bernice brightened. "That would be nice."

Later, when the doctor found she'd awakened, he brought a little doll for her. It was the first doll she'd ever had. She tucked it in under the blankets, its painted face sticking out from the covers. "A doll of my own," she said, over and over.

As Bernice began feeling better, she took to teasing the doctor. Her brothers always liked her teasing, and she thought maybe he would, too. "You should cut off that mustache," she told him.

The nurse, standing by, picked up the theme. "Some day," she told Bernice, "we're going to put whipped cream on his mustache, and turn a kitty loose on him, and the kitty will lick his mustache off."

Bernice laughed so hard her side hurt. "That's just silly," she giggled.

A few days later the doctor came into Bernice's room and she noticed his mustache was gone. The nurse who was with him said, "Well, Bernice, we did it. We put whipped cream on, turned the cat loose, and look — no mustache!" She was tall, blonde, and pretty, and she winked as she smiled at Bernice.

"Oh, doctor, did it hurt?" Bernice asked in mock sympathy. He ruffled her hair and laughed. She smiled up at him; she decided she liked this man.

And then one day, Bernice was told there was a visitor to see her. Her dad.

"Hi, Bernice," he said, tiptoeing into the room, holding his derby in front of him with both hands.

37

Bernice took one look at this once-loved face, this person who had hurt her so deeply, and silently turned her face to the wall.

"I heard by the grapevine you were sick . . . you were sick real bad. I just wanted to come over and say hello. Are you feeling better?" There was only silence.

"Bernice, speak to me. You know you were always the apple of my eye. My oldest daughter. My helper." No reply.

Mitzi watched the drama in amazement. She saw the man standing patiently, humbly. And each time there was no answer to his remarks, he slumped a bit more. The derby sagged, too.

Finally, Mitzi spoke up. "Bernice! You stop that! You look at your daddy! Talk to him. He came here to see how you're doing."

But she wouldn't. The ache inside was even worse than the pains from her surgery. Bernice just kept her face turned to the wall and bit her lip. The tears trickled onto her pillow. Finally the man turned, and still holding the derby with both hands in front of him, he tiptoed toward the door.

For a long time Bernice kept her head averted. Her heart was breaking, but she knew better than to hand it back to him to hurt again. She said very little the rest of the day. When Mitzi questioned her about her behavior, Bernice said only: "He hurt me so bad. I don't ever want to see him again."

❦

"Where are you taking me?" Bernice's brown eyes were wide with uncertainty.

"A convalescent home," answered the man who was waiting for her.

Her friend, the doctor, was seeing her off. He explained, "That just means you'll be at a place to help you get stronger, with other children your age, too." He kissed her goodbye. "You get better quick," he called after her.

She was delivered to the Home, which was an estate-like mansion with large gardens around it. As Bernice was being admitted, she met another little girl about her age, a black child, Ruth.

One day, when the two were cleaning a bathroom, her friend said to Bernice, "I wish I was white, like you are."

At six, Bernice felt it was all a matter of scrubbing. "I tell you what I'll do," she said, "I'll get soap and a rag, and I'll wash you real good, then maybe you'll get white, too."

38

Bernice sat her down on the floor and she scrubbed and scrubbed the little black arms and legs. Then they went to look in the mirror. "I think you're a little bit whiter," Bernice nodded.

They went back to scrubbing, but a rough voice interrupted their efforts. "What are you doing?" boomed a supervisor.

"I'm trying to make her white, like me." Bernice stepped back from the woman, confused at the question.

"You'll be punished for this," the supervisor said with a deep scowl.

Bernice grew to fear the staff at this home, because these and other disciplinary actions were never explained. She began to fantasize a life different from the one she was living, and unlike her past. Figuring strongly in this fantasy was a little angel, whose picture hung on a mantel in the large sleeping room.

One night Bernice's yearning for the beautiful angel — for anything pretty and happy — became so strong that she decided to climb up and take it. After the others were asleep she shoved back the covers and stealthily sneaked past the other beds. She crept to the mantel where she began stacking chairs, one on top of another. She hoped she could climb high enough to touch the angel — to make it her own. But as she tried to balance on her homemade ladder, the chairs toppled, and down she went. She wasn't hurt, but there was a terrific clatter.

The other little girls sat up, rubbing their eyes. Some began crying, asking, "What happened?" The housemother rushed in, quickly surveying the situation. "Get back in bed, all of you," she ordered. "Bernice was climbing on some chairs and she fell off."

She took Bernice's hand and ushered her back to bed. Tucking her in, the housemother asked, "Why did you do that? You could have hurt yourself."

"I wanted to touch the angel."

"But it's not yours, Bernice. It's there for everyone to look at."

Bernice began to weep. "I'm so lonesome," she whispered. "I miss my brothers and my baby sister. We've always been together and now I'm all alone."

"Don't you like to play with the other children here?"

"It's not the same, ma'am," she shook her head. "Not the same as famb-ly."

"So you miss your family. Perhaps we can arrange a visit with your brothers. They're not far from here. I'll see what can be done. Now you get to sleep."

6

"We're together!"

A sleek black car swept over the bridge into the city. Grownups in the front seat were talking to one another, while the other little girls in the back seat entertained themselves with chatter and games. But Bernice just stared out the car window. More and more she was beginning to realize that the grownups held control of her life and her hopes. She listened to their talk for hints of their plans. How she yearned to be home again in Corning, with all her family! But at least she was on her way to spend the day with Cliff, Harold, and David.

Abruptly the car swung into a tree-arched brick drive and chugged past wide green lawns toward a mansion. Bernice saw children playing in a side yard and caught a glimpse of rose bushes in bloom.

"There they are!" she called happily when she spied her brothers sitting on the stone steps of a smaller building. Their bare feet dangled idly as they waited for Bernice.

"Cliff! Harold! David!" she dashed from the car to greet them with a hug.

"Hey, little sis," Cliff said affectionately, holding her at arm's length. "You're gettin' awful tall!" She giggled and answered teasingly, "And you got glasses!"

"How long can you stay, Bernice?" Harold wondered.

As if in answer, a woman called from the car, "We'll pick you up at three so you'll be back for dinner. Have fun. And not too much sun!"

"Are you all right?" she asked the boys in a hushed tone, as she put her arm protectively on little David's shoulder. "I have a lot to tell you."

"Us, too," Harold confided.

"I get to be first," Cliff announced proudly. "I want to show you the corn I hoe. Come on." He led the others behind the buildings to an open space with waving green leaves. "Here it is," he beamed. "I do this whole patch by myself. And I ain't never hoed before."

Bernice wasn't sure what "hoeing" was, but she said enthusiastically, "It sure looks good!"

"Let's walk on the trail into the woods a little ways," Cliff suggested. "They have a bunch of city kids up here for the summer, so it's pretty crowded." He looked around carefully; he did not want eavesdroppers at this reunion.

Bernice held David's hand and followed her two brothers down the dusty path. "I couldn't have come today if those other girls hadn't had brothers here, too. I wanted to come real bad." She began relating her experiences at the hospital and told about the doctor she liked so well. They came to a bench and sat down. Then she said: "And Dad came to see me in the hospital!"

"He did!" Cliff exploded. "When? What'd he say? Think he might get us back?"

"No. It was a long time ago," Bernice said sadly. "I would not even look at him. He'd hurt me so bad." She tried in vain to describe the sadness she felt.

But Cliff pressed for more information. "You mean you never even looked at him?"

"No," she said simply. "He went away."

"I guess that's the way he wants it," Cliff shook his head.

"But it wasn't long till I got out of the hospital, and went to a place for sick girls to get well. Now I'm feeling lots better. But I still miss all of you so much," she finished sweetly.

"Tell about us now, Cliff," Harold prompted.

"Well, after you went to the hospital, Ma told us we was goin' to the orphans' home. I guess she was waiting for you to get better to send David, because he didn't come here for quite awhile. But she took Harold and me to the train. When we got to New York a man took us to a great big office building while somebody typed up a lot of papers. There was about eight kids there, all going to the same place. Pretty soon they took us down to the subway and put us all on a train and told the conductor where to put us off.

41

"The train run along underground awhile, then we popped up out of the ground and run quite a ways on the top of the ground. Then we stopped here at Valhalla and the conductor put us off."

"Wasn't nobody to meet us," Harold put in. "So we just walked around together."

"And we saw this wooden thing with a big steel ring hanging there, and a steel bar laying on it," Cliff continued. "Well, one kid picked it up and started hammering the ring with it, and gee, it rang out something terrible! Made an awful nice noise. Well, people came a-running from all over town. Wanted to know where the fire was! It was their fire bell! Made 'em pretty mad," Cliff giggled with mischief. "They wanted to know where we was going, and we said 'orphans home.' They said, 'Just walk up this road and you'll come to it,' " He pointed to the road Bernice had just traveled.

"So we started walkin' up the road, and a guy in a car come down, stopped us and wanted to know who we was and we told him. He said, 'Get in — I was s'posed to meet the train but I was late.' He turned around and took us here. There was about a hundred kids all around."

"What's it like?" Bernice wanted to know.

"Strict." Cliff summed up their months in one word. "When we got here they took our clothes, and made us take showers, and checked us for lice. Then they put their own clothes on us. These aren't much, but I guess they can't get none better for orphans. Then they put us up in Brown Cottage, over there," he motioned.

"Do you work? I do." Bernice wanted to compare chores.

"Heck, yeah. We all do chores. Scrub floors, make our beds, work in the garden," Harold put in.

"Seems like it don't make much difference what I do," said Cliff. "Good or bad, I get bopped on the head or slapped. Mealtimes, even. The faculty members sit at the head of the table, and they have the right to reach over and cuff you if you do something wrong."

"He eggs 'em on, Bernice," said Harold.

"Well, maybe I do," Cliff admitted. He dug his toes into the dirt under the bench before continuing his story. "I been working in the kitchen. That's nothing new to me — I been cookin' for you kids since you was babies. Here they don't allow the kids no sweets — not even sugar on their oatmeal, even though the faculty members get pie and cake. But I pulled a fast one on 'em." He chuckled with satisfaction. "Once when I was cookin', I dumped sugar in the oatmeal while it was on the stove. The kids really liked that."

"But Cliff, are they really mean to you? They don't treat me bad at my place," Bernice persisted.

"Let me tell ya!"

"But you do like hoeing. You said so." Bernice tried to look on the bright side.

"Yeah, I've learned a lot about farming. We work in the field most of the time."

"Cliff gets to lead the mule for the others while the boys cultivate the corn. Sometimes we get to ride the mule." Harold added. "And when we whitewashed the inside of the barn, I got a white face," he laughed.

"We get all the milk we want," Cliff went on, "cause we got a dairy here. The older boys milk the cows. Wanta see the cows, Bernice?" He jumped up and led the way, following a path that led past a gray cottage, a white cottage, and over to a big barn. In the gloomy atmosphere, Bernice wrinkled her nose at the smells of cows and hay. Her brothers bravely stood on the mangers and patted the cows' faces, but she held David back at a safe distance. At last Bernice was able to lure them to quieter places. "Show me the big house," she begged.

They trudged back to the main house and swarmed through the enormous wooden doors of the mansion. Bernice found herself in a wide hallway. "It's so pretty — everything shines," she said with awe.

"Ought to," Cliff was quick to explain. "We scrub the whole place every morning. They give out little wooden buckets, scrub brushes, and rags. We use soap they make right here. And we kneel on little boards while we scrub."

"I help scrub at my place, too," Bernice nodded.

"In here's the rumpus room," Harold said. "Look at this piano. It has a lay-down top. When it's cold, the kids all bunch up together and get under the piano. Kinda like baby chicks."

"Who takes care of David?" Bernice asked. David had been strangely silent during the tour. "Do they make him work?"

"He's too little. He gets a lot of spankings down in the furnace room, 'cause he wets his pants."

"Oh, David," Bernice reproached him. "You shouldn't." She looked down at David, who'd settled on the couch and was playing a solitary game of "eensy, weensy spider." He made no reply.

"I work in the sewing room and the laundry, too," Cliff bragged. "That's how I got my glasses. This supervisor wanted me to fold towels so the stitching matched, and I couldn't do it right. They took me to a doctor in New York a couple times, and I finally got glasses. Well, then I could fold the towels right, and this supervisor, she told me, 'See, I knew you could do it if you wanted to.' She acted like I was just lazy."

Harold said to Cliff, "Don't complain too much, buddy. Tell Sis about the surprise."

"Oh, yeah," said Cliff. "Well, Mr. Nelson — he's a nice guy here — lets me help him with things like painting, tinkering, fixing stuff. Guess he thinks a lot of me, 'cause not too long ago, know what he said?"

"What?" Bernice responded.

"Said he'd miss me when I go away. I said, 'You mean when I go back home?' He said, 'No, when you go out to Texas on the train!' "

"What does he mean?" Bernice asked, fearfully.

"Well, I says, 'Who's going?' and he said, 'Some other kids from this place. The two redheads and some others.' And I said, 'I ain't goin' nowhere without my brothers and sister.' And Bernice, he said, 'Don't you worry. You'll all be together.' "

Bernice felt confused.

"Texas? Why would they send us to Texas?" asked Harold. "I can't figure it out."

"If they want to get rid of us, why don't they send us back to Ma?" Bernice wondered.

"No. Mr. Nelson said we'd never go back home. We're wards of charity now," he said, "whatever that means."

None of them knew whether this was good news or bad. The children looked at one another wordlessly, and instinctively huddled in a close circle, with David in the center.

The bell rang for lunch. Their family was always being pulled apart by the orphanage's ways, Cliff grumbled. "But maybe if we all go on a train somewhere, it'll be nice. It just has to be." He and the others joined the crowd of children already streaming inside to eat.

The day passed quickly. Soon the black car wheeled up the drive and whisked Bernice from her brothers.

The children's lives went on as before. As the weeks passed, preparations were made to take them West, but they knew nothing of these plans. Mr. Nelson gave no more hints to Cliff. The children could only wait and hope.

❧ ⚜ ☙

"Hey, Bernice! Over here!" Cliff jumped to wave his arm high above the crowd as he shoved his way toward Bernice. Her face lit up when she saw him. Jammed with milling travelers, the station was hot and grimy, and a layer of soot seemed to cover everything. Jostled and pushed by the crowd, Bernice finally managed to move near Cliff, who had Harold and David with him.

"We're together!" Cliff grinned. "I was afraid they weren't bringing you. Look, they gave us back our own suits. The ones the social worker bought for us." Cliff proudly pulled back a tattered coat to show Bernice his corduroy suit. "It's tighter this year, but still looks like new."

"They just gave me what they had," Bernice looked down at her second-hand outfit. "My shoes are so big I have to curl my toes so they don't fall off."

She turned to David. "Hi, David. You sure look nice. Aren't you excited, honey? You're gonna get a new mommy!" David's plump cheeks dimpled. His brothers had also been telling him about a new mama.

"Better hurry," Cliff said. "I don't want to miss the train." He herded them toward the long, dark green cars that hissed puffs of steam.

They stood at the back of a group of children gathered around a tall woman. She was waving a list and calling to be heard. "I'm your escort, Miss Hill! Is everyone here? Please answer when I call your name!" And she began reading from the list.

Cliff guessed that there must be about thirty kids. He knew there were eight from his own orphanage. That woman with Miss Hill was probably her assistant, he thought. Suddenly, Cliff recognized Miss Hill. "Harold," he whispered, "that's the woman who took us to dinner. Remember? When we were on our way to the Farm School last year?"

"Yeah," Harold answered. "Hope she don't remember us!"

"Why?" Bernice wanted to know.

" 'Cause we embarrassed her," Cliff explained. "She took us to a fancy restaurant and we grabbed at the food like usual. Made a big mess. She scolded us for it. Said we didn't have no manners. Heck, what can you expect?" he muttered defensively.

45

"Well, she doesn't look like she'd hurt us," Bernice surveyed the woman.

As the children clustered on the platform, two men carried a stack of large boxes to Miss Hill. "Oh, the sandwiches. Good." She peered into a box. "And the bakeries' donations of sticky buns. Put them in our car — right there." She pointed toward their coach. Abruptly, the two women began directing the children onto the train. Confused by the noise, the crush of people, and the fear of becoming lost, the youngsters stumbled and shoved their way toward the steps as the conductor called out: "All aboard for all points west."

❧ ❧ ❧

Thirty children. Two chaperones. A hot, sooty, fifteen-hundred-mile train ride was under way. It was September 17, 1920.

❧ ❧ ❧

At intervals, cheese and butter sandwiches were brought out. Each child was given an orange, and cups of milk were distributed. That night the children curled up on the seats to sleep.

Cliff's sleep was restless, for once again he dreamed his terrible dream — that his mother abandoned them in a swirling flood. When he awoke his throat felt dry and his fists were clenched. The dream strengthened a feeling that had been growing in him. He stared out at the passing landscape, deep in his own thoughts.

From the moment Cliff's mother had told him she was sending them all to an orphanage, that she was not going to try to keep the family together, a coldness began to wrap around Cliff's heart. He did not know it, but that deadly coldness was hate. Cliff had begun to hate his mother for her weaknesses, for her indifference to their plight. He made no effort to curtail its growth. And each time something at the orphanage had gone wrong, each time he was punished, humiliated, or ridiculed, he allowed the arrow of guilt to whisk past him, and lodge in the figure of his mother. Cliff's thoughts continually accused her. *She* forsook her own flesh and blood; it was *she* who had started this whole long, miserable chain of events.

Cliff was just eleven years old, and didn't realize that this bitterness would cling to him, affecting his life in many ways. Like any child, he did what came naturally, and hating his mother had begun to seem very natural. Soon he was unable to rid himself of it, to let it go. Like a shield, he clutched his bitterness, afraid of a new rejection, or of a very old one.

But Cliff did not share his feelings with Harold, Bernice, and David. As he sat with them, he vowed to become the father they'd lost. He, the oldest, had always taken care of them, and he always would. Harold cried and cried and that tore at Cliff's heart. Bernice comforted little David, telling him over and over that he'd find a new mama when they got off the train. Cliff's protective feelings surged, and he repeated his promise to them: "No matter what happens, I'll always know where you are, and I'll take care of you."

Miss Hill tried to keep everyone's spirits up, too. If she remembered Cliff's and Harold's behavior in the restaurant, she did not let them know it.

In Missouri, many of the children got off with the other chaperone, leaving just eleven with Miss Hill.

"Might as well finish the sticky buns," she told them. "We'll be getting off soon."

As they devoured the rolls, Miss Hill took note of their appearance. It was time for a general cleanup. "Look at you" she chided gently. "You're not fit to meet anyone that way. Porter — can the children wash up now?"

"Sorry, ma'am," came the reply. "Water's all gone."

"Alright, then," she responded. "We'll do the best we can. Take out your handkerchiefs — you each have one — and spit, then scrub your hands and face. You can't get new germs from your own saliva," she explained, "and you shouldn't be seen until you're cleaned up."

Then they were told to gather their things. They were getting off the train.

"Texas?" Cliff wondered aloud.

"Abilene, Kansas!" shouted the conductor as if in answer. The train wheezed to a stop.

"Right over there," said Miss Hill, pointing to a two-story white frame structure beside the track. "The Union Pacific Hotel. That's where we're going."

7

Homes in Abilene

The old Sealy Theater was wide, and seated many spectators. A heavy rain had prevented farmers from plowing that day. Row upon row of people filled the main floor, and the crowd spilled into the balcony.

All eyes focused on the stage, which was framed with elaborate gilded scrollwork. On each side frosted tulip fixtures held flickering gas flames. Across the stage were eleven chairs, and the spectators gazed at the children seated in them. Even the most charitable observer would have to admit that this was a motley group of youngsters. Their clothes were ill-fitting, and their faces showed the ravages of poverty, disease, or simple sadness. Indeed, these orphans from the east looked far more than pitiful. Some might have thought them undesirable.

Cliff perceived this as he viewed the mob of unknown faces. He felt uncomfortable and self-conscious. "Here we sit — just looking at them all staring at us," he whispered to Harold.

He had understood that he and the others were going to find homes, but he wondered why they had to be on stage. Perhaps they were supposed to give a performance. As far as he knew, that's what stages were for.

"Do you s'pose they want us to put on a show?'" he whispered.

"No," came a whisper from down the row. "They just want to look us over and pick out the kid they want."

Picked by looks? Nothing could be worse! Cliff glanced at his brothers and sister, and a rock grew in the pit of his stomach.

Miss Hill began to speak to the crowd. She told about each of the children. Cliff thought it was sort of interesting, learning about those little redheaded boys' background, and hearing how the others had come to be here. Then Miss Hill began talking about the Switzers. "None of the children has attended school," she said, apologetically, and Cliff cringed. That would not help them find homes, he thought. But it was the truth.

Cliff heard a familiar sob — Bernice was crying. Oh, no! Now what would people think of her? Would they assume she was hard to handle, spoiled, troublesome? Cliff's anguish increased.

Miss Hill went quickly to Bernice and asked, "What is it, dear?"

Bernice wailed loudly, "I just don't want any of those mamas out there. I want my *own mama!*"

Bernice knew her wish would never come true, for her mama had let her go. That was what made her cry so.

"Please, Bernice," Miss Hill tried to control the child. "If you just stop crying, I'll buy you a little gift."

"You will?" Bernice asked, sniffing.

"I sure will. Today."

The proceedings went on.

***

The air was humid and heavy. Men wiped trickles of sweat from their temples, and the women dabbed discreetly at their foreheads. Miss Hill had requested that interested persons come forward. The thick air seemed to blanket the audience and those on stage. No one stirred.

Then one couple stood up. "We'd sort of like to have that little boy," they said, pointing to a child, "but we're just not sure about his past . . ."

"Well, come on then," Miss Hill invited, "let's just sit down here and talk about it." This meeting was requiring more than the usual amount of persuasion. She'd found other audiences in general much more interested in children.

David, unable to sit still, had quietly scooted to the edge of the stage, where he began playing with the darkened footlights. Several more people stood up and began moving toward the front.

A stout, friendly-looking man of about thirty-five pointed toward David. "I think I'd like to take that chubby fellow there," he said. "But I'm not sure. My wife's been sick, and couldn't come today. She said, 'Go and pick out a girl,' but I can't resist that lit-

49

tle boy. If you could take care of him a few days till my wife can see him, we'll settle on it then."

"I think we can arrange that, Mr. — " Miss Hill hesitated.

"Weber's the name. J. J. Weber."

"All right."

After a lengthy session, only two children, not counting David, had been offered permanent homes. Miss Hill began asking if people would be willing to care for a child temporarily, until further decisions could be made.

A tall, handsome man with thick, graying hair stepped forward. "Afternoon, Miss Hill. I'm Ott Callahan, and my brother-in-law, John Middleton, took one of your orphan kids last time you were here. I heard Mr. Weber needs a place for the little boy. I'm offering our home to him for the weekend." He turned and smiled toward David.

"And if you don't find a place for her," he added, "we could keep his sister, too — the girl who was crying."

Miss Hill thanked him. Many more offers were heard, while the children squirmed anxiously. Finally Miss Hill was ready to announce the results: two of the children were placed, several more had temporary homes, and the futures of the rest were still to be decided. When Harold heard his name and Cliff's mentioned, and realized they had nowhere to go, he began to cry.

A quiet, dark-haired woman immediately arose and marched with determination to the stage. She explained that she could not stand by if she could be of help. She introduced herself as Mrs. Will Collins and said that although she couldn't keep a child permanently, "I'd like to take this little boy for a few days." She put her hand on Harold's shoulder. "I want my brother to come along!" Harold responded quickly.

"Well, which one's your brother?" the woman asked patiently. Harold pointed to Cliff.

"All right. We can take him, too."

Mr. Callahan took David and Bernice home with him, as Mrs. Collins escorted their brothers off in the opposite direction. Cliff was so confused he felt ready to scream. But he kept silent and did as he was told.

<hr>

It was Sunday afternoon when the Webers came to the Callahan's door. Bernice had tried to brace herslf for this moment when she would have to give her baby brother over to strangers. She spoke brightly to him about his "new mama."

50

When the door opened, and David looked up to see them, he smiled and lisped charmingly, "Well, hello, Mama!"

Mrs. Weber immediately bent down and hugged him. "Well, hello, son!"

Mr. Callahan laughed. "I promise you we didn't tell him to say that. It came natural!"

"No matter. He's perfect," she said. "He's everything I ever hoped to have. We waited so long for a child, this is our last chance."

Bernice watched out the window as the Webers carried David away. She suddenly felt empty and helpless.

"It's so sad," she tried to explain to the Callahans, but they had no idea what the children had gone through. "He's been mine to look after all our lives. I'll miss him so." She started to cry.

"Come, Bernice, let's go for a walk," Mr. Callahan suggested.

As they walked, Bernice looked up at this strong, kindly man, and took his hand. "I wish I could call you Daddy," she said impulsively, for she had long yearned for a father like him.

"You can," he answered slowly.

Item from the Abilene Journal:

MORE HOMES FOR THE LITTLE ONES
Half the Children from New York
Have Found Homes in Dickinson County

Four of the eleven boys and girls who were brought here from New York under auspices of the New York Orphans Society have been placed in homes in the county. Besides the two who were adopted the first day, others who have been placed are Bernice Switzer, age 8, taken by Mrs. Luther Otto Callahan, E. 24th St., Abilene, and her brother, David Switzer, 4, taken by Mrs. J. J. Weber, E. 7th. There are still five boys and two little girls for whom homes are to be found.

The children are among the older ones. One girl is ready for high school and is very bright and advanced in school work for her age. Her younger sister is a bright, attractive child 1-1/2 years younger. Two of the boys are redheaded, blue-eyed fellows, old enough to be helpful. The other two are brothers also old enough to be helpful wherever they are. They are all intelligent, bright-eyed, well-behaved children who would make some home very happy. Several people are considering taking the various children but have not yet decided.

Bernice tiptoed past the closed door of Grandma Stowitz's room. Every day at this time, Grandma and Aunt Frances gathered for a prayer session. "Dear Lord," she heard Aunt Frances say, "Please bless Bernice. Help her to grow up strong in her faith, and tireless in good works. Guide her steps and protect her. Lord, thank you for sending her to us."

Bernice paused. She'd heard those prayers many times as she played over at Grandma's, and they moved her deeply. Although she had never set foot inside a church, or even a public school, until she was almost nine, Bernice responded to the idea of a personal God. She sensed this God had protected her even when her life was in danger for weeks and weeks, and when she'd had no place to go, no home to return to.

Bernice was a tomboy, and was Mr. Callahan's "shadow." Whenever he was out on a construction project, she was never far away. She climbed high beams, stepped carefully along narrow catwalks, and scaled shingled roofs. She was sometimes rowdy and mischievous, and laughter went before her like fanfare. Her sense of humor attracted people. Bernice was flourishing in Abilene.

She tiptoed down the hall to Aunt Frances's room to begin a favorite pastime — looking at the bits of finery in the dresser drawers. She never tired of trying on gloves and jewelry, and examining pieces of lace, pretty combs, ribbons.

After prayers, Aunt Frances joined her. "Up to your old tricks?" she laughed, and helped Bernice put things away.

"I just love pretty things," Bernice explained.

"And we just love you," Aunt Frances replied. She was a beautiful young woman with a slim figure and delicate features. The younger sister of Cora Callahan, she had lost her fiance in a freak electrical accident just weeks before they were to be married. Aunt Frances made her home with her parents and worked at the local department store. It was she who purchased many of the

52

fabrics for Bernice's new wardrobe, and, along with Mr. and Mrs. Callahan, set a Christian example for the girl.

Several streets away, at the Webers', David, too, was being outfitted for a new life. Of all the Switzers, he was the only one who found instant acceptance. The childless Webers doted on him and showered him with new clothes, affection, and everything a boy would want. David had indeed found his "new mama."

But at the Will Collins residence, their older brother was in turmoil. Things were not settled for Harold and Cliff, and Cliff was worried.

"I said I'd keep track of them," he told Mrs. Collins, "but already we're starting to get separated."

Mrs. Collins was an even-minded person with a logical approach to life. She suggested, "Keep track of everything, Cliff. Start now. You told them you'd always know where they are. Well, just write it all down. Make it a point to check on them now and then. When each of the children comes of age, send them the addresses of everyone else — even the family in New York."

"I can't write very well," Cliff began.

"I'll help you get started."

Mrs. Collins cared for the boys, doctoring the eczema on Cliff's face and sending them to her brother, the barber, for haircuts. When they weren't in school, they rode around with Mr. Collins in his truck delivering fuel oil.

After a few weeks, Miss Hill came for Harold. She had a home for him in the country. But Cliff stayed on at the Collins'. He stayed so long that he began to feel as if it were home. Then came a day when Mrs. Collins told Cliff, "I have to run down to the neighbors' and see about a dress I'm making."

"Why'd she go?" Cliff asked, suspicious.

"Well, son," Collins replied, "she had to go down there to get some information."

Then there was a rap at the door and Miss Hill appeared. She announced, "Cliff, I've got a place for you on a farm."

"But I want to say goodbye to Mrs. Collins!"

"She said she couldn't bear to tell you goodbye," Collins explained sadly. "She said she loves you."

Cliff packed up his things and went with Miss Hill. Encouraged by his stay with the Collins, he told Miss Hill, "I'll tell 'em what a good worker I am! I learned a lot about farming at the Farm School."

8

Dutchman's Justice

Mr. Schmidt hoisted a heavy bucketful of milk in each hand. He gripped the lantern handle in his teeth. The eerie light flickered on his flat face and spread a small yellow arc in the pitch darkness as he turned toward the milkhouse. Cliff, struggling along with his two pailsful, followed the wavering light and remembered the prophetic words Mr. Nelson had told him at the Farm School months earlier.

"Farm work's tough, son. When you hire out to a farmer, you might as well trade your bed for a lantern right at the beginning, because you're going to see a lot more of the lantern than the bed."

True enough, Cliff thought to himself. All the work was done with horses, so he got up early, went out with the lantern, and got the horses in to curry, harness, and feed them. Then he had to get the cows in and do the milking, still working with the lantern since it wasn't yet dawn. He felt he did half a day's work before the sun came up.

After a week on this German farmer's place, Cliff was bone tired. He usually finished up the barn chores about daybreak, and he'd go in for breakfast, then hurry out to hook the horses to whatever job he was going to do. He stayed in the fields all day and left just before sundown.

After that he took care of the horses again, fed and cared for the cows, and ate supper by 8 or 9 p.m. Then he'd go to bed, and it was the same cycle again the next day.

Most farmhands were paid wages for this work, and farm

boys did chores before and after school. Cliff received neither pay nor regular schooling. Schmidt was a hard taskmaster.

On his first morning there, Cliff was instructed to milk a certain cow. When he got good enough, he was assigned to two, then three, then four. Soon, he was working right alongside Schmidt. They did all the work by hand.

The milk was separated on the farm. Turning the separator was Cliff's job. He fed the skim milk to the hogs and calves, and stored the milk and cream until Saturdays, when it was taken to the creamery in town.

When threshing time came around, he helped cut the wheat with a binder and shocked it, then got together with Schmidt's brothers' crews to thresh it.

"Ever drive five horses at once, Cleefie?" Schmidt asked one morning. "You learn now." Eleven-year-old Cliff gulped when he saw the five huge horses, enmeshed in a tangle of lines.

"You only use two pair of lines — you drive the team in the middle,"the man went on."The others are on jockey sticks and tie-backs." He showed Cliff how the jockey sticks fastened to the hame of one horse on the team, and connected to a line at the other horse's mouth. The tie-back line came from the outside horse to the belly back of the one that the jockey stick is tied on. This prevents the outside horse from crowding in or out and he can't go faster or slower than the others, He explained. "Now, take the lines."

Cliff made one round by himself, circling from the outside in, throwing the dirt out, with the heavy plow. When he turned around, Schmidt had disappeared, and Cliff was left alone. Soon he was plowing, harrowing, drilling, doing a man's work.

Although he wanted to leave, he felt no real compulsion to do so until Schmidt began mistreating him. It happened when Cliff was out in the barn, washing the separator. Ingeniously, he thought of pounding some nails in the wall to hang the separator parts out to dry.

Schmidt came in, saw what Cliff had done, and boiled up angrily. "You vaste nails." He doubled his fist, knocked Cliff to the floor and shouted, "I'll learn you to vaste nails." Cliff laid on the floor until the farmer went into the house.

"I know Miss Hill wouldn't want you to beat on me," he said quietly when he came in. "When I tell her, she will take me away from here."

Cliff never learned how, but the Schmidts had a method of learning about Miss Hill's visits before she got there. Someone telephoned them. Then they'd start in on him. "You tell her that you're being treated real good and you like it here. Or, you get a real bad vipping ven she leaves."

So each time Miss Hill came, Cliff pretended all was well. He was afraid not to.

"The understanding is," Miss Hill pointed out to the Schmidts as she prepared to leave, "that you're to send him to school, raise him till he's eighteen, then give him a team and wagon and harness, so he can start farming on his own."

"Yah, ve do that."

Cliff watched with sinking heart as she drove away. Life went on as before, an endless assortment of farm chores, even on Sundays. The only time he left the farm was to go with the Schmidts to town on Saturday nights, but he had no money to spend and no one to chum with.

Then one day things came to a head. Cliff was bringing some mules into the corral when one mule broke loose and ran into the barn with the cows. All the cows were finding their stanchions, and Cliff sprinted along behind them. He was trying to chase the mule when a cow suddenly kicked him in the ankle. His yell frightened the mule, who jumped over a gate and broke it down.

Schmidt raced in with a pitchfork and jabbed it into the mule's neck and the mule, streaming blood, raced out. The farmer paid no attention to Cliff and went on tending the horses while Cliff did the milking. Suddenly, Cliff saw Schmidt advancing on him with a strip of tire. Schmidt beat him for the broken gate. The next day, Cliff, barely able to move, was sent to school.

Clarabelle Comstock's eyebrows shot up in surprise. She'd been friend and co-worker of Anna Laura Hill for over fifteen years, yet she'd never seen her so incensed. But anger didn't interfere with Miss Hill's sensibilities, Clara noted. She nodded encouragement as Anna Laura Hill stood before the judge, arguing her cause.

"Madam," the judge spoke sarcastically, "for some time now, your organization has been bringing ruffians and ragamuffins into our county, and dumping them on unsuspecting citizens. You call it welfare work. I call it — disposing of garbage. Now you want me to remove one of these unsavory children from the custody of a fine couple. And after they were kind enough to take in this little criminal."

"He's no criminal," Miss Hill's voice was controlled. "His only crime, if you want to call it that, was having had the misfortune of being born to a couple who cared nothing for their responsibilities. This boy has worked hard in the fields and barns of Mr. Schmidt for many months. He does everything that is required of him, yet I have learned that the Schmidts have beat him regularly. They have threatened that if he tells me about it when I come round on my visits, he'll receive worse treatment."

"Do you have proof of these charges?"

"Would I stand here before you if I did not?" she flashed back. "I have a witness — the young man's teacher, who says he had bruises and welts all over his body when he came to school. He was unable to sit down at his desk because of his injuries."

"I suppose in the interests of justice, we must listen," the judge sighed wearily. "But surely you realize that there is strong feeling against these wild orphans you keep dragging in here. Did you not see the editorial in the paper recently? Even the editor feels it. He said, 'Take your children back to the slums; we don't want them out here.'"

"Most of these children are not from the slums," Miss Hill retorted, stepping close to the judge's chair. "But if they were, they'd still need help. I've tried to tell you that these are children of immigrant families, children of destitute parents, the offspring of deceased persons. Each case is different. The one constant factor is that these children need a chance. They need loving care, a foster mother's love, a foster father's good government, to make them useful citizens."

At last the judge backed down. "All right, Miss Hill, you may take the boy."

"Come, Cliff," she said, putting an arm around him. "We'll find a place for you."

9

The Gift of Courage

"Get the principal! Tell him to come here quick!" The Sterling High School principal heard the shrieks of one of the women teachers, and bounded up the stairs two at a time. He followed the sound into a second-floor classroom to find the teacher, flushed and excited, pointing toward — a cow! A cow in the classroom!

"How'd it get here?" she howled. "Just look at this place! Oh, why'd I ever want to teach here?"

The cow advanced toward her and she ran out the door, slamming it, leaving the principal alone with the cow.

It was so silly — the principal had to laugh to himself. The cow was coming down the aisle between the rows of desks, like some overgrown, ignorant student. It's tail swished and knocked small items off the desks.

"Come on, Bossy," he coaxed, removing his tie and slipping it around the cow's neck. "We'll get you out. I can guess who put you in here — I'd bet it was that Bill Bishop again."

He led the cow out the door, and called to a few early students to help him hold her as they started down the wooden staircase.

"Whose cow is it?" asked one of the boys.

"I want you to find out," the principal replied. "You are excused from class, and I want you to lead her around town until you find the owner. Someone will be looking for her by now. It's past milking time."

"You," he instructed another boy, "go help clean up upstairs."

The princpal asked himself, "What can I do this time? If Bill did it, I'm afraid he'll have to go. Bill and his hooligan friends have gone too far! After he put the skunk oil in the furnace pipes, I told him he'd better watch himself. I'm afraid we'll have to expel him this time."

❧⟐❧

"Bill, you're smart, and you're ambitious. Why do you get into all this trouble?" Ida, sympathetic but confused, wanted to know.

"I just don't know, Kid," Bill answered. "You know I like school. But things get dull and I want to liven them up. The gang of boys was just looking for something to do . . ."

"The folks aren't going to like this. How will you tell them?"

"Oh, I expect the neighbors will be kind enough to do that job for me. Maybe they already have," Bill added, sarcastically.

"Things were fine till you finished grade school," Ida reflected.

"Yeah. Our eighth grade teacher was sharp. Started us in Latin, Algebra, and Geometry. And since there were only three eighth-graders, we got a lot of training. And we loved it."

"I was real proud when you won the top academic prizes at the county eighth-grade graduation in Hutchinson," Ida put in loyally.

"Yeah, I guess the trouble started at Sterling High. I wrote that paper for a junior girl, and she got an A+, but when I turned in the same paper, I got flunked. That didn't make a bit of sense to me."

"Maybe they thought you copied it."

"I told them I didn't. Well, even going back to Union 5 and spending another year with that good teacher didn't help . . ."

"You could go to Nickerson, to Reno County High School, next semester."

"I might just try that, Kid," Bill said with a sigh.

❧⟐❧

Bill Elder Bishop was proud, and bright. He could see faults — in himself, which he tried to correct, and in others, which he found hard to tolerate. He particularly hated dullness, laziness, excuses, and mediocrity.

Bill had taken pride in his own heritage, and looked to his father as a guide and a pattern. But he'd had to alter that pattern, and style himself anew, after being placed out in the West.

The transition to the new culture had been hard on Bill. He treasured learning, but it seemed to him that Western people placed greater value on brute strength and physical accomplishments than they did on knowledge. Of course, it had taken back-breaking work and tremendous stamina to tame this country. Only the strong had survived the perilous life on the prairie. But instead of identifying with them, and finding likenesses between their struggle and his own fight against the forces that had struck his family, he felt alienated.

Bill wrote to Miss Hill from time to time, and she always wrote back. And whenever she was nearby, she would stop in and visit him. She tried to impress on him the need for keeping his energies channeled, and she made it clear that she believed he would "amount to something."

When Bill entered Reno County High School, he found he could not keep his opinions to himself. He was outspoken, and daring.

One day he drew a cartoon of an administrator. He told his friends, "You see, he's henpecked. His wife really runs things. I think I'll draw a monkey on a string. That'd be appropriate."

Bill left the drawing in an obvious place, and soon he was called into the office.

"Did you draw this?" asked the official, holding up the drawing.

"I did," Bill answered.

"Well, what do you have to say about it?"

"Pretty poor drawing, if you ask me."

The official grimaced at Bill's cockiness. "You know I could literally thrash you for this?"

"I question that, too," Bill answered insolently. "I don't scare easily."

The official started to get up, but Bill just stepped back, removed his jacket, and laid it aside as though he were preparing to fight.

The official turned pale and sat down. "You may go," was all he said.

"I'm not scared of a fight," Bill explained it all to his friends later. "Never have been. But I never pick one either. If someone yells at me, I just grin and give 'em a soft answer. Makes them mad. Then they either have to start the fight or back down."

"You know this isn't your first offense here," one of his friends assessed the situation. "Does the administrator know it was you who organized that holiday from school, and got all the kids to come out for a picnic on the island in the river?"

"He's got a pretty good idea," Bill answered. "They all came back and went to school, all except the principal. But he knows how he happened to be left on the island, all alone, with no boat."

"Who called his wife, and told her where she could find him?"

"Oh, someone," answered Bill, sheepish.

"Know what I think, Bill?" a friend suggested. "You ought to leave, before they kick you out."

"Thought of that myself, pal," Bill answered.

It wasn't too long after that a field representative from McPherson College happened to stop by Sterling and visit with a neighbor of the Bishops.

"I wish you'd do something for the Bishop's boy, Willie," the neighbor said. "He's one of the brightest kids I ever saw, but somebody's got to help him before he goes bad. He's headed for trouble."

"I'll see what I can do," the fieldman answered. "Is he ready for college?"

"Hardly. He's been in and out of two high schools."

"Well, if we could get him into the academy, we could start there, and see how it works out. Two years at the academy and he could enter college."

"Good luck," the neighbor added. "He sure needs something."

"Phone call for you, Bill," the matron in the dorm called out.

"I was expecting it," Bill answered, rushing to take the receiver. "My advisor told me I'd be getting a call. What ever it is, he told me not to turn it down."

"Bill Bishop?" A woman's voice spoke firmly. "I'm from the McPherson Community Hospital, and we just can't take any more flu patients; we're full. We need somebody to handle the YMCA. The Y is being turned into a 'pestilence house' to deal with flu cases. We want you to take charge. We understand you did a good job managing the men's dorm on campus when it took in flu cases during the last influenza outbreak."

"Yes, I did it," Bill said. "We had beds in every hall, and plenty of volunteers."

"We'll be doing the same thing at the Y," the woman said. "We'll put beds in the offices, the gym, and even the empty swimming pool, if we have to. But we need a supervisor. Will you do it?"

"I guess someone has to," Bill answered tentatively.

"Come on down, then," she responded.

***

The sounds of tortured, rasping breathing filled the room. Bill looked on in anguish, his own breath catching in sympathy with the young doughboy's struggle.

Bill sat beside the soldier they'd brought in off the train that morning, burning with influenza. He was even younger than Bill, and desperately ill. His forehead shone with sweat in the dim light, his mouth hanging slack to catch the life-giving air. His slender body tossed about occasionally on the narrow cot. Out of the corner of his eye, Bill saw the shiny gym floor on which the cot stood. Shaking his head, he hated the incongruity of it all. This building wasn't meant for death. The Young Men's Christian Association building had been meant to help folks live fuller lives, he thought, not as a place for them to lose the fight to this terrible disease. Suddenly Bill leaped to his feet and ran to find the nurse who shared duty with him.

"Oh, Betsy," his eyes refelcted pain. "Isn't there something more we can do for them?" He motioned toward the figures lying on pallets and cots all about.

The nurse, young, well-trained, but weary and defeated, turned and looked up. She hadn't experienced an epidemic – she was used to duties in which life and death were more defined – looking after mothers-to-be, and placing the newborn in their arms after the struggle. Or emergencies she would never forget, as when a mangled farmer had been brought in. He had died in her arms, saying, "It doesn't hurt so much anymore."

This was different. Anyone might die. She and the others were pitted against a horror that lurked in the shadows around the cots, a terror made more powerful by their own exhaustion and lack of facilities. The nurse suddenly slumped down and looked in defeat at Bill.

"I don't have anything to give them," she said, "and you know there's no cure." She shook her head.

Bill touched her shoulder. "I'm sorry. I know you're doing your best. Everyone is. But I can't stand being so helpless."

He turned and threaded his way back through the bed-filled building. He heard a mother soothing her child. His mind jolted. What suffering and desolation! He went back to the soldier and sponged his burning forehead with a cloth. As head of this temporary "Pestilence House," Bill agonized over the pain he saw here. Children, parents, old folks . . . wasting away hour after hour. It was a nightmare.

But night was always the hardest. The dawn brought hope . . . for those who lived to see it.

If only he could make it through this night. Bill willed the thought to the young soldier silently. Noticing the war medal on the boy's folded uniform jacket, Bill turned cold inside. What irony! This soldier came through the war, perhaps only to die here in a strange town.

The soldier was struggling to speak; he raised himself on an elbow. Bill eased him gently back onto the cot. "Just rest now. Get strong again," he whispered.

How odd, thought Bill, as he walked to a window and looked down on the furious storm whirling along Main Street three stories below. It's so cold out there, but people are burning up with fever in here.

There was a "flu ban" on in McPherson now. No gatherings of any kind were allowed, as a measure to contain the epidemic by reducing the chance of exposure. It was as though the town were under siege.

Another wave of weakness overcame Bill and he thought his knees would give way. The pain he saw clutched at him in unexpected moments. He often felt he could not stand it another minute. But then he would find the strength to go on. Where did it come from — this inner strength? Where did he get his courage? From being a slum kid? Is that where he had learned how to survive? Did slum life make him tough? Having to fight for everything he got, even for respect? Nothing had been handed to him. Whatever he got, he'd had to grab for himself.

He had always been intolerant of others with less strength than his own. Yet, he wondered, could he really blame weaker

63

people any more than he did these helpless, hopeless forms he tried daily to aid? He'd had experiences others hadn't, but that was neither their fault nor his credit. Maybe that's why he'd been given his courage — to encourage and advance those around him, advise and guide them. At last he realized it. His courage then was partly his experiences and partly a gift.

Bill Bishop during college days.

10

Pressure from Above

"Well, Ida, I see you're wanted in the office for another talk; your name's on the list again," Joanna said, her eyes sparkling as she watched her friend's face.

"It'll be the same old thing," sighed Ida as she absently combed her hair before the mirror in the girls' lounge of the administration building. She lowered her voice to imitate the one they knew she would be hearing. " 'Why aren't you a church member, Miss Bishop? Sterling College is church-related, you know. You must join . . . ' I get so tired of it." Ida's large, wide-set brown eyes reflected her indignation. She turned to her friend. "I just won't give in, though, simply because he's pressuring me. I believe I ought to be sure, before I join a church."

"Don't be too hard on him," Joanna answered with a smile. "He just isn't used to dealing with young women with such a deep sense of justice and principle. He *preaches* principle, but he does not expect to find it in us, especially on a subject such as this!"

"I don't know how to explain it to him, Joanna. What do you think I ought to say? I'd like to tell him how confused I felt when I was little, after Mother died. Father was Protestant, but apparently Mother was Catholic. Bill and I never knew for sure. But anyway, all the relatives began squabbling over who would bring us up and what religion we should have. When Father decided he couldn't keep us, he stowed us away in the orphans' home, and then put us up for adoption. I think he was afraid that if something happened to him, the Catholic relatives might get us, and bring us up Catholic.

"The whole thing left a question in my mind. Does God love one group more than another? Which people or denominations of people will go to heaven? Whose religion is the right one one? And why are religious people so hateful to one another? I'd heard terrible and ridiculous things about Catholics versus Protestants, but I couldn't believe them! Weren't they all praying to the same God? Wasn't each group as devoted and faithful as the other?" Ida's eyes reflected her puzzlement. "I want to be sure before I make a lifetime decision. I wasn't sure then, and I'm not sure now."

"I know," Joanna nodded. "We all had to adjust when we came out here on the orphan train." Joanna paused. "We'd been raised by one set of rules we'd been taught was right, and then we came out here, and suddenly lots of things we'd thought were okay, weren't. I'll never forget how confused I felt then."

"You'd think my brother Bill would be feeling this way, too, but he went forward at a Dunkard tent meeting, and he seems to have found peace preparing for the ministry."

"You shouldn't feel guilty about your doubts, Ida." She patted Ida's hand. "You want to do the right thing, I know. Besides, joining a church just to get a teaching recommendation from the president is hardly a good enough reason." Joanna hesitated. "You do believe in God, don't you, Ida?"

"Oh, yes. I'm sure there is a God, although I did doubt it when we first came out here. We felt like such outcasts! Didn't you? I remember how the other kids laughed at us at school, and how much I missed my father, and everything familiar. I thought: 'What kind of God would take away someone's parents and dump her in such a strange place?' But then I began to see that God was still with me, and I could see Him in the beautiful sunsets, in the kindness of strangers, oh, just lots of ways!" Ida said. "But I did rebel for a while. Oh, not in big ways, like Bill did. He got himself kicked out of two high schools — he even ran away from home. I guess I was more quietly rebellious."

"That's generally the way it is with girls, I think." Joanna sat down on the couch and patted the red leather seat. Ida put her comb into her purse, closed the latch, and sat down beside Joanna.

"At first I planned and schemed to get back to New York," Ida confided. "I just *hated* being out here, and I wanted to get back to my own father. I was going to run away, and I was sure if I just showed up at Dad's door, he wouldn't have the heart to send me away again. But before I could get back there, he died. Then the Bishops adopted us. And I knew I'd stay out in the West."

"Oh, Ida! I never knew you wanted to run away. I did, too! But I thought you were happy here. Whenever you came to town with your folks, you seemed so content. You got such a nice mother."

"I did, didn't I!" Ida smiled and shook her head. "I didn't realize it at first, but now I know that I couldn't have found a better mother if I were still looking."

"She's so sweet. And you're the apple of her eye. I always thought your mother had more time for you than mine did for me."

"Oh, she did fuss over me," Ida laughed. "I remember how she put Vaseline on that short hair of mine to make it grow out faster. I think she kind of doted on me. Maybe she still does." Ida looked thoughtful. "You know, if I *had* run way, it would probably have broken her heart. But I guess kids don't think of things like that."

"Well, anyway, are you glad you stayed?"

"Yes, and I got over my bitterness at God."

"Do you think about God quite a lot?"

Ida answered slowly. "Yes. I try to follow the Ten Commandments, and be a good Christian person. I just don't belong to a church yet. It seems so phony to join a church because somebody is making you do it. It's more honest to keep on searching until you find what's right for you."

"Searching?"

"Yes. I always feel like I'm searching for something to belong to — to be a part of — where I fit in."

Joanna thought a minute, then said, "That's part of being an orphan, I think. Feeling set apart. Not like everybody else. Alone."

"Well, I'd better get down the hall to the office." Ida started to get up.

"Ida?"

"Mmmmm?"

Joanna offered an encouraging smile. "Do whatever you think is right."

"Oh, I will."

"Say, if you want to show him how it feels to have come into this community as an outsider — help him see the way religion looks when it's forced — you could tell him what happened to my sister and me when we first came here."

67

"What's that?"

"Maybe I never told you before. Well, you know our folks were Reformed Presbyterians, and very strict. We had prayers and devotions on our knees every night."

"A lot different from that Brooklyn orphanage you were in . . . "

"It sure was! Well, it was the first spring we were here, and a nice evening, and the chickens that had been penned up all winter were out scratching in the yard. Sis and I were kneeling in front of the big bay window, but we didn't have our eyes shut. And we saw the rooster take out after the hen. We thought he was trying to kill her, and so we got up and rushed out to save that hen! It was the first we'd seen of chickens, having come from the city, and of course we didn't know one chicken from another. We thought we were doing right . . . "

Ida was laughing.

" . . . But our folks came tearing after us, and wanted to know what we were doing. We told them, and we got sent to bed right then, without any supper. We had been disobedient, and irreverent, and I guess we'd offended their strict moral code by noticing what went on between the chickens . . . "

Ida chuckled, "I really don't think I should tell that to him."

"Well, maybe not. But this time why don't you just try listening to him? Tell him you'll think about what he says. Don't give him any arguments. And Ida . . . "

"Yes, Joanna."

"Remember, you might be pushing your luck to graduate without a recommendation. Jobs *are* hard to come by. Maybe you'd like to come and visit my church. You said he didn't care which church you joined, any good Protestant denomination would do . . "

"Thank you," Ida answered, feeling full of affection for this understanding friend. "I appreciate the offer. And you're right. They've even threatened to take the achievements award away from me. But you know what? I don't even care anymore. I know I earned the award. Getting the pin isn't that important anymore. As for visiting your church, well, I might just see a chicken while they're having prayers." Ida grinned ruefully, opened the door and went down the hall.

Ida cranked up the Model T and turned down the road to-

68

ward town, mulling over the conversation with the official. It had not gone well, and she was angry. Oh, he was so high and mighty! He was going to use all his power to try to make her conform.

She tried to imagine herself in his shoes — what would she have done? It was hard to tell. But surely, church people must know they can't force anybody into faith. So why did they try to force the outward signs of faith, such as church attendance and baptism? And even that was hotly disputed, Ida reminded herself.

She wished she could talk it all over with Bill. He had such a grasp of all the complexities of life, Ida thought. When he came home next time, maybe he could answer some of the questions that bothered her.

She had found it useless to try to express her doubts to Mom Bishop. It seemed her mom had climbed from her cradle into a full-grown faith and commitment. But Ida knew Pop Bishop would argue against enforced church membership. Maybe she'd picked up some of his doubts.

She wheeled in and parked in front of the grocery store where she had worked after school, and during the summers. It hadn't been easy, but she'd made it through college this way. The Bishops had agreed to let her live at home, and use the family car to get back and forth to Sterling College. Each morning for almost four years, Ida had arisen early to milk the cows, hoping her hair would not take on the fragrance of the cows she leaned against. Then she drove off to school, attended classes, participated in debate, choir, and all the other activities, worked after school at the store, and arrived home in time for supper. The Bishops did her evening chores to give her more time for work and studies.

Ida loved learning. She hoped to become a librarian someday, after teaching elementary school. She wanted to help other children to learn as she had.

She opened the grocery store door and heard the familiar jingle of the bell. She took down her starched apron and tied it on, and began stocking shelves.

Before long, her beau, a fellow student, popped in from across the street where he worked at a battery shop.

"How'd it go?" he asked, with a deep look of affection at Ida. She was so pretty, so slender and graceful, he thought. He loved her quiet assurance and confidence in herself and her abilities. Even when things were rough, she maintained a beautiful dignity. But now her heart seemed heavy.

She answered his question dismally, "Like usual."

"Hey, don't feel so bad. In a few weeks nothing can stop my favorite teacher-to-be, and," he added shyly, "my best girl. Maybe then we can . . ."

"Now . . ."

"Look, it's not so terrible. Even if you don't get the achievment award, we all know you earned it. And you believe in God, you believe in yourself, and I believe in you! So — things are gonna work out. Hey, I've gotta run. See you at school tomorrow."

Ida smiled as she watched him dashing across the street back to work, before she could fend off another of his many proposals.

Ida Bishop worked at the grocery store, which she called the "Prune Parlor."

When there was a break in the store's business, Ida hurried next door to the Mercantile.

"Well, here comes my favorite customer," Mrs. Cantwell

70

greeted her as she swung open the door. Mrs. Cantwell was as much a fixture at the Mercantile as the glass counters. And she never seemed to grow any older.

"Hi, Mrs. Cantwell. Can you match buttons to this swatch of material? Mom Bishop's sewing up a storm of a spring wardrobe for me."

"Of course, dear. How are you lately? Still dating the same boy?" Mrs. Cantwell's eyes reflected friendly concern? she was not a gossip.

"I am," Ida replied, "but my plan is still to become a teacher, and then a librarian. I want to teach until I get my lifetime certificate before I make any other changes in my life."

"Good for you, Ida; I could tell you were a spunky one the first time I ever saw you, even though you were a little shy then." Mrs. Cantwell paused, "Tell me, do you ever think back to that time?"

"Yes, sometimes," Ida answered with a look of pleasure.

"And Miss Hill was bent on outfitting you in hairbows."

"Oh, yes, she gave that high priority," Ida laughed. "Once in a while I wonder whether I would have found a home if I hadn't had that beautiful headdress you two made for me. I wonder if the Bishops would have wanted a homely little girl like me."

"Why, of course they would! Why, this whole town took the orphan train kids right to their hearts."

"Yes, I guess they did. They sure got stuck with us. We all stayed!"

Suddenly Ida noticed a little girl who'd come in with her mother. She was standing in front of the ribbon counter, absorbed in the banquet of colors and designs. She was petite, dark-haired, and very pretty. Soon the mother took the little girl by the hand and they left.

"Did you notice that little girl at the ribbon counter?" Mrs. Cantwell asked.

"Sure did."

"She reminded me of you, Ida. Pretty as a picture."

Ida paused with her hand on the door and looked quizzically at Mrs. Cantwell. Why, she hadn't been pretty! Surely Mrs. Cantwell's memory wasn't fading, was it? Then she understood. Mrs. Cantwell and the others didn't remember her past, or her pitiful first appearance. No, that was as distant as yesterday's clouds. All they saw was the young woman she had become. They loved and accepted her as she was. And this was home.

71

11

"Feeling Respectable"

Cliff sat down at the table and scrawled out a letter, as a plainly-dressed young woman stood over him, helping him with the spelling.

May 1924

Bernice Switzer
Luther O. Callahans
Abilene, Kansas

Dear Bernice,

Guess you haven't heard from me in awhile so I better tell you how things are. I found a good home at last, but it took three years of hell before I got here. The last you knew of me, I was at the Schmidts. But Miss Hill came and got me and took me away from them because they were mean and they beat me. Well, she put me on a train for Marion, Kan., which is about forty miles southeast of you. A doctor Jones met me. He is in charge of orphans around here. He found me a temporary home with some real nice people in town.

One winter night when it snowed real deep they asked me about my family. Told them I didn't know where they was. Wanted to know about my grandparents. All I could remember was Ma's dad's name was Moss. That's because my middle name is Moss after him. I couldn't remember his first name but I said he lived at Savona, New York. So they said I should write to Grandpa Moss, Savona, N.Y. Well, I did. They helped me spell out the words. And what do you know, I got a letter back from him in a few days. Grandpa was glad to hear from me. They are ok and Ma lives close. No one knows where Dad is.

One day these people thought of a friend of theirs that would like to have me. They came and got me on a bobsled. But it turned out to be hard work and no fun. I milked 15 cows morning and night, fed the hogs and separated the milk and lived on bread and cream. They never did take me to town. Just once, and they gave me one dime to spend. All I did was work. But he never beat me like Schmidt did.

I was there about a year then one day his neighbor wanted help with the threshing, so I went to them. This man knew I wasn't happy where I was, so he invited me to live with them, and I lived there quite awhile. I went to school then. And I met a kid at school who asked me to come over to his place.

Cliff went on to detail his experiences in Marion, living on one farm after another, and moving on when he became uncomfortable or restless. He described how he had come to the present . . .

Went over to another party I knew, he had a farm about five miles away. Asked if I could work for him. Well, this guy said he could use my help, but he wouldn't take me just for room and board. He said he'd seen enough of my work along the way, he'd pay me $25 a month plus room and board.

Well, we went over to the other place and asked if it was alright if I lived with them and they said ok. So that night I moved over here with Ben and Ella Reents. He is about 35 and she is younger. They have a baby. It's the nicest home I ever had. They treat me real nice, and I feel respectable.

I know you ain't heard of me in awhile, but I been keeping track of you, so I know you and David are getting along okay in Abilene. Harold ran away and went back to New York, then came out this way again. I expect you've seen him from time to time. He rides the railroads a lot. I told him if he'd had to pay the railroad what he owed them in free rides, he'd be paying a long time.

Well, I'll be sixteen this fall, and so you're gonna be thirteen. That's a rough time. Just don't cause your folks no trouble.

Your brother,
Clifford

Cliff finished the letter and laid the pencil on the table. The young woman could not help but know the contents; there were so many words he'd wanted to use but hadn't known how to spell. She was shocked. When Ben had brought him home she'd thought of him as a farmhand, not as a mistreated child.

"Cliff," she began, "if all those things are true that you wrote to your sister . . . "

Cliff cut her off. "What do you mean? Of course they're true! You think I ain't been shoved around? Think I tell stories? I put up with stuff you ain't never dreamed of. And someday I'm going back and I'm gonna show that Schmidt and his wife what I think of them."

A look of bitterness crossed his face. He had had to put up with senseless beatings, and second-class treatment all over the country, and now she thought he was a liar on top of it. He didn't give Ella time to reproach him, but burst out with his frustrations. "Do you know how I found out I was gonna get a beating once? From a four-year-old kid! The Schmidts' little girl. I come in at night from working all day, and she said to me 'du brecha' and pointed to the daybed. Well, I knew du brecha means whip in German, and I looked under the daybed and sure enough, there it was!

"And that ain't all," he went on, savagely. "The one time somebody was nice to me, Schmidt tried to ruin it. I went into town with the Schmidts one Saturday night, and I was hanging around the hardware store. A fella said, 'You got a pocketknife, boy?' and I says no. He says, 'Every kid ought to have a good knife. Pick out the one you want. I'll buy it.'

"So I picks out a nice brown-handled one, and I says thanks to the guy, and on the way home I says to Schmidt, 'Look at this nice knife a fella bought me.' Well, he didn't believe me. Said I had to take it back. So he turns around and back we go to the hardware store."

Cliff mimicked Schmidt's accent, " 'I vant to return the knife dis boy stole' he says, real righteous. But lucky for me, it was the same clerk who'd waited on us and he says a gentleman paid for that knife and gave it to the young man. Schmidt was fit to be tied. Never said another word all the way home. But he let me keep it."

"Cliff . . . " Ella tried to interrupt.

"And the beatings. I'll never forget them." Cliff's fists clenched. "Just wait till I get full growed. I'm gonna go back to Schmidts, if it's the last thing I do, and bust his head."

Ella was alarmed at the violence she'd provoked. "Let me tell you something I learned myself a long time ago," she said firmly. "It doesn't help to be bitter, Cliff. Bitterness only ruins your outlook on life, makes you jumpy, and suspicious of people.

74

Sure you remember those awful things, but don't repay evil for evil. Do you know why? Because then you give evil a chance to dwell in you. You don't want that. Didn't your family . . . ''

"There you go again," Cliff burst in. "Family! You read my letter where my family is. Strung all over the country. Our ma didn't care about us. She just let us go. If it wasn't for me, we wouldn't even know where each other was. She's another one I'm gonna fix up someday. 'Course I wouldn't hit her, but I'm gonna show her she don't amount to nothin' in my book. Someday . . .''

Suddenly Cliff found his wrists locked in Ella's strong grip. "You listen to me, Cliff Switzer! You haven't had it so easy, but look at you! You're still alive, and able to make your own way. And you aren't the only one that's been deserted. I'm going to tell you something I never admit to anybody, except that a lot of folks know it anyway. I was deserted, too. My ma couldn't take care of my brother and me, and she left us with a relative. Some folks say we were abandoned on a streetcorner, but I don't remember that. So I know how you feel. You think the mother is responsible for the child, and she's supposed to be. But not always. Things happen. Then the natural burden shifts from parents to someone else. And of course it hurts to think I was abandoned, and you hurt because you think your ma doesn't love you. Well, that's not always so. When you grow up, you might understand it better. Now that I've a child of my own, I can sort of understand how our mother felt. See, if I didn't have Ben to keep up with the chores, and make a living for us some way, I'd try real hard to keep my child. But I'd have to admit that if I had *six* kids, like your ma did, and no husband, I might think it was better for the *kids* if I gave them up.''

There was silence as Cliff pondered Ella's outburst.

"You was an orphan?"

"That's right. Just like you. An orphan with a mother."

"How old was you?"

"Just a little tyke."

"And you don't hate her?"

Ella let go of Cliff's wrists. She smiled faintly and her voice was patient. "How can I hate someone I don't know or understand? I just thank the good Lord for keeping me in his care when I was homeless, and for sending me a good husband like Ben."

"Well," Cliff said stubbornly, "You don't know nothing about getting beat up and pushed around."

"That's true. But I do know that you can't make right out

75

of two wrongs," Ella answered quietly. "And if you don't change your ways, neither your sis, your brothers or anybody else is going to be proud of a fella that goes around with a chip the size of a log on his shoulder. Think it over, Cliff," she added. "I'll see that your letter gets mailed tomorrow." She turned and went to pick the baby from his crib to prepare him for bed.

Cliff was suddenly very tired. He headed upstairs to his room and fell wearily into bed. But he didn't sleep. He folded his hands behind his head and stared at the ceiling. He guessed he didn't mind Ella lecturing him like that. Maybe he had it coming. But he sure wasn't ready to forgive his ma. Or Schmidt. Not yet.

He lay thinking back over the wandering, back-tracking path that had, at last, led to the Reents' farm, and security. Then he reflected on his favorite memory — the first day at Reents, when Ben had taken him to town. That day he'd begun to feel like a respectable person.

All during the time he'd lived with farmers around Marion, there had been one place in particular that represented acceptance, prosperity, and everything wonderful to him. His yearning was centered on a certain cafe.

The Cubby Hole was a locally famous hang-out, and its modest size took nothing away from its standing as THE place to eat.

It was appropriately named. The narrow, lean-to structure was tucked under a flight of stairs beside an old two-story limestone building around the corner from Main Street.

Not much wider than the stairway, the cafe barely accommodated a counter, stools, and a work area for the cooks behind the counter. Customers would come in one door, holler out their order, and pick it up and pay for it before they went out the other door. If there was space at the counter, they could sit down to eat. The menu ran strong to hamburgers, homemade pies, coffee and cokes, and good milkshakes. Everything was homemade except the line of Tom's Peanuts.

Many a time Cliff had stood, hands shoved into the empty pockets of his old clothes, inhaling the heady fragrance of sizzling hamburgers and fried onions, and listening to the friendly chatter as folks went in and out. He was sure those hamburgers were the best, most tantalizing, mouth-watering burgers ever made. But he never had any money to go in and buy.

Lying in his bed, he remembered how he had arrived at Ben's on a Sunday night, barefooted. They'd put him up, and he'd started work the next day. He helped Ben haul two wagon-loads of hogs into Marion. Then Ben took him into a store and outfitted him with new overalls, shoes, and a plaid mackinaw. For his first day's work, Ben gave Cliff a silver dollar, and told Cliff to come along with him. Of all things, Ben headed right to the Cubby Hole Cafe! Just stepping inside the door was a milestone for Cliff, who looked with wonder around the hallowed place as they slid onto stools at the counter. At last he could see, not just imagine, the way the cooks flipped the burgers. He could see the selection of pie slices lined up on a display. A huge pot of coffee dispensed steaming liquid into heavy white mugs.

"Order all the hamburgers you can eat," Ben had told him generously, not realizing how much this experience meant to Cliff. So Cliff doused his hamburgers in catsup and downed as many as he could hold. Then with his silver dollar he bought a corncob pipe and two cans of Velvet smoking tobacco.

"Always wanted to try this, but I never could get anything to smoke," he explained to Ben.

When Ben turned the team and wagon toward home, Cliff sat beside him, puffing on the pipe. By the time they'd gone the nine miles, Cliff felt mighty sick. The hamburgers and catsup roiled round and round, and his tongue was so sore from smoking the pipe that he could not even talk. But as he looked up at the bright stars, and listened to the quiet creak of the wagon wheels, he knew it was the greatest day yet in his life.

🙢⚜🙠

One morning, a few weeks after Cliff had written to Bernice, Ben called up to him as he dressed, "Put on your best over-alls, son. I want you to come with me when the morning chores are done."

"Where we headed?" Cliff asked later as they started out in the wagon.

"There's a farm sale across from here. Might be something we can use."

Cliff had never been to a farm sale and he was surprised to see a huge gathering of vehicles — horses, buggies, wagons, and autos — parked along the narrow dirt road around the farm. A crowd stood circling the auctioneer, who was calling out in a melodious voice words too fast for Cliff to understand.

Cliff looked around the place. The front yard of the old farm house was set out with furniture, room by room, creating a strange effect of an outdoor living area.

How shabby the front room furniture seemed in the bright sunlight. How pitiful the faded cabbage-rose patterned rug looked. The old ice box and flour cabinet leaned at angles on the uneven yard, and the dining room table and chairs seemed eerily set up for a party of ghosts. Cliff shuddered.

"Come on back here," Ben called to Cliff. "Look at this." Cliff walked around the edge of the crowd, past the row of farm machinery lined up at one side, in a nearby field, and followed Ben's tall frame toward the corral beside the barn. They climbed up on the fence and looked at the stock. The cattle would be sold one by one, probably to neighboring farmers to increase their herds. Ben explained. Cliff noticed one other animal in the pen — a spotted pony, not too tall, but sturdy-looking.

"How'd you like to have that pony, Cliff? Then you'd have a way to get to school, and over to your friends' houses, and into town, all on your own."

Cliff was speechless. He'd worked horses on several farms, but those were huge draft horses, wide and cumbersome, and not much fun to ride. He had seldom been allowed to sit on a farmer's riding horse.

No thrill in the world could compare with the prospect of a pony of his own. He breathed reverently, "He's a dandy. Looks like a tough little nut, don't he?"

"Probably weighs about 850," Ben figured. "What do you think?"

"You know I ain't got no money, Ben. I ain't worked for you long enough to have any income yet."

"That's all right, son. I'll just deduct a little each month from your pay. It'll be like a loan."

When the auctioneer got around to the stock, the crowd gathered along the fence. Cliff was wound up like a top in anticipation as a man hooked a bridle onto the pony and led him around the corral. The pony lifted his head proudly and stepped high, nostrils flaring. What a beauty! But when the bidding began, Cliff was unable to watch. Anyway, it was too confusing; the bidding seemed to be done by magic.

"Sold to Ben Reents for twenty-five dollars!" he called at last.

Cliff looked at the pony — his pony — and then at Ben. "Thanks, Ben," he grinned. Ben's wide hat dipped in reply.

"You ride him home," Ben said as he paid the clerk at the little table set up in the shade.

The farm wife came up to them as Cliff was taking the reins. "His name's Prince," she said, in a faraway voice. "He belonged to my boy. Take good care of him." She reached up and stroked the pony's neck. Cliff nodded and leaped onto Prince's bare back.

As he swung up he felt a sense of exultation. He kicked his heels lightly into the pony's flanks, and they swept off into a gallop down the lane. Mane flying and hooves digging in, Prince carried Cliff along the first of many miles they would travel together.

⚬⚬⚭⚬⚬

Cliff decided to take Prince home by way of the scenic route — through the nearby Flint Hills. The Reents' place in the Youngtown community was on the edge of this strange outcropping of closely-spaced, high ridges and valleys which had been cut by ancient ocean currents and glacier movements.

Cliff galloped Prince across the pastures and over cattle trails, feeling an exhilaration of carefree joy he'd hardly known. He reined Prince in at the edge of a high escarpment overlooking a valley of green, dotted with Black Angus cattle. There wasn't a town in sight. He thought back to a year earlier when he'd stopped in another pasture, over on the other side of Marion, and held a pistol to his mouth. Suicide, he felt, was the natural solution to the despondency, the utter frustration of trying to stay alive when no one cared. But he'd put the gun down, mostly because of his promise to his brothers and sister. Who would look after them if he was gone? Now he was glad he'd held on when there seemed to be no reason to hold on.

As he studied the beautiful scene before him — the serene cattle moving slowly as they grazed, unusual misty haze fusing everything with glowing color — his heart soared.

In the months and years to come, he would sometimes leave the Reents' place, when the toot of a distant train whistle stirred the wanderlust in him. But Ben's patient reassurances provided the perfect response. "I understand you got to see something of the country," he would say. "But when you get tired, come on back. There'll always be a place for your feet under our table, and your bed will always be turned back and waitin' upstairs. You're like a son to us."

And so it was, that in the Flint Hills, Cliff found peace at last.

12

Saving the Children

Rain pelted the cab as its headlights pointed the way along the city's darkened avenues, wending a path among the hansom cabs, teams and wagons, and automobiles. It was 1924, a transition age, as the assortment of vehicles on the streets of New York City attested. The changes were threatening . . . invading every part of life, and people had to struggle to keep up with them. In little more than three decades, America had come through the financial panic of the 1890's, through a brief period of elegance, and then it was plunged into the peril of a world war. Now, as if in response to the austerity and uncertainty of those times, came the Jazz Age. Mad gaiety concealed much as mechanization, industrialization, and social conditions created drastic changes in people's lives.

Yet inside the cab, passengers were jovial. There was laughter and bantering.

"Most people returning from a month's vacation to the Southwest would want to rest, Auntie, but not you."

Anna Laura Hill answered her young nephew, "Yes, John, I can't wait to get back to work. The next group goes out tonight. I don't want to be late."

"Tell us again, Auntie, how you got that stubborn old mule to back away from that canyon precipice." John's eyes crinkled and he chuckled at the vision of his portly, sedate, but afraid-of-nothing aunt meeting a long-eared mule in a war of wills. And on a trail in the Grand Canyon.

"Really, I think you'd have that memorized by now," she teased him gently.

"To tell the truth," Clarabelle Comstock put in, "I don't think that mule was any more ornery and stubborn than some of the officials Annie Laurie's met up with out West. What do you think, Annie? Didn't that mule sort of remind you of that judge back in Kansas . . . the one who tried to keep you from taking a child out of an abusive home just because of the family's good name? Seems to me," she went on, "you handled them about the same."

"Oh, Clarabelle." Miss Hill answered humbly, not wishing to speak of her crusades.

"Yes you did. I saw them both. You just held your ground and that old mule knew you had your mind made up harder than he did. Same with the judge, near as I can remember."

"Well," Miss Hill admitted modestly, "I always said I never could sing a note, but I sure can take my own part."

Everyone burst out laughing.

"Oh, you missed the annual Ladies Tea," said the fourth passenger, Caroline Petersen. A worker at the Society's Five Points House of Industry, she was Miss Hill's friend, and had come along to see her off, just to have a chance to visit. "What a pity. You'd have enjoyed it so much."

"Would I?" Miss Hill quipped, turning to Caroline.

"No, I guess you wouldn't have," Caroline admitted ruefully. "It might have been just like last year. I'll never forget how you told those two old dust chasers what you thought."

"Well, everyone's entitled to an opinion. I just got tired of them whining about leaving their housework undone. Ruined the day for everyone."

"What did you say?" John wanted to know.

"As you know," Miss Hill began her explanation, "If I want to go someplace, I go. I've never had a mess spoil yet. But they kept carrying on about how they shouldn't have come, they had cleaning to do at home. I just asked them, 'Well, then that's where you belong. What did you come for?' They said they came because it was the day to come. I said, 'If I felt I needed to be home, I'd be there. But if my dishes aren't done, I just run water on them until I get back. And I look at the dust kittens under the bed, and I tell them to stay there and not move till I get back, and they never run away. If I go out I enjoy myself, and I don't think I should be at home.' It's a matter of priorities."

"You keep a pretty home," Clarabelle put in loyally. "You make it sound like you don't care about it, but you're a good housekeeper."

"Thank you, Clarabelle," Miss Hill replied softly. "I guess phonies just raise my hackles. And those two are phonies."

"By the way," John injected, "have you seen the latest issue of your favorite magazine?" He knew the reaction he would get. He liked his aunt's spunk.

"No. Why?"

"They started carrying liquor advertisements," John informed her.

"Oh, no. Well, that magazine will never come into my house again."

"Now, Auntie. Why would a good Methodist give up her favorite magazine because of a liquor advertisement?"

"Principle, John," Miss Hill answered, her chin lifting and shoulders squaring. "Too many times I've seen the results of liquor on helpless children to tolerate it. If that magazine wants liquor ads, it doesn't need this reader."

Caroline, in an effort to switch to a more comfortable topic, asked Miss Hill, "Don't you ever get tired of traveling? Aren't you ever afraid? Or tired?"

"Oh, goodness no. I've been traveling the country with orphan children for over twenty years now, and I never expected anything to happen to me, and it hasn't. The only thing I mind is the cold. I do believe the cold is more bitter out West. And it bothers the arthritis in my knees. But I just wrap up warm in this old fur coat I got years ago. It's the only sensible thing to wear out West, especially when we have to travel in open liveries, and any type of auto I can hire."

"Do you think the Society is going to stop sending orphans out West?" Caroline asked. "Seems like the times are changing."

"I suppose so," Miss Hill answered with a sigh. "Someday. When they do, I want to retire. Those children are my life. All those precious young lives that need love and care."

"What will you do if you retire, Auntie?" John asked.

"I don't know. Maybe I'll be just like that old man back in Burlington, the one who lost his mind. But when they put a fiddle in his hands, he could still play the tunes he'd played for barn dances and parties fifty years ago. I suppose I'll be like that. Just put knitting needles in my hands and I'll start to knit, even if my mind is gone."

"That'll never happen," Clarabelle stated vehemently. "You've got what they call a strong life force. Besides, after you retire, you'll still have all those letters to answer from the children you've taken West."

"Well, never mind supposing. Here's the railroad station. John, you see that Clarabelle and Caroline get home safely. I must go. The children will be waiting."

She climbed out of the cab and waved goodbye. Suddenly she turned. "Oh, Caroline. When I get back, I want to introduce you to my brother, John's father. He's a widower now, you know."

"What a wonderful woman," Caroline said admiringly, shaking her head. "Always concerned about other people's happiness."

"That's Auntie!" John exlaimed as the cab pulled away.

◦❦◦

Settled in the railroad car with her charges, Anna Laura Hill assessed the situation. There were eleven this time. Eleven years old down to two years. When there were children under two years, she always had her hands full, because the little ones required more care, cuddling, feeding. Yet it was a joy to take them, because she knew from experience that the youngest ones almost always found loving homes. It was as if the Heavenly Father had his arms most closely around the youngest ones, "the least ones," as some folks called the babies. She loved the youngest, but she did more praying for the older ones.

◦❦◦

"Pardon me, ma'am." A neatly dressed gentleman of about forty stood before Miss Hill in the train. Of medium build, he had sharp blue eyes behind glasses. An unlit pipe was clenched in his teeth. Miss Hill had just finished tucking the baby in for a nap.

"Yes?" She spoke softly so she wouldn't wake the sleeping baby.

"My name's Morton. Ben Morton. I run a newspaper out in Colorado. Been watching this crowd you're traveling with. Fine group of children. Well-mannered. Are they yours?"

"Oh, no, sir." Miss Hill smiled and shook her head.

Morton was still balancing in the aisle. "Then might they be orphans such as I've heard about, traveling West to find homes?"

"They are, sir. In a matter of days, and with good luck, these children will have new homes and the hope of a brighter

83

future." Seeing that he wanted to talk, she asked him to sit down.

Morton slid gratefully into a seat across from Miss Hill and smiled his thanks.

Miss Hill had often been approached by curious passengers, and she tried to answer any questions courteously without upsetting the children or allowing her concentration to be diverted from them. But she could hardly cut short a conversation with a newspaper editor, of all people. They figured prominently in the Society's whole placing-out system.

"Many a time I've depended on assistance from those in your profession," Miss Hill told Morton. "Not only is the newspaper's cooperation necessary for advance notices, but a follow-up story after the meeting helps to find homes for those that weren't chosen right away."

"I hope you don't mind my asking a few questions," Morton said, bringing out a small notebook, "Miss . . . er . . . "

"Hill. Miss Anna Laura Hill, agent for the Children's Aid Society of New York City." Miss Hill suppressed a smile at his persistence. "I don't mind, if the story you write will be helpful to the children."

"Tell me, why is there a need to bring children from the city to the West?"

"That is basic information to many New Yorkers, Mr. Morton, but outsiders are seldom aware of it. New York has been troubled by child vagrancy and juvenile delinquency for many years. Seventy years ago, the problem was acute. Great numbers of homeless children were running the streets — begging, stealing, and causing trouble for others and themselves. There were many reasons for this. European immigrants died, leaving children with no relatives to care for them. Some children were lost by migrating families. And the slums, with their poor conditions, alcoholism, and disease, took a toll on adults who left dependent children. It became a great problem."

"If I recall the history of social work, there were few charities to care for homeless children."

"Correct. The Children's Aid Society was formed in 1853 specifically to help such children. It was founded by Charles Loring Brace, a young clergyman. He dedicated his life to helping the homeless children. He discovered sorry conditions. Children literally roamed the streets, begging, stealing, committing all kinds of crimes. They slept in alleys, doorways, dumps, wherever they found a place to lay their heads. And," she lowered her voice, "many girls were forced into a life of prostitution for lack of any other way to survive."

"But one tends to think of New York City as so cosmopolitan, the ultimate in modern living."

"It was also the ultimate in misery for many innocent children. There were no facilities at that time to look after them, and child vagrants were confined in jails and other institutions. They were cold, disease-ridden, and the food and sanitation were appalling. Some were no more than babies — under six years of age."

"How did Reverend Brace get the inspiration to start the Society?"

"It began with a report by the New York City chief of police, a Mr. Matsell. In 1849 he described the crimes committed and arrests made by police. It included information about the so-called 'child criminals.' Matsell called them a 'constantly increasing number of vagrant, idle, vicious boys and girls who infest the public thoroughfares, hotels and docks.' He said they were destined to lives of misery, shame, and crime. And he predicted that this blight would continue to spread over the entire business section of the city."

Morton observed, "Then it was a vicious cycle. The children were destroying the business environment and the city was destroying the children."

Miss Hill nodded. "The city's population was about 500,000 at that time. Matsell said there were at least 10,000 delinquent and dependent children wandering the city. Horace Greeley, the newspaperman who published Matsell's report and brought public attention to the problem, predicted that 'the pit of infamy' would not remain unnoticed by press or pulpit. And he was right."

"Go on."

"The clergymen responded with sermons to arouse public awareness, and plans to redeem the neglected children. Matsell had suggested educational and vocational training, but the clergymen proposed religious training and character building."

Morton drew on his unlit pipe and scribbled on his notebook as Miss Hill described the orphan boys' rejection of religious services.

"Then Matsell issued a second report. He said that of the city's 16,000 prisoners, one fourth were minors. Of these, 800 were between nine and fifteen years of age. It was then that Reverend Brace became involved. He had just been graduated from seminary, and he wanted to serve God by working with the poor. He

85

studied the situation and realized that the work of the city missionaries was only a start at reforming the vagrants. He felt there should be an organization designed to aid homeless children, and he placed primary emphasis on education. He said, 'In this country, education is a sure means to livelihood, and nothing breaks up vagabond habits like a taste for intelligent occupation.' "

"True enough," Morton agreed.

"The Society was organized in 1853 and Brace was the director until his death in 1890. His son succeeded him."

"How was the Society financed?"

"Public donations," Miss Hill explained. "Wealthy people were solicited. The churches also helped fund the work. Mr. Brace felt the Society should have conventional industrial schools, reading rooms, and lodging houses with paid agents to care for the children, because most of them wouldn't or couldn't go to regular schools. He traveled all over Europe to study their methods in handling homeless children. One of his ideas was a plan to remove homeless children from the city, to find them work or homes in the country. That was the start of our placing-out department. The Society contacts farmers, manufacturers, and families in the country who can use an extra hand or are willing to take in a foster child. Public meetings are held to find homes for the children. Some call it 'giving children away' but that is misleading. The system is actually 'placing out,' and the agents have to approve every home and visit the children regularly."

"Who takes the children? Is any money involved?"

"No. Mr. Brace insisted the foster homes should be for free. Older children who go to jobs are to be paid for their labor."

"Do you know how many children the Society has placed?"

"Yes, I do. Since the placing-out work began in 1854, over 90,000 children have been placed. The first children went to homes just outside the city. Later, they were sent to midwestern farm communities. You see, the Society wanted to send the children West to avoid the industrial areas."

"Do you ever encounter young criminals in your groups?" Morton asked, looking over at the crowd of children.

Miss Hill smiled and shook her head. "I can't imagine comparing these dears with thieves and crooks. Of course, some of those taken West years ago had impressive criminal records. But nowadays, the children come from orphanages and charitable organizations. Very few are street kids now."

"I didn't mean to imply anything, Miss Hill," Morton apologized. "I just wondered. You're right, of course. They do look like good youngsters. But I do notice an extraordinary look of maturity on their faces."

"Yes, they often look older than their years. That's because their faces reflect the experiences they've endured."

"Of course, not all of my charges are little saints. There's a quality of self-preservation in young ones thrown out on their own. I've met a few children that had a mind for trouble. Not many, though. Most of them just need a fair chance."

Morton was fascinated with the story he was getting. His town had never received a trainload of orphans, but he was sure his readers would be taken with the human interest angle. "What about the costs of travel?"

"It's cheaper to take the children out to find homes than to support them in orphanages. The railroads have been very cooperative in giving discount rates to our groups. A child can be placed in a home for under fifty dollars. But saving money isn't the important thing, Mr. Morton. It's saving the children that matters."

"I suppose you have good response at your meetings?"

"I've never had a presentation that wasn't well attended, unless, of course, there came a blizzard or something." She went on to outline the adoption procedure and her follow-up visits to the children.

At last, satisfied, Morton stood and thanked Miss Hill for the interview. He returned to his own seat, and unknown to her, began the lead for his story. "Today I met a brown-haired, middle-aged angel of mercy."

13

California Dream

Anna Fuchs jerked awake as the train jarred on rough road-bed. She sat up feeling stiff and cramped, so she stretched her legs out straight on the hard leather seat. Although they'd been traveling all day, Anna had dozed most of the trip. The flu had made her so weak and shaky she could only lie back and be jostled by the wagging train.

As she looked around, she remembered that she and her sisters were aboard an "orphan train." Sadness overwhelmed her. She wanted to cry.

If only she could sit on Mother's lap, the way she used to when she was small. Mother would stroke her hair and sing a Hungarian lullaby. But just thinking about it made things worse. She could never do that again. Mother was gone.

Anna realized that she must try to be brave. She could not cry. She'd been taught at the sanitarium never to cry unless she was hurt, or really sick. With Margaret and Helen on the seat opposite her, she had to put on a good front. She had promised herself she would never let them see her cry.

She turned and looked out the window, blinking quickly to clear her eyes, and concentrated on the scenery. Browned corn-fields, barren trees, and sleepy, snow-covered villages slipped past her smoke-streaked window.

Anna realized that everything had changed, especially herself. She knew she was different, for she felt she could not trust anyone. She remembered when she was happy, carefree, and loved. Now there was no one left to take care of her, and maybe she would even be separated from her sisters. She heaved a heavy sigh.

It seemed a long time before the sadness began to lift. But at last she tried to find some comfort by daydreaming. It had been her salvation.

Anna was so immersed in her dreams she hardly realized she was tapping her toe in time to the rhythmic click of the wheels on the rails beneath their car. At last, very quietly, she began to sing one of her favorite tunes to the rhythm.

"Cal-i-fornia, here I come! — "

Margaret glanced up, surprised. "You must feel better. All you've done since we left New York is sleep."

Anna stopped singing and looked at Margaret. But before she could answer, Helen interrupted. Putting down the doll she had been holding, she looked over at Anna trustingly, "Where are we going, Anna?"

"To California," Anna replied.

"You don't know that," Margaret countered.

"I heard Miss Hill say she was taking the children West, and West means California," Anna said with authority. "In all the movies and books at the sanitarium, whenever somebody went West, they went to California. It's real pretty there. Warm, sunny . . ."

"Anna!" Margaret cut in and shook her head.

"Tell!" Helen broke in. "What's it like? What's going to happen to us?"

"Well, the way I have it figured, it'll be much nicer than in cold New York. And we'll find nice homes with friendly people, and we'll have new clothes — not second-hand things, and," she paused for breath, "maybe we'll even get horses!" The deep longings she'd felt as an orphan these past months fed her imagination.

"You mean like the delivery teams in New York?" Helen frowned.

"No! Pretty horses. Riding horses." Anna's emerald eyes sparkled with the vision. "Nice and gentle, to ride through meadows . . ."

Margaret wasn't impressed. "I don't believe that stuff. You're just one year older than me, but you have to act like you know everything. All the time you were in the sanitarium, I was the biggest — taking care of Helen, helping Mama. Now you just take over."

"Well, I've been places," Anna tried to explain. "I've lived in a sanitarium and been with lots of different kinds of people. It's scary, going somewhere new, but I've done it before."

"But we haven't!" Margaret's stoic attitude suddenly dissolved and her pent-up fears broke through. Tears welled up in her blue eyes. "Oh, I want to go back to the orphanage. I wish we could have stayed there."

"No," Anna insisted. "Take that back! This is better. Remember Lucy, my friend? She stayed at the orphanage until she was eighteen, and then she had to take an awful job in a factory. That would have happened to us, too. This way we're together, and we'll probably get to go to school and we'll have a chance to be the kind of young ladies Mama was teaching us to be."

"Don't talk about Mama," Margaret whimpered. "I miss her so much."

"Me, too." Helen's lip trembled and a tear rolled down her cheek.

Anna put her hands to her face in dismay. Now she'd made her sisters cry.

"Girls! What's all this about?" Miss Hill moved into the seat beside Margaret, facing Anna and Helen. "Why the tears?"

"My sisters are afraid, and they miss our mother," Anna explained sadly.

"I see," Miss Hill nodded. "Well, sometimes it helps to talk." She gave a handkerchief to Margaret, then lifted Helen onto her lap. "I've taken lots of orphan children out West, and tears are just part of the trip sometimes."

"I hate being an orphan," Margaret said fiercely. Her eyes were still wet. "It's so--so lonely."

"Yes," Anna added. "How I wish Mother and Father were still here. If we were all going, it would be perfect!"

Miss Hill wanted to divert their attention. "Tell me about your father. What was he like?"

"He was a butcher. His name was Stephen Fuchs, and he came over from Hungary when he was a young man, and married my mother. Her name was Katherine. We lived in a Hungarian settlement in New York. We were very happy until Dad got sick," Anna said, "with tuberculosis."

"Were you at the sanitarium long?"

"Five years," Anna answered. "Dad and I were together a lot, and it was pretty in the Catskills. But he died after two years, and I missed him. They kept me there until after Mama died."

90

"Then they sent Anna back and put us all in the orphanage."

"And there weren't any relatives?"

"An aunt!" Anna began, and Margaret continued, "an aunt came to see us in the orphanage, but she was Catholic; Mama had changed right before she died, so we're Presbyterian."

"I know. The agencies don't allow people of one faith to take children of another faith."

"I'd have gone with our aunt," Margaret said, "even though we didn't know her. Somebody said she was from the old country."

"But see — Mama didn't want us raised Catholic," Anna explained. "We don't know why. She and Dad went to the Catholic church."

Margaret was big-eyed. "All I know is, just before she died, two nuns came to see us in our apartment, and it was the only time I ever saw Mama get mad. She ordered them right out the door!"

"So we all got baptized Presbyterian!" Anna explained. "I was last. They did me when I got back from the sanitarium."

"I'm sure all this confuses you. And I know you miss your parents," Miss Hill said slowly, holding Helen close and seeking the right words. "There comes a time in everyone's life when we are tested and life seems very hard. Right now you are feeling unsure and untrusting. But you'll feel good again sometime soon. I promise you that."

Anna smiled at the sweet-faced woman with the soft voice. She had put her finger on just the way Anna was feeling. Without warning Anna had been thrust into the adult world of responsibility, pain, and frustration. Her happy-go-lucky feelings were swept away. She had been forced to grow up very quickly in the past few months. In spite of the cheerful front she showed to her sisters, she was overwhelmed by the fears, frustrations, and distrust so common among orphans.

Anna knew she was the least adoptable of all nine children in Miss Hill's care. She was the oldest, and she had physical deformities as well. A crippled leg caused by a congenital hip defect forced her to walk with a limp. Two operations had not repaired it. And she was missing the first two fingers of her right hand. Only a webbed stump remained where those fingers should have been. Although she seldom thought about these deformities, Anna realized that adoptive parents might not want to take a child who was different. But over and over she'd told herself, "I'd rather go on the orphan train — no matter what happens — than stay at the orphanage." She'd begun reading early, and her years in the sanitarium had developed an appetitie for movies, books, even daily newspapers, a stimulating intellectual life for a child. She sensed that an open-ended opportunity was far more valuable than the dead-end of orphanage life.

When Miss Hill went to look after the other children, it had grown dark. Anna watched the reflections of herself and her sisters in the window.

The heavy door between the passenger cars opened, letting in the rushing sound of wheels on steel. A handsome black porter in white coat and dark trousers entered with an armful of linens.

"Bet you children want to go to bed," he said, and with that he began to transform their moving auditorium into a portable hotel.

The children moved across the aisle and watched him turn their seats into a bed. With a flick of his hand, he pulled the upper berth down from the panel overhead, and maroon velvet curtains appeared. The air-fresh scent of crisp, ironed sheets and pillowcases filled the car.

The girls readied themselves for bed in a little dressing room, then squealed as their bare feet touched the steel ladder to their upper berth. Anna found that sharing the accommodations was fun, but it wasn't the best arrangement for sleeping.

"Quit jumping around, Helen," she ordered, growing more stern as an elbow jabbed her side. "Please lie still. Let me tell you a story." The small girls in their long white flannel nightgowns squirmed to find a comfortable spot.

"Do you remember that painting of the Good Shepherd in Mama's bedroom?" Anna asked. "Sometimes when I was little, they'd let me lie on their bed, and I'd watch that picture. When I'd get sleepy, it seemed like the sheep came to life and started to chase each other. And then the shepherd would reach out with his crook and bring them all back again. Just be brave," Anna cautioned them. "And wish real hard that we get to stay together."

At last her sisters fell asleep. Anna was relieved. Now she could daydream her troubles away. She pictured the three of them in a nice home with foster parents who were like their own parents. But just thinking about that, Anna realized that foster parents wouldn't be the same . . . it would never be the same as with her own parents. She suddenly missed the sanitarium. She yearned for the security and friendship of being there with Mother D'Jacoma, Sophia, and Amanda.

As she drifted off, it was hard to hold onto her thoughts. In her daydream, her father was there at the sanitarium with her. Dad! She remembered when he'd made some beads for her. She recalled that autumn day when she'd come out to see him as he sat in the shade, the sunlight filtering through those huge trees. It was a blue and gold day and she had skipped happily to find him. He'd held up the necklace he was making from beads he kept in a cigar box. He said he was making one for each of his girls. She had chosen the blue beads.

Then she remembered her rosary beads. Dad had given her those, too, and he told her to use them every night before she went to sleep.

She could even use them when she was afraid or sad, he'd told her. Now she wished she still had that rosary. But after Dad had died, there was no one to remind her to use her rosary. Now she wished she had something she could touch to remind her of the past she'd belonged to but had to give up. As she slipped into sleep, she tried to think how the Hail Marys went. She couldn't remember any of them.

Finally, all three girls were asleep, and the train carried them on through the black cloak of night.

Chicago. Anna wondered if it was as windy as she'd heard. She watched the steel factories of Indiana belching gray smoke and studied the frozen ruffles of the Lake Michigan shoreline.

The train edged past tenements that reminded her of the poor sections of New York. Finally it pulled into the depot.

The children huddled around Miss Hill as they made their way through the steam of the trains to the marble-columned lobby. After a short wait, they boarded another train, and were on their way again. How far was it to California? Anna wondered.

"Let go of it!"

"Why should I?"

"Because I said so, that's why."

"Aw, come on, Anna. I just want to see what's in it."

"Listen, August — you get your hands off right now, or else," normally gentle Anna spit out the words through clenched teeth, her eyes glaring.

The object of this contest was Anna's doll valise, a little round-topped, imitation leather case with two hinges. August, the oldest boy in the group, had decided to find out why Anna grasped that tiny trunk as if her life depended on it. He noticed that she was either holding it on her lap, or had her foot on it, or had it braced between herself and the train wall, all the time. He had grabbed it from under her feet while she was looking out the window, but she'd been able to hook her fingers through the handle. They were locked in a duel to the finish.

The other children looked on amazed, for Anna and August had never quarreled.

Miss Hill stepped in. "What's this all about?"

"He tried to take my case," said Anna, near tears. There was a tremble in her voice, but her fingers were still entwined firmly around the handle.

"I just want to know what's in there — she keeps it with her every minute."

"I'm very disappointed that you two, the oldest, are quarreling, and setting a poor example. Give it back , August. You may not look in it without Anna's permission. Give it back and tell her you're sorry."

At last Anna regained the valise. She sat down with it on her lap. It seemed like hours before her heart began beating normally again. She had succeeded in keeping possession of it, but she knew she would have to keep an even closer watch on it.

On Friday afternoon the train pulled into the Rock Island depot of a small town. Miss Hill stood up and said, "Boys and girls, we get off here. Please gather your things. You older ones help the littler children. Just bring your bags to the platform and someone will take care of them."

Miss Hill picked up the baby and rested him on one hip, took her luggage with her other hand and moved toward the exit.

Smiling in anticipation, she stood at the door beside the trainman. She was ready to help each child, giving instructions and encouragement.

Anna got up with the others. All she could see was a plain village and a flat, snowy landscape. Suddenly she felt confused and afraid. She gasped, "This can't be California! What is this place, Miss Hill?"

Unaware of Anna's expectations, Miss Hill cheerfully answered, "This is a nice, friendly town called McPherson, Kansas. It will be your new home."

Anna's face lost its color as she stared in disbelief.

"I thought we were going to California. I don't see why we have to stop here," she protested. "Who ever heard of Kansas! Oh, Miss Hill, why can't we keep going — to California?"

"California? No, child. This is our destination. I know many people here, and they're expecting to meet you all." She climbed down the stairs. "Come along, Anna."

"Whatever made you think we were going to California?"

"Isn't California 'West'?" she asked, biting her lip.

Anna stood at the top of the steps. The conductor reached for her hand. She stumbled onto the platform, and began to cry. Of all her disappointments, this was one of the worst. Blindly, she gave her small suitcase over to the baggageman; but she held onto her valise for dear life.

The others were following Miss Hill up the snow-covered street away from the depot. "It's just three blocks to our hotel," Miss Hill was telling them. "We'll walk so we can all stretch our legs. Our baggage will be brought to us." Turning, she noticed Anna, still standing by the train, flanked by Margaret and Helen. "Anna, bring your sisters and come quickly."

A terrible feeling of dread and despair engulfed Anna as she saw that all her dreams of California were lost.

Finally, seeing it was useless to resist, she took Helen's hand, and the little trio trudged into the frigid breeze and followed the others up the barren street.

Margaret and Helen, who had begun to believe Anna's tales about California, were shocked at this sudden turn of events. Margaret, fully grasping the situation, couldn't resist a caustic comment to Anna.

"California, hah! You made it all up. This looks more like the North Pole. We'll probably all freeze to death here. And you thought the orphanage was bad!"

In spite of her deep dejection, Anna bristled. She snapped back: "Listen, Margaret, I've got enough problems without your remarks. If you say one more word, I'll *never* speak to you again!" The girls trudged on in silence, the snow crunching under their feet. Finally, Anna spoke. "At least we're all still together."

Flat. Gray. Cold. Desperately, Anna searched for something good about this barren place, something to be cheerful about. There! Down the street, off in the distance, she spotted a movie theater! It was a small encouragement, but Anna took it to heart.

McPherson looked like hundreds of other farm communities

they had passed through on the train. Sturdy brick and limestone buildings lined the modest main street. Most of the homes were neat frame structures, very different from the tenements of the city.

As they walked along the brick sidewalk, shoveled clean of snow, Anna thought that the bricks were an improvement over some of the boardwalk villages along the train route. A few automobiles grumbled up and down the street.

She noticed some horses and buggies being driven by men wearing simple black suits and beards. Women in black dresses and bonnets rode beside them. She had never seen anything like *that* before. She would ask about them later, she decided.

The group came to the McCourt Hotel on the corner of Main and Marlin Streets. Anna stared up at the vertical sign which spelled the letters. Miss Hill held the door open for the Fuchs girls.

"Just wait while I register," she told the children. "You can warm up over there by the stove if you want," she added, pointing to a cozy-looking fat black stove in the center of the room. The lobby had tile floors, brass spittoons and ferns on stands. A few old men sat in the wicker rockers that circled the stove.

Behind the desk stood a young man, his hair parted in the middle. "Hello, Miss Hill!" he exclaimed. "I'm glad to see you made it. Folks are expecting you!" He smiled at the small, silent tribe gathered behind her and added, "Looks like you brought some fine youngsters!" Anna Fuchs didn't smile back.

Miss Hill registered for four rooms, then led the children up the stairway. Anna and her sisters were shown to a room by themselves where they were to freshen up and rest. The hotel room had a large iron bed covered with a quilt, an oak bureau with a mirror above it, and walls bright with pink flowered wallpaper. A dark green shade was at halfmast at the only window.

As Margaret and Helen began settling in, Anna put down her valise and went to the window. She knelt on the floor and propped her elbows on the sill. Silently she surveyed the wintry scene below her, the small stores, the light traffic, those bearded men and bonneted women in their black buggies. There was no building over three stories high in the whole town. And everything looked cold and bleak.

"What a place!" she said finally, her voice as flat as her spirit.

Later that afternoon, tipped off by a newspaper article, several McPherson people appeared at the hotel to ask if they might invite a child out to dinner. Miss Hill handled the arrangements and coached the children on their behavior.

Margaret received an invitation from a Mr. and Mrs. Runyan. He was a typesetter at the newspaper office, and while setting the type for the story, he had made up his mind that he and his wife should look over the children for a possible addition to their family.

Margaret got dressed with Anna's help, and went out with the Runyans. Helen, too, received an invitation, so when she left, Anna was alone.

Anna pretended not to care. She hung up her two new dresses, put on her nightgown, and brushed her hair. Then she opened her valise.

But her mind was in turmoil. Tomorrow was the day of the adoption meeting. What would happen?

Eventually her thoughts traveled back to the sanitarium. What was it Mother D'Jacoma, her friend there, had said when Dad died? "You must believe that God has a plan for your life!" Yes, that was it.

"And if I watch and pray, that plan will be unfolded," she remembered aloud. She sighed. Here she was — alone in this hotel room, in a strange little town in Kansas, a state she'd never even heard of.

Trust. That was the only thing to do. She would just have to trust that this was really the way it was supposed to be. Hadn't her mother trusted when she had left her own parents to cross the ocean and come to America with Dad? And hadn't Dad trusted, when he knew he was going to die, and told her goodbye for the last time? Perhaps this Kansas town *was* where her future would lie.

There were schools, even in Kansas. She could still get an education! Snow and cold weather weren't strangers to her. She had been looking forward to California sunshine; yet she had loved playing fox-and-geese and other winter games at the sanitarium.

By the time Margaret and Helen returned, Anna's spirits had lifted. And the harsh words with Margaret were forgotten. She felt sorry for her sisters. They were all in this together. Being older, she would have to help them. The girls were bursting with stories of their dinner out and the people they had met. Anna listened to them with interest. Then she hurried her sisters off to bed and kissed them goodnight.

14

"Welcome to Kansas!"

When his roommate tossed a copy of the McPherson *Republican* into his dorm room, Bill Bishop was deep into another of his self-designed research projects — the study of pedigreed chickens. He had already completed studies on suicide, and education of the supernormal. He looked up from the stack of books surrounding him, put down his coffee cup, and stretched to pick up the paper from the floor.

He glanced idly over the news items. Suddenly his eye was caught by a page-one headline: "Hoping to Place All Here."

> The Presbyterian Church is expected to be crowded tomorrow afternoon when Miss Anna Laura Hill, representing the Children's Aid Society of New York City, presents nine orphan children, ranging in age from two to eleven years, whom she has brought from New York for adoption by families of this community.
>
> Four of the children are boys and five are girls, and it is hoped that all will be placed in homes in this vicinity. It is the policy of the Society to place these children in homes with religious leanings in keeping with the early training of the orphan children. Of this party, eight came from Protestant homes and one from a Catholic home; and Miss Hill is planning on taking the latter child on to northern Kansas points if she fails to find a place for her in a Catholic home here.

Bill's mind was jolted with old memories — the early struggles without a mother, the time at the orphans' home, and the train trip west with Miss Hill and the others. He remembered the trip as though it were yesterday — running up and down the aisles, sitting and talking with Miss Hill, getting off at stops to buy food for their group, sleeping on the converted seats.

Then another memory jabbed him — the way he felt on that stage in front of hundreds of curious eyes, "up for adoption." His heart wrenched at the thought, even though it had been thirteen years ago, and he was now a mature twenty-four.

After being taken by the Bishops, he'd struggled through difficult growing-up years. No school seemed to capture his interest and after leaving several, he was finally taken under the wing of a field representative of McPherson College. The man had seen him through the Academy, a high school equivalent, and into college. Bill's life was busy by necessity and his own design. He worked night and day, studying and holding down several part-time jobs. He'd washed dishes, unloaded coal cars, and served food in the cafeteria. He wanted to learn all he could about everything, and this led him to read at least ten books a week. He spent every cent he had on more books.

Remembering his past, he felt he owed a debt to those who'd helped him. But he had learned that the only way to pay back those who've helped you is to help someone else. Kindness spreads and flourishes as it is shared with others in need.

Bill felt deeply for other children who were in the awkward position he once was, and he was determined to do something for them. Folding the newspaper under his arm, he left his room and went down to the cafeteria. There he found his two closest friends, Harry, who played in the college band, and Mercedes, nicknamed "Chick," a pretty student teacher.

"Look here," he said, spreading the paper and pointing to the article. "You know how I told you I came out here on an orphan train and was adopted by the Bishops? Well, another orphan train has come — it got to town today. I sure wish we could help those kids."

"But how?" Chick turned in her chair to face Bill.

"Maybe we could get together and adopt one of them ourselves," Bill suggested. "Sometimes it's hard to find a home for one or two of them. Maybe we could take a leftover child. They need a chance."

"But we don't have any money," Harry pointed out. "We're all barely paying our way now. You know how broke we are."

"And where would we keep a child?" Chick asked. "In a dorm closet?"

"I don't know," Bill replied, "but there must be a way."

During dinner, the three friends mulled over their plans. Harry was realistic. "Bill, you're holding down all those jobs to pay for your school. I bet you don't even get four hours sleep a night, and you don't have two dimes to rub together."

Reluctant to give in, Bill suggested, "Well, let's think about our assets and where a child might stay. We could take turns taking care of him."

"We could play ball with him on Saturdays, and Chick could take him to Sunday school," Harry offered hopefully.

"You know it won't work," Chick admitted at last. "We just can't do it. If we were out of school and had jobs, then maybe. But not now."

"My dad always told me I was born with my mind made up on all the important issues," Bill smiled ruefully. "And I say I won't give up on this idea. Someone may need us."

"They may need us, but what can we do for them?" Chick said.

Shoving his plate aside, Bill stood up. "I'm going to give Miss Hill a call at the hotel and ask if there's any way we can help."

"We'll go along with that," Harry nodded. "Just don't sign us up for something impossible."

Later Bill rang the hotel and asked to speak to Miss Hill. "Hello, Miss Hill," he said, the warmth of her memory encouraging him. "This is Bill Bishop. You placed me and my sis Ida in Sterling about thirteen years ago. Remember?"

"Bill!" Miss Hill exclaimed with pleasure. "How good to hear from you. How are you and Ida?"

"Ida's fine. She's in college at Sterling, living at home with Mom and Pop Bishop. I'm a senior at McPherson College here. I might even turn out to be a preacher. Can you imagine that, from an ornery kid like me?" he chuckled.

"Of course," she replied confidently. "The ones who kick up their heels in their youth often turn out to be the pillars of the church in later years."

"Miss Hill," began Bill, changing the subject, "I read in the paper how you brought those orphans to town. I'd like to help any way I can. And I have two friends who'll go along with me on it."

"What did you have in mind, Bill?"

"Actually, I'd like to adopt one, but I guess that's not possible. We can't seem to find a way. But I want to do something."

Miss Hill was ready with a suggestion. In fact, it was an answer to prayer. "Well, we have a couple of children who have special needs," she began.

❦

Anna opened her eyes and sat up in bed. Today was the day! What would it bring? Resolutely she got up and began dressing for breakfast. "Get up," she called her sisters. "We have to get ready."

The girls had just finished preparing for breakfast when there was a knock at the door. "I'll get it," Anna called.

Miss Hill greeted her. "I didn't forget! Happy birthday, Anna!" Her eyes sparkled and she looked pleased as Anna grinned. "I want you to meet an old friend of mine. This is Bill Bishop."

Anna hadn't noticed anyone else in the hall until a young man with dark eyes stepped from behind Miss Hill. He wore a coat, a sweater, and corduroy pants, and he was smiling broadly.

"I brought Bill to Kansas when he was about your age," Miss Hill explained. He wants to have a birthday party for you. I told him I thought you'd like that."

"A birthday party! Oh, yes! But where? When?" Anna gasped in surprise.

"Across the street, as soon as you're ready," Bill answered, pleased at her response.

Margaret and Helen heard Anna's exclamations and ran to the door. But Miss Hill was firm. "This party is just for your sister," she told them. "You went out to dinner last night while Anna stayed in. You may stay with me this morning while she goes out."

Margaret and Helen stepped back.

"Get your coat," Bill told Anna. She ran to the closet and slipped into it. "I guess I'm ready," she announced.

Anna hurried along beside Bill as they crossed the street to Smalley's Art Shop.

"I work here part time," Bill explained, opening the door.

Anna noticed that there were many paintings done in pastels, with a certain style. Bill saw her pause before one of the paintings, so he said, "That's by Birger Sandzen. Mr. Smalley thinks Sandzen (he pronounced it Sand-ZEEN) is going to be famous someday. He lives in a nearby town."

He directed her toward the back of the shop where Anna could see two people seated at a small table.

101

"It's a little place Mr. Smalley has for college kids to get together and have snacks. He knows the students will be customers someday, and I guess he likes our company, too."

He led her up to the couple seated at the table. "I want you to meet my friends Chick and Harry. This is Anna."

"Hello," Anna said uncertainly.

"Sit down," Chick invited, and Anna slid into one of the round-backed chairs. Then Bill brought in a pile of presents and put them before her. And Chick got up and came back with a birthday cake, frosted in pink. Anna put her hands over her mouth in surprise.

"Happy birthday, Miss Anna Fuchs!" Bill said formally. "Welcome to Kansas!"

"Happy birthday, Anna," echoed Chick and Harry.

"Well, go on," Bill urged, eyes twinkling. "Open those presents! Then we'll have some refreshments."

Thrilled, Anna set about unwrapping the packages, her face smiling as her fingers flew to untie the ribbons. Even her deformed right hand could not slow her down. She peeked into the first box and beneath the white tissue she saw something blue. She drew it out — a tiny teacup of deep blue china.

"A tea set!" she exclaimed. "I've never had one!" Gently she unpacked the four cups and saucers, the teapot, the creamer and sugar bowl and set them all on the table.

In the next package she found a strand of pretty red and green beads. "I'll help you put them on," Chick offered, smiling.

The third package contained a book, *Heidi.*

Anna thumbed through the pages. "This is the first book I've ever had — for my own," she told them. Then remembering her manners, she looked around at her three new friends. "Thank you very much. I'll always remember this party."

"I baked this last night," Chick said, slicing the cake onto white china plates. "Hope you like it." Bill quickly poured up four cups of hot chocolate.

As they ate, Bill set about fortifying Anna as best he could. "You can call me Uncle Bill," he began, "because we're sort of related — we both come from New York."

Anna laughed. "Sort of related," she repeated.

"You and I are just two of the hundreds of kids Miss Hill brought West," he went on. "Some of them have become famous — governors, senators, teachers, judges — really important people."

"Henry Jost, the Missouri congressman, was an orphan kid

who came West years ago. He got to be mayor of Kansas City. Now he's in congress," Harry spoke up.

"Really?" Anna was impressed.

"Sure. And lots of other people came out and made good lives for themselves. It's no different now. You can still do whatever you want to do. It just takes some time to get used to things here."

"Did any of the orphans get to go to California?" Anna asked.

"Not that I know of," Bill replied. "Most of the kids were taken to Kansas, Missouri, Nebraska, Illinois — the farm states. Seems like the Society wanted to get kids out on the farms. Why?"

"I'd read all about California, and I thought when Miss Hill said 'West' she meant California. I wanted to see mountains and the ocean. I never thought we'd stop here."

"Oh, I see," Bill chuckled. "I suppose Kansas seems pretty dull, compared to California. But I like it here. Someday you'll grow to love the big sky and the feeling of freedom in these open spaces. Spring and fall are pretty seasons," he went on encouragingly. "The trees are like bouquets of flowers in spring, and in the fall everything is golden. Too bad it's so cold and dark now. I came out in December, too."

"I guess the Society wants to make sure that farm families can come to the meetings," Harry observed. "Most of the year, farmers are busy in the fields," he turned to Anna, "but in the winter, they can get away from their work for awhile."

"Is everybody around here a farmer?" Anna asked.

"Not everybody. We're all college students. And there are business people, teachers, and laborers. But it is a farming town. I was adopted by farmers in Sterling, west of here. Someday maybe you can come out and meet the Bishops. Things worked out okay for me, and they will for you, too, Anna. Miss Hill says you're smart as a whip, and you'll do just fine."

"What do you want to be when you grow up?" Chick asked.

"A nurse," Anna answered quickly. "I want to help people."

"I hope you get to," Chick responded. "I'm going to be a drama teacher, myself. Would you like to ride out and see our college?"

"Sure," Harry added, "it's not far. We can ride out in my car."

"Maybe you'd like to invite a friend, Anna?" Bill said. "How about taking that little Catholic girl along?"

"I'll go get Hope,"Anna said, slipping into her coat. Because she was the only orphan on the train who had come from another orphanage,Hope had been a stranger to the others, and had kept to herself on the trip.

Anna brought her and they all climbed into Harry's old roadster and toured out to the campus, on the east side of town. After looking through the library and main building, the three guides led the girls toward the cafeteria. "You can have lunch with us," Bill told them. "Miss Hill said it was alright."

After everyone had been served meatloaf, mashed potatoes, and biscuits, and was seated at the big table, Bill stood up to introduce the two orphan girls.

"Hey, everybody," he called out to the other students as they ate. "I'd like you to meet two friends of mine." He leaned over and lifted Anna to the tabletop so she could be seen. "This little lady is Miss Anna Fuchs," he said, "and she's just come out here from New York City. Today's her eleventh birthday! How about a big hand for her?" Politely the students applauded and cheered.

"Anna," Bill said, "Would you like to say anything to the kids — sing a song, recite a poem, or anything?" But Anna shook her head. She suddenly felt shy and nervous. This was a new feeling for Anna, for when she was younger she was almost fearless. She dared to swing higher than all her friends, and almost knocked herself out while sliding downhill in the snow, riding in her own washbasin. Once she had even cuddled a snake. She had performed in many programs at the sanitarium, giving readings and doing solo dances. But recent experiences had subdued her exuberance and shaken her confidence. Bill lifted her down from the table.

When Bill introduced Hope and asked her the same question, he was surprised to find a born performer. She did a little jig and sang a song as heartily as though the tabletop were a stage.

The cafeteria was filled with applause, but Bill looked at his watch. "We'd better be getting back. I promised Miss Hill the girls would be back in plenty of time to get ready for the program this afternoon."

When Anna got back to her room, she showed her gifts proudly, and told her sisters everything she had seen and done. Echoing in her ears was the happy farewell from "Uncle" Bill.

"Goodbye, Anna!" he had called. "Good luck."

15

A Spinster's Struggle

"Hold still, Margaret. I'll never get your hair combed if you don't hold still. You don't want to go out looking like you've never seen a hairbrush!" Anna exclaimed in exasperation.

She picked up the box with her birthday beads and handed it to Margaret in hopes she'd stop squirming. Margaret suddenly grew quiet as she carefully inspected the contents of the box, hardly noticing that her head was being jerked backward with every one of Anna's hurried tugs and strokes.

"Helen, you put your dress on now," Anna reminded her once again, for Helen had become distracted with her teddy bear.

"There," Anna pronounced, finishing Margaret's hair. "Now I'll get ready. Don't you two get messy."

"Don't be so bossy," Margaret countered, seating herself on the bed innocently.

Anna ignored the comment and laid the blue velvet dress out on the overstuffed chair, packing her other dress into her train case. She pulled on the long black stockings, wiped her good high-topped shoes with a sock she'd worn yesterday, and slipped the shoes on, admiring their shine. She put the dress on over her head. It was so big it almost fell onto her when she raised her arms. But she quickly busied herself fixing her hair, firmly brushing the natural curls in an attempt to make the Buster Brown cut lie flat. But the ends of her bob and bangs sprang up every time she brushed them.

Miss Hill had instructed Anna to wear the red sailor hat the orphanage staff had bought for her. She hadn't had it on since she'd modeled the clothes at the orphanage. She had been sick with the flu and couldn't go out with the others to get new things. When they'd returned, she had climbed out of bed long enough to try hers on. Unfortunately, the shopping for her had been done according to her age rather than her size. Nothing fit.

Now Anna dutifully put on the hat and tied the string under her chin. She tilted the dresser mirror and backed across the room far enough so she could survey her entire image.

"My dress is too big, my bangs go up instead of down, and this hat looks terrible!" she lamented, tears welling in her eyes. She didn't want to upset her sisters, and she had been able to hide her feelings until now. But this was too much! Surely no one would want such an awful sight, she thought dejectedly.

There was a sharp rap on the door and Anna realized it was time to go, ready or not. She sniffed, struggled to wipe her eyes, and concentrated on the wonderful birthday party she'd had. "I'll wear my beads," she said to herself. She grabbed them off the bed and put them on, slipping them inside the collar of her dress since they didn't match. Only she would know they were there; they were her secret reminder of the first good thing that had happened to her in Kansas.

Helen opened the door and Miss Hill stood in the doorway. "Everyone ready?" she asked brightly. "Yes, yes," said the girls as they hustled into their coats and hurried out of their room to join the others. Everybody looked shined and polished to a new finish, Anna noticed. But the group of normally lively children were strangely quiet. Miss Hill led the way, with the children filing silently behind.

⁂

Despite the raw December wind and driving snow, local interest in the orphans from the East ran high. The churches in and around McPherson had encouraged support for the event, and the publicity in the newspaper had been helpful. Farmers, business people, and many others, some from as far as twenty miles away, were gathering to see the children. Well before the scheduled program time the large, red brick Presbyterian church on South Main Street was jammed.

Miss Hill and the children arrived at about five minutes before two, and paraded up the wide cement steps of the church. They quickly hung their coats in the back and filed down a side

106

aisle amid the crowd of curious onlookers. As Anna came into the sanctuary she noticed a beautiful sight — a large, round, stained-glass window. The colors were deep and rich, illuminated by the daylight. The Virgin Mary held her baby Jesus as the three Wise Men knelt in adoration. Anna caught her breath as she gazed up at it. The scene was one of motherly love. "Is this a sign?" she wondered. Would she, too, be held close and lovingly in a mother's arms again?

Anna walked forward and took her seat with the others. The folding chairs on the platform faced the audience who had come to have a look at them. Aware that she was the oldest, Anna attempted to set a good example. She tried to smile, and she sat very straight. But that sea of strange faces was frightening. Her heart pounded. Every pew was filled, and the people in the audience craned their necks this way and that, attempting to get a better view of the children.

Miss Hill stood up, still holding Arthur, the littlest child. The crowd grew quiet.

"Ladies and gentlemen," she began. "I represent the Children's Aid Society of New York City, and I'm glad to see so many people interested in these children! They are about as bright a set of youngsters as anyone could find anywhere . . . each and every one. Though the two-year-old here isn't old enough to realize what the excitement is about, all the others are full of their big adventure . . . their trip from New York City to the Great Plains of Kansas."

Anna kept her eyes on the familiar and reassuring Miss Hill. The woman stood very straight, looking directly at people in the audience, her face pleasant, her voice strong, yet gentle. She had on a black dress and her dark hair was swept into a wide-brimmed hat that bobbed up and down as she spoke.

Miss Hill explained the how and why of the orphan trains and the extent of the work of the Society's placing-out department. She said that anyone interested in adopting a child should inform the local adoption committee members standing at the rear of the church. The committee would consider each request and announce the results at the end of the session. Then the children would enter the homes for a year's probation period. After that, they could be officially adopted if all parties were satisfied.

Miss Hill turned to face the children. Anna grew nervous when she realized that the people in the audience, too, had taken their eyes off Miss Hill and now gazed at her and the others. But

Miss Hill continued her talk. "I'll introduce each child and tell you something about his or her background, health, education, and interest." Now she spoke directly to them. "Children, will you please stand when I call your name? Remain standing until I have finished telling about your background.

"Ladies and gentlemen, may I present to you . . . the children . . . "

As Anna was introduced, she automatically folded her crippled right hand into a fist. She drew up her small body, with the shorter leg on tiptoe to make herself appear normal. As Anna heard Miss Hill relate the facts of her hip operation, the years in the sanitarium, and her parents' deaths, she grew uncomfortable. She removed her red sailor hat and began to swing it by its string. Now her once-awkward bob was revealed as a thick mass of attractive dark curls. Although Anna did not realize it, by removing the unbecoming hat she had greatly enhanced her appearance.

Anna began to pray. "Please, God! Let somebody choose me! Somebody who is nice, and friendly, and . . . " She continued her silent supplication even after she sat down.

Although several couples had gotten up from their seats and were moving toward the rear of the church to talk with the committee members, no one had stood up after Anna's introduction.

Anna swallowed hard. It seemed entirely possible that no one would choose her. Every passing second brought Anna a greater struggle to remain on that platform, trying to look confident. She was trembling inside.

◦≈⊶☙⊷≈◦

Anna's obvious discomfort caught the eye of a certain spinster in the audience. She had arrived too late to find a seat, so she stood at the rear of the church. She was middle-aged, of medium build, with auburn hair twisted into a knot and secured at the back of her head. A few stray wisps of hair framed her face.

"Aunt Jennie" Bengtson had almost not come to the church that day. After all, she had many chores to finish. But her neighbor, Dr. Heaston, was chairman of the local adoption committee, and he dropped by and invited her to come. So, at the last minute, she had taken off her apron, donned her old coat, and walked to the church.

As the drama of the orphan children unfolded before her, Jennie couldn't help but recall her own feelings as a motherless child. Her heart went out to each of these children. How well she remembered the loneliness she felt after her mother had died when she was just nine and her sister Minnie was seven. Their older sister had done the best she could, and their father had tried to help, too, but nothing could fill that emptiness.

Jennie Bengtson had come today strictly as a spectator; but now, without warning, she was being drawn into the drama before her. She loved children, and was like a second mother to her nieces and nephews. She'd taught Sunday school classes for many years. But she had never dreamed of actually being a mother!

"I'm too old — and unmarried — how can I even *consider* . . . " she cautioned herself.

But something greater than her own mind seemed to be moving within her. She felt that God was speaking to her, telling her that if she could act on faith, He would uphold her. It didn't matter that she was living alone on a small income and knew nothing about being a mother to a child. She must do something!

What was it she'd been teaching her Sunday school classes for years? Could she not practice what she'd taught about faith? Her mind whirled with conflict. "I'm forty-nine years old — and set in my ways." An answer came back: *Suffer the little children to come unto Me.* "I wish I could talk to my sisters about this, but they aren't here." *Whatever you do for the least of these . . . you do so unto Me.* "How in the world would one raise a child who's had a completely different background?" *Train up a child in the way he should go, and when he is grown he will not depart from it.* "I do love children, but who would look after a child if something happened to me?" *Trust in the Lord. Trust Me.*

Jennie studied each child in turn, searching for some sign of guidance. Her eyes kept returning to Anna. Jennie saw a handicapped child in an ill-fitting blue dress, swinging a red sailor hat, but she also noticed a look of courage and spirit about the girl. Jennie was a good judge of character, and this child had character, she was sure of that.

As Jennie watched Anna, the child caught her eye across the room and offered a hesitant smile. Jennie felt her resolve grow stronger. Suddenly she stepped from her place and made her way through the crush of people to Dr. Heaston, who stood in the narthex doorway.

"Doctor Heaston," she began. She addressed him formally as always, though they were long-time friends and neighbors, "I would like to adopt one of those children! I'd like to take Anna, the older girl in the blue dress."

The committee soon retired to a vestibule to consider all the requests. The audience waited impatiently and the children squirmed in their chairs. Anna looked down at her hands in her lap, continuing her prayer.

Then Dr. Heaston strode to the front and stepped onto the platform. He was a short, dark man with a bristling mustache and a commanding presence; the entire town respected him.

"I am very pleased to announce the committee has approved the placement of seven children." As he spoke, Anna grew panicky. "We also think we have found homes for the other two! The committee wishes to thank everyone for coming out today and supporting the program."

Then, one by one, he began reading off the names of the children and the families who had taken each one. The audience seemed as excited as the children, and there were nods and murmurs of approval with each announcement. The Fuchs girls were last on the list.

"Margaret Fuchs will go to the C. T. Runyan home," the doctor said as Margaret's face lit up. Anna, seated next to her, reached out and squeezed her hand.

The doctor went on: "Helen Fuchs will go to the home of Reverend and Mrs. W. L. Horton of Moundridge, and their older sister, Anna, has been taken by Jennie Bengtson."

Anna looked up at Dr. Heaston with surprise, then joy spread over her face. She had not been passed by! Someone had wanted her!

"Walter will be temporarily cared for by a couple here in town, although we hope to have a permanent home for him in a few days. A family from New Gottland could not make it to town today, but they asked us for a boy his age. And our one Catholic girl, Hope, is expected to find a home with one of the twenty Catholic families here in town, although we can't make an announcement just now."

Suddenly the tension broke with an explosion of applause from the spectators, and the children jumped from their chairs in relief and curiosity. Anna stood up, too.

"It happened. It really happened," Anna whispered to herself. "I've been adopted." Although she still hadn't seen who had taken her, she hugged her sisters, telling them, "Now don't you worry! Everything is going to be fine. I'll be able to see you both often." Then, repeating the words Bill Bishop had spoken to her

110

just a few hours earlier, she added, "You'll like it here. You'll see."

While the crowd was dispersing, Jennie Bengtson edged her way toward the platform. Miss Hill met her and arranged to bring Anna to Jennie's house personally. The other adoptive parents were to pick up the children at the hotel, after the paperwork was finished and the children's luggage collected. But Jennie pressed on through the crowd; she wanted to speak to Anna *now.* She had noticed the child's apprehension and wanted to reassure her. And she could not pass by the other children without giving each of them a friendly word of encouragement and a smile.

Then she came to Anna. Reaching out, Jennie took Anna's right hand and held it. Jennie's gray eyes looked deeply into Anna's bright green ones — Jennie saw intelligence and wit in them.

She said, "Hello, Anna. I'm Jennie Bengtson. You'll be coming to live with me. I hope you'll be happy here." Then she added, "I understand Miss Hill wants to bring you over to my house, so I'll see you then."

Anna smiled. It was good to know that she wouldn't have to go back to the orphanage. But this was only one fear that had been taken care of. There still remained the worst type of fear — what kind of home was she getting? She was afraid of stepmothers because of the stories she'd read about them. And also — Miss Hill would be leaving. She would be left alone with strangers! Anna tried to calm her own thoughts.

Jennie Bengtson turned and, buttoning her coat and fastening a scarf over her head, made her way out the church door. She was dumbfounded by what she had just done, and her first impulse was to tell someone — her sister and friend, Minnie Swanson.

Minnie lived on Elm Street, just a few blocks east of the church, and it would not be much out of the way to stop by on her way home. "I hope she's there," Jennie murmured to herself as she strode through the snow. Her heart thudded and her thoughts were still awhirl.

She arrived at Minnie's front porch and rapped on the door before opening it. "Yoohoo! Minnie! Are you home?" She stepped inside and brushed the wet snow from her coat.

Minnie appeared in the kitchen doorway, an apron over her old green dress. "I'm here, Jennie. Come on back here, I've got my fingers in pie dough."

"Oh, Minnie," Jennie blurted, "you'll never guess what I've just done! I took a girl from the orphan train!" Jennie's eyes sparkled, her face was flushed.

Minnie stared at her in surprise. "Adopted a girl from the orphan train?" she repeated dumbly. "Jennie! I read in the paper about that group of orphans coming to town. There was a meeting this afternoon . . . and you took one of the orphans?"

Minnie now gave up on the piecrust and wiped her hands on a towel.

Jennie waited expectantly for her sister's response. At last, Minnie collected her thoughts. "Well, isn't that wonderful," she began, smiling reassuringly. Then, "Why did you do that?"

"I don't really know," Jennie answered. "It seemed the thing to do. Her name is Anna and she's eleven years old, and she has two little sisters. They found homes here, too. She's a very nice girl," Jennie went on, watching Minnie's face for approval. "She has dark hair. She's polite, and very smart, I'm sure." She did not mention Anna's handicaps.

"I'll need your help and advice, Minnie," Jennie went on. "I don't know anything about being a mother, and you have four children. You'll help me, won't you?"

"Of course I will. Whatever you need," Minnie responded. "The child will probably be good for you. You don't like to be alone, and you've had no one to care for since Dad died. If anyone can bring up a girl, you can," she stated firmly. "But where is she?"

"She went back to the hotel with the others, but Miss Hill, the agent, will be bringing her over to my house soon. I should go, but I wanted to tell you about it. Would you like to meet her tonight?"

"Well, the poor child is probably exhausted after the trip and the excitement today," Minnie observed, quickly assuming her role of advisor. "It would probably be better to let her rest up and get used to you and your home. You'll bring her to church tomorrow, won't you? Why don't you bring her here for dinner afterwards? We can all meet her then. You say her name is Anna? That's a good Swedish name."

"I'm glad you approve, Minnie. I'm counting on advice from you."

Jennie left hurriedly and walked as fast as she could toward home. She wanted to have everything ready when Anna arrived.

16

The Brave Front Crumbles

Miss Hill called to her milling charges above the din of the disassembling crowd. "Children, follow me. Get your wraps. Cars are waiting to take us back to the hotel."

The children, nervous and anxious, chattered and jostled one another, but finally formed a single line and filed toward the back of the church. Helen leaned around to tap Anna.

"Come here," she whispered, crooking her first finger. Stepping out of line, Anna let others pass and again caught a glimpse of that circular window above the altar. "I hope . . . " her thought trailed off as she joined Helen and Margaret.

"Who took you, Anna? Was it the people who gave you the party? I couldn't see!"

"No,'" Anna replied as the girls clustered together and shuffled slowly down the aisle. "It was a lady named Jennie. She came to say hello to me. Aren't you glad it's over? Now everything's going to be fine!" She spoke with much more confidence than she felt.

After the children had fastened their coats and tightened their mufflers, Miss Hill pushed open the front door. It was caught by a strong wind that banged it open and strained its hinges; the storm had not yet subsided. As the children scurried down the steps and climbed into smoke-sputting automobiles, Anna saw that people were standing around outside the church watching them. She hopped into a back seat with Margaret and Helen.

"Did you see the Runyans, Anna?" Margaret leaned forward to see Anna's face. "Aren't they nice?"

113

Anna nodded. "You're lucky you got to know them last night." She turned to Helen. "And you had supper with the Reverend and his family. You know you like them already," she stated encouragingly.

As Anna turned to gaze out the window, she reflected that she knew nothing about her new family. "What if they don't like me, or I do something wrong?" Fear began to well up inside her. "No!" she thought. "It will be all right. It just has to be."

At the hotel Miss Hill stood in the wide lobby, already bidding goodbye to some children and talking with foster families.

"I'll be taking you over to your home when I'm through here, Anna," she said, catching sight of the Fuchs girls stamping snow from their feet. "Margaret and Helen, your families are waiting. Get ready quickly." They nodded and hurried to their room. Anna helped them collect their meager luggage.

"We'll see each other often," Anna said, hugging her sisters as she walked down the staircase with them. She waved goodbye and watched them leave with their families.

When all the others were gone, Anna picked up her small case and her valise and followed Miss Hill. "Five-twenty Marlin Street, please," Miss Hill told the driver.

Anna was so excited she could hardly sit still. What would the new home be like? How many sisters and brothers might there be?

They hadn't gone very far when they veered into a driveway. The driver had apparently misunderstood the address, for Jennie, who'd been watching from her front door, leaned out and called from the porch next door. The car's gears clacked as the auto bounced backward and then pulled into the next drive.

The white frame, two-story house had a front door in the exact center and one window on each side. There were three windows across the front of the second floor. The porch, trimmed with lattice-work, ran the width of the house, and empty flower boxes sat on the railing. Every window gleamed, reflecting the scene across the street. Somehow, these shiny windows seemed beckoning and homey to Anna.

"Welcome, Anna," Jennie smiled, holding the door open wide. "Please sit down, Miss Hill. Anna, follow me and we'll put your things away." Anna climbed the stairs behind Jennie.

Jennie put Anna's coat on the bed in the smallest of the three bedrooms, set her suitcase on the rag rug, and reached for Anna's valise. But Anna placed it beside the case herself.

"This is a boarding house, Anna," Jennie explained, "and this is how I support myself. I'm not married, and you'll be the only child in the house." Anna's face fell, so Jennie quickly added, "But two of my boarders are high school students. They are also my niece and nephew, Ruth and Ted Anderson. They live out in the country, so they stay with me during the school week and go home on weekends. They'll be your cousins," she added smiling.

Anna was confused, so she just nodded shyly. She followed Jennie downstairs.

They returned to the parlor, where Miss Hill had approvingly looked over this home situation from her vantage point on the loveseat. She gave Jennie the one-page adoption agreement to sign. "I'll mail it to you, Miss Hill," Jennie said. "Just leave it with me."

"Well, the car is waiting. I must go." Miss Hill got up. She turned to Anna and kissed her cheek lightly. "Be sure to write to me," she said, then she swept out the door. Anna followed her to the porch and Jennie stood behind her, waving goodbye. As Anna watched Miss Hill climb into the sedan and drive away, she suddenly burst into tears.

"What is it, dear?" Jennie said, alarmed, putting her arm around the girl. Anna just shook her head and sobbed miserably.

"I know this has been a big day for you," Jennie said comfortingly. "Come to the kitchen with me. We'll have a snack. Do you prefer gingersnaps or sugar cookies?"

Anna made no reply; she sobbed louder and harder until her breath was coming in gasps and her eyes spurted huge tears. But she obediently followed Jennie out into the kitchen.

This spacious room with its scrubbed wood floor, big black wood-burning stove and bright yellow curtains was Jennie's center of operations. And she knew youngsters could be comforted with food. But Anna refused to sit down at the kitchen table with its cheerful checkered cloth. Instead, she found a little stepladder in the corner and sat down, weeping.

"Please, Anna," Jennie began, "everything will be all right. Just give things a chance. Will you tell me what's wrong?"

But Anna wept as though her heart were breaking. Wild thoughts began to flit through Jennie's mind. Could it be that Hungarians had volatile temperaments? Was the girl well? In a matter of minutes, Jennie felt she was already in over her head with this sudden leap into motherhood. "I could call the Runyans and have them bring your sister over. Would that help, Anna?"

But just at that moment, the kitchen door opened and a tall

young man stamped the snow from his feet and began removing his wet galoshes. He looked up in surprise at the sound of Anna's sobbing.

"Oh, Ted!" Jennie exclaimed. "I'm busy with Anna, and I haven't had time to put your supper on the table. Will you talk to her and see if you can get her to stop crying? I'll call the Runyans and ask them to bring her sister over. I'll put your supper on when I finish calling."

"Sure, Aunt Jennie," said the blond, handsome, sturdy young man. "I heard all about it. People have been coming into the grocery store all afternoon to tell me my aunt adopted a girl from the orphan train." He turned to look at the newcomer, who was still sunk in misery.

"Oh," Jennie murmured, "this is Anna. Anna, this is my nephew, Ted Anderson. He's a big tease." She went to the telephone, leaving Ted to talk to Anna.

Catching the hint, Ted said, "Hey, is this any way to treat a fella? Are you trying to drown this kitchen in tears?"

Anna still wept.

Ted kept trying. "Hey, let me tell you about this town. Or are you gonna be a big-city snob and not even speak to a country cousin?"

Anna thought Ted reminded her of her sanitarium friends, always teasing. She tried to smile through her tears, but she could not stop crying long enough to even say hello.

"Well, let's see," Ted went on valiantly. "I know that song, 'East side, west side, all around the town.' That's about New York. What side of town do you come from?"

Jennie hurried into the kitchen. "It's going to be all right, Anna. The Runyans are bringing your sister right over. Please try to stop crying now, and have some cookies and milk."

Anna sniffed and nodded. "If I can just stay here on the step-ladder," she whispered. Jennie turned to get the snack.

Anna realized she had to stop crying before Margaret arrived. She had succeeded so far in keeping her sisters from seeing her cry. Her brave front, put on for their benefit, had been intact. Any minute now, Margaret would walk in the door. It wouldn't do for Margaret to see her bawling like a little kid. Desperately she wiped her eyes with her hands, then wiped her hands on her skirt. She bit her lip and her body shook with unvented sobs. Gradually she calmed down. At last she took a big gulp from the glass of milk Jennie had put beside her.

116

Ted hastily ate his supper, then got up. "I have to hurry back for the Saturday night rush at the store. Bye for now," he said to Anna as he swung out the door. "Take good care of my aunt. See you tomorrow night when Ruth and I come back from the farm."

Anna was brushing cookie crumbs from her skirt when Margaret and the Runyans appeared at the door. Jennie knew instantly she'd had a good idea when she saw Anna rise from the stool and speak to the visitors.

She exchanged small talk with the Runyans while the two girls visited quietly. At last the Runyans were ready to leave and Anna said goodbye to her sister again. The visit had helped all of them.

Jennie tried to put herself in Anna's place. She could see that Anna needed time to adjust to the day's developments, the new surroundings, and to Jennie herself. "Why don't you go look around the house," she urged Anna. "I'll finish my chores here."

Timidly at first, Anna began to inspect her new surroundings. On the first floor were two living rooms, a dining room, a big kitchen, a front and back porch. The dining room table was spread with a white lace cloth and in its center was a beautiful Christmas cactus with red blooms. Floral patterned rugs, potted ferns on stands, lace curtains, colorful paintings on the walls, and a pretty chandelier pleased her. But it was the parlor loveseat that appealed most to Anna. Upholstered in beige with a mahogany frame, it seemed to symbolize this new life, for it looked like a perfect spot to curl up and read books.

While Anna was still exploring, she heard footsteps on the porch. A warmly dressed woman with a full figure, and a beaming smile came in the front door just as Jennie entered from the kitchen. "Hannah," Jennie announced to the woman, "This is Anna Fuchs. She's come to live with me. Anna, this is Hannah Johnson, the school nurse. She boards here." Hannah grinned cheerfully, disguising her surprise.

"Do you suppose we could move things around so there's room upstairs for Anna?"

"Sure, I'll get the folding cot," Hannah offered.

That night, as Anna went to bed, she pondered the events of the day, and tried to understand more about this woman who'd chosen her. There was nothing about Jennie that reminded her of her own mother. Nor was she like Mother D'Jacoma. "Why did Jennie pick me?" she wondered as she drowsed off to sleep.

Jennie stayed up late. She had a special task to accomplish —

117

remaking Anna's blue velvet dress so it would fit properly. She knew just what was needed . . . taking in the side seam and a deeper hem. Perhaps a tuck at the shoulders.

As she sewed, she thought. She believed she'd done the right thing in taking Anna. Surely, God wanted them to be together. That feeling had been so strong, there was no mistaking it. That did not mean it was going to be easy, she realized. But it could turn out to be a blessing for both of them — the homeless girl and the lonely woman. Not since her aged father had passed away had Jennie had anyone to care for.

But the many demands required of a mother! How would she, a spinster, cope with them? Minnie and Ida would give advice and help, she knew. But much would depend on Jennie herself.

Then, as she rethreaded the needle, she bowed her head. "Lord," she whispered. "What have I done? Did I act on impulse? If so, I just put my trust in You."

She finished her sewing and went to bed.

17

New Cousins

As the Kansas winter sun streamed through her window and spread gently across her bed, Anna began to waken. It was a cozy feeling to be warmed by the sun, especially in winter. She smiled lazily and stretched. She opened her eyes. Suddenly she remembered yesterday's events, her crying spell and the heartache she'd felt. She looked around, her throat tightening. She was alone in a strange house, with a woman who spoke up for her at the adoption meeting. The woman seemed nice enough, of course, but many others had, too. Anna had learned that people could not be trusted — her safety and welfare were up to her alone.

For now, she realized, she was here, and she had to make the best of it, but she would watch her adopted family closely. With this decided, she found it easier to get out of bed and start to dress. That baggy blue velvet dress was on the chair beside her bed. She quickly pulled it over her head and looked down in surprise. It didn't hang limply on her — it fit! The shoulders no longer drooped, the waist was just right, and even the hem had been taken up.

"You fixed it!" she exclaimed to Jennie as she came down to breakfast. "Thank you!"

"I want you to look nice for church today," Jennie answered. As long as she lived, Jennie would never forget the sight of the orphan girl in the too-big dress standing on that platform.

Anna's dark head was bent over her plate. She ate sparingly and daintily. Jennie spoke brightly of the day's plans, but Anna said little.

They walked together to the Swedish Lutheran Church on

the corner of Marlin and Elm Streets. Anna noticed it was built of red brick, like many of the buildings in New York. But she could tell by its tall steeple and beautiful stained-glass windows that it was a church. Anna had not been in a church since she had been baptized as a Presbyterian five months earlier, back in New York.

A tall, elderly, balding man in a black frock coat waited at the door. "Ah, Reverend Anderson," exclaimed Jennie, "I want you to meet my girl, Anna Fuchs! She's come to live with me. Anna, this is Reverend Erland Anderson."

Bending slightly, the pastor took Anna's right hand. As he did so, he noticed her handicap. Without a flicker of surprise he said, "Oh, look, Anna. We have something in common. I'm missing a finger, too." He showed her his hand. "Mine was lost in an accident when I was a boy."

Anna answered shyly, "I was born this way, Reverend."

They went into Jennie's Sunday school class in the basement where Anna sat quietly, observing the activities. When it was time for church, Jennie was one of the last to come upstairs, so they took seats on a crowded side aisle. This day's sermon was in Swedish, for as Jennie explained, "Each week alternates, one week is in English and the next it's in Swedish. Many of the older folks want to hear the sermons in their native language. On special occasions, both languages are used."

Afterwards, several people came over to meet "Jennie's girl." Anna tried to act ladylike.

"We'll walk over to Aunt Minnie and Uncle Joe Swanson's for dinner," Jennie said. "They have four children, Ingeborg, Kenneth, Oscar, and Elizabeth."

Anna was introduced to her new relatives. She stood with her hands folded behind her back, her eyes down. She was not accustomed to being around families, for at the sanitarium and the orphanage she'd been with other children and young people. But the Swanson children shared their Sunday comics with her, and she began to feel comfortable.

When they sat down for dinner, the food was passed around and each child was allowed to take as much as he or she wanted. This was a new experience for Anna, who was used to having her food dished up for her in the institutions. She quickly learned that although she could help herself, this did not mean she could pass up anything. Instead, Jennie quietly instructed her to take a very small portion of the foods she didn't care for, and more of the things she liked. It was a pleasant feeling to be able to have some control over this aspect of her life.

After dinner, the children were still looking one another over before becoming too friendly. The Swansons brought out their favorite books, sharing them with Anna. They all sat quietly reading.

As Minnie came into the living room, still drying a dish, she noticed that things were very quiet. She knew that reading was not a good way for children to get acquainted, so she took Jennie aside. She had a huddle with her in the kitchen.

Minnie came back to the living room and announced, "All right, you bookworms, you need some fresh air. It's a nice, sunny day so bundle up — we're going outside for some fun!"

To Anna's delight, they fixed the circle for Fox and Geese, a game she loved to play. She knew it required hollering and laughing if one was going to have fun, so she joined right in.

As the children giggled and teased, Anna began to feel more at ease with her "cousins." When they got too cold and came back indoors, they asked her if there was anything else she'd like to play. She blurted out, "Hey, do you have a deck of cards?"

They did, although most card games were forbidden in Swedish Lutheran families. Kenneth got the cards out and gave them to Anna, who shuffled them with such expertise that her cousins' eyes seemd ready to pop.

"Hey, how do you do that?" asked Kenneth, impressed.

"It's easy," Anna answered, pleased that she had their interest. "What shall we play? Rummy? Pinochle? What'll it be?" There was a stony silence.

Finally Ingeborg spoke up. "We're not supposed to play cards, except Old Maid and stuff like that," she admitted. "Our church doesn't approve," and she shook her blonde head for emphasis.

Anna was puzzled. By asking many questions, she also learned that the children were not permitted to attend movies or to dance.

No one could give her an explanation that satisfied her. Eventually they all began playing dominoes. Anna vowed to herself to learn more about this religion that kept people from doing things that were fun.

This was only the beginning of a serious problem for Anna . . . the adjustment to a narrower lifestyle, for standards were different in the East than in the conservative Midwest.

Anna also decided that at her first opportunity, she was going to show these country cousins how to dance the steps she had learned at the sanitarium social events. There couldn't be any harm in that, she told herself, and then they'd find out how much fun they were missing.

As the Swansons, Jennie and Anna sat around the dining room table after supper, everyone started telling Anna about her new relatives.

"Uncle Eddie, Aunt Jennie's oldest brother, lives in California," began Ingeborg. "But he brings Aunt Esther and the cousins — Carol, Marjorie, Evelyn, John, and Ann — to Kansas every year on the train because he gets free passes."

"That's because he works for the railroad," Oscar broke in.

"But Uncle David and Aunt Edith — they live north of McPherson — they have the biggest family," Ingeborg went on. "Seven children!"

"I'll name them all for you," Kenneth volunteered, and not waiting for Anna's reply, began: "Let's see, there's Ralph, Edna, Arthur, Ann Marie, Margaret, Paul, and baby Joan."

Anna began to giggle. "Wait . . . wait!" she cried, shaking her head. "I can't keep up. So many names — I'll *never* remember all of those cousins! Until I meet them," she added.

With all of Jennie's relatives a jumble in her own mind, Anna would have been amazed to know that one of the cousins she'd never met, Ruth Anderson, had had a dream about her the night before.

After Ted had met Anna in Jennie's kitchen and tried to comfort her, he went home and talked about Anna to his fifteen-year-old sister, Ruth.

"We have a new cousin, Ruth," Ted announced. "Aunt Jennie adopted one of the girls from the orphan train!"

"Really?" cried Ruth. "How exciting! What's her name?"

"I can't remember her name!" Ted looked thoughtful. "All she did was sit on a stepladder and cry while I was there," he said. "But she looked about ten years old."

When Ruth went to bed that night, she couldn't stop wondering about the girl Aunt Jennie had adopted. When morning came, she told her family that she'd had a dream about her.

"In my dream, her name was Emma Jane. Isn't that pretty?" she said.

"Nope," said Ted, shaking his head. "I don't think so."

"Well, don't waste your time arguing, you two," their mother told them. "It's Sunday and you'll be going back to Aunt Jennie's tonight. Then you can find out all you want to know about the orphan girl."

When the Andersons pulled up in front of Jennie's that night, Ruth was the first to dash up the porch steps and burst into the house. Jennie and Anna were waiting for her.

"Hello, Ruth," Jennie said. "Anna, this is Ruth." The two girls smiled at each other. *Look at those dark curls,* thought Ruth, staring at Anna. *What beautiful hair. And a velvet dress, too!* She was impressed and pleased with her new cousin from the East.

Anna, too, looked at the other girl with shining eyes — Ruth had a lovely face and long, blonde hair. She could see that Ruth was older, too, and probably knew about things like dancing and movies and cards. Anna told herself that when the two of them were better acquainted, she would ask her about those things.

Anna was introduced to Aunt Ida and Uncle Alfred, too, and everyone sat down around the living room, chatting. Then Ted offered to take Anna around the block on the sled. When they returned to the house, they were laughing and ruddy-faced. Jennie invited everyone to have some hot chocolate with marshmallows before Aunt Ida and Uncle Alfred left for home.

Later, while Jennie and Anna were putting the dishes away, Jennie complimented Anna on how well she had done, meeting so many new people that day. "Everyone likes you, Anna. They can tell you're a bright, well-mannered young lady. I'm proud of you."

"Thank you," Anna said shyly. She wanted to say so much more, but somehow, no words would come.

The next morning, Jennie took Anna down to Park School, where she was enrolled in the fifth grade. Now Anna began to feel like she belonged. She soon made friends with some of the girls in her class, and for the first time in months she began to feel that maybe her education would be completed in the way she had hoped.

Jennie's friends and acquaintances would stop Jennie and inquire about "her girl," and many questioned her about Anna's crippled hand and hip. There were quietly-posed questions about how she expected the child to make a living and someday take care of Jennie in her old age.

"All I want is to be able to give her a home, because she needs it," Jennie would answer. "I'm sure that girl will always be able to take care of herself," she said.

18
Secret Photographs

Anna bent over two small photographs on the marble-top table in the corner of the living room, her hands clasped behind her as she leaned forward to study them.

"Those are my parents, Anna," Jennie explained as she entered the room. She pointed to the faded picture of a young woman in a dark dress. "That's my mother. She died when I was nine, so I understand how it feels to be motherless." Motioning toward the picture of a white-haired, bearded man, she added, "And that's my father. He passed away just two years ago. I took care of him, kept house and all."

"Did he ever get married again? Did you have a stepmother?" Anna's eyes opened wide.

"No. No, he never did re-marry," Jennie reflected.

"That's good. Stepmothers are awful people!"

"Why, Anna! Where'd you ever get an idea like that?"

"From the movies. And books. Stepmothers always treat little kids real mean."

"Well, I don't think that's true. But I do remember that once my father told my brothers and sisters and me he was going to get us a stepmother, and we were scared, even though she lived in Sweden and we'd never met her. Then Dad told us that the lady wasn't coming to our house because she didn't want to leave her country. And we were glad."

Anna wanted to know more, but didn't know how to begin. "What happened to your mother?" she finally asked.

"Mother wasn't very strong after she had so many children, and she just wasn't well enough to live the hard pioneer life. My older sister — that's your Aunt Ida — took over the housework, and I tried to help, too. Your Aunt Minnie was only seven then, but even so, she worked hard to do her chores. And I got an early start on cooking. Ida tried hard to make a good home, and Dad worked to keep the family going."

Jennie adjusted the two photographs, and absently straightened the lace doily. "Anna," she said, "I'd like you to feel at home here. I know I can't take the place of your parents, and I don't want to. I just want to give you a home because you need one. So, if you want to put up some pictures of your family, that's fine with me. Do you have any photographs?"

Anna hesitated. She didn't know if she should divulge her secret. Did Jennie know? Should she tell her?

"You see," Jennie continued, "it's a natural desire of everyone to have a keepsake or memory from loved ones. I'd like you to put your parents' pictures right here on the table beside mine."

Anna looked at Jennie intently. Jennie had already proved to be loving and concerned. If she were going to be living here, she might as well confess her big secret — the secret she'd kept even from her own sisters.

"Yes, I do have some pictures," she whispered.

"Where are they? Let's see them!" Jennie smiled warmly.

Anna took the stairs two at a time, grabbed the valise from under her bed and brought it down. She joined Jennie on the loveseat and opened the valise.

"My dad gave me this valise for Christmas when we were at the sanitarium," Anna said. "I used to have a doll, too, but it got lost somewhere. Everybody tried to take this valise away from me, but I didn't let them." She did not add that her tactics had included a tantrum, and an all-night crying spell at the halfway house. The staff there had finally decided that their attempts to remove the valise were the cause of all her wailing, and one had told another: "Whatever you do, let her keep that case." So, in spite of all rules to the contrary, Anna had arrived in Kansas with one of her own possessions.

She lifted the lid and rummaged under the doll clothes and books, then drew out a packet of photographs.

"I had to keep these hid. All the way out here I was afraid someone would find out. At the halfway house, the orphanage, on the train, everywhere. Not even my sisters know."

Jennie raised her eyebrows: "You mean the authorities didn't want you to have pictures of your family?"

"No. The rule is, no possessions — too many memories. But I wanted these so bad. I knew it was all I'd ever have to remind me of my parents."

"Oh, Anna! But how did you get them in the first place?"

Anna took a deep breath, then looked straight at Jennie. "I stole them."

"Oh, my . . . "

"Well, not really. See, I got them out of my mother's apartment after she died. But I wasn't supposed to have them."

"Tell me about it."

"When I came back from the sanitarium after Mother died, I stayed with her neighbor, Mrs. Rawald, for about two weeks. My sisters were away at camp. When they came back we went to the orphanage. Well, one day, Mrs. Rawald took me to Mother's apartment, and I was halfway happy for the first time since I'd left the sanitarium."

Anna paused to catch her breath, trying to think how best to explain things.

"Go on," Jennie said with an encouraging nod.

"While Mrs. Rawald was checking on things in the kitchen and front room, I went to the bedroom and headed for the trunk. I guess Mother had let us do that, because it seemed natural, even though I hadn't been home for five years. I was in the sanitarium, you know," Anna paused and smiled nervously.

"I even had an idea what I was going to find there — pictures. And I started looking at them. I sorted them into three piles. The ones of the family I put on a stand near the trunk. The ones I wasn't interested in, I put in the lid of the trunk, and the ones I wanted to look at again, I put on the bed. There were two pictures I wanted to know about — one of a man in a uniform holding his gloves in one hand. The other was of a pretty woman in a fancy dress holding a parasol.

"Then I found a picture of two babies sitting on a rug. I thought maybe it was me and my twin brother — someone said I was a twin — and I took the three pictures to Mrs. Rawald." Here Anna paused again.

"What did Mrs. Rawald say? Are you a twin?" Jennie's eyes were warm and interested.

"Well, she got real mad . . . She took the pictures away from me, and she said, 'Where'd you get these?' I asked her who the

126

people were and if I could keep the pictures. She said no, and she didn't have time to tell me about the people. And she said it in a voice that meant *no*. So I showed her where I found the pictures.

"She took those three pictures, and the ones I'd put on the bed, and the ones in the trunk lid, and put them all in the trunk and closed the lid and latched it. She told me not to open the trunk again, and not to touch anything else, either. She said we were going back to her apartment."

"Then how did you get these?" Jennie enquired.

"I saw that she'd missed the pictures I'd put on the stand, so I said, 'okay' and I walked real slow behind her, and grabbed the pictures as I passed the stand. I slipped them in my dress pocket and then I followed her."

"And she didn't notice?"

"No. She knew I felt bad, and let me go in the back bedroom when we got to her apartment. She made some hot chocolate to cheer me up, but I had to hurry and find a hiding place for the pictures. I decided the valise was the best place, because I could keep it with me. And I did. All the way out here."

Jennie's gentle face reflected no condemnation. And she felt very small. The girl had pluck, just as she had surmised. Considering the crime, Anna seemed sorry enough about it. Probably Mrs. Rawald sold or gave away all of the Fuchs' possessions, anyway. Why couldn't a child have a picture of her parents? Jennie put her hand on Anna's. Sometimes she wondered about the wisdom of decisions made by some people that had such profound effects on the lives of others, especially little ones.

"Let's see them," Jennie urged.

"I only have two pictures with my mother in them," Anna said, deftly sorting through the pile. "Here she is with my little sisters. I guess this was taken when I was at the sanitarium."

127

Jennie studied the photo of an intense, dark-eyed, dark-haired young woman seated beside two little girls in white dresses.

"Your mother was a beautiful woman. Refined looking." Jennie commented.

"She always told me to use my right hand," Anna confided. "She'd say, 'I want you to use it in the normal way.' Here she is with the whole family." Anna flicked another picture from the stack. "This was taken the day Dad and I left for the sanitarium. I remember how excited I was to be going on a train ride. I didn't know I'd never see Mother again."

Jennie noticed that the family had been seated in a cardboard boat with the name *Mayflower*. How ironic that this little immigrant family had posed in a boat with such a name. She saw a frail-looking, darkly handsome man sitting in the bow, a lovely young woman with a huge hat, white blouse and dark skirt at the other end of the boat, and between them, three little girls. Anna was in the middle, her huge hairbow standing high above her hair.

"This one's my favorite," Anna said, "because it was the last time we were all together." She tucked it away, and laid four more photos in Jennie's lap. "This is Dad when he was very young. Look on the back, the writing is Hungarian, I guess."

Jennie could trace the progression of Anna's father's illness in the pictures. The last three, all taken at the sanitarium, showed a man whose health had failed swiftly. One photograph showed Steven Fuchs and his little Anna, at age five or six, together, their arms around each other affectionately.

"And these were Dad's friends," Anna poined out. "He's standing in front of the shacks at the sanitarium. We called them

128

shacks — but they were sleeping porches with dressing rooms inside."

"He was handsome," Jennie said, "and I'm sure he was a loving father, too."

There were five more photos in Anna's collection, depicting activities of the sanitarium and showing Anna posing happily on a pony, playing in a snowsuit, waving an American flag, and squinting cheerfully from the front row of a group of children on a hillside.

"All of the children look older than you," Jennie observed.

"Yes, I was the youngest. They let me stay because Dad was there."

Jennie noticed the girl behind Anna had her arm on Anna's shoulder. "That's Sophia, my friend. Her family escaped from Russia, but she was crippled. And there's Amanda." She pointed to a black girl. "She was my friend, too. We held a snake once, and we used to slide down snowy hills in our washbasins."

"You were happy there, weren't you?" Jennie surmised.

"Yes. Until Father died. We played outside a lot and only had school half-days. There were movies every week, and lots of things to do. Dad and I saw each other every day. Sometimes he would hoe the flower garden. A certain kind of flowers — nasturtiums — remind me of Dad," Anna said. "And he'd talk to me after supper every night before we went to our shacks."

"But you never got to go home — even for a visit?"

"No, Dad told me he was going home, but he didn't. He only told me that because he knew he was going to die, and I guess he thought if I believed he was at home I wouldn't be sad. But he died, and I knew it. After he died, no one would tell me, but I found out."

"And then you stayed there until you were ten years old, and then came back to the city after your mother died?"

"Yes."

"Well, Anna, you have been taken out of one situation and put in a different one, but I know you'll make the best of it. If you can be happy in a sanitarium, you can be happy in Kansas," Jennie chuckled, trying to cheer the girl.

Anna grinned.

"When we go to town Saturday, I'll buy frames for your pictures. Which ones are you going to put up?" She sensed that Anna was uncomfortable with the memories and needed reassurance.

Anna's fingers nimbly sorted through the stack and she chose three — the family in the Mayflower, the one of her father and herself at the sanitarium, and one of her mother and sisters. "These," she said.

Since Anna had used the handicapped fingers with such dexterity, Jennie decided she should bring up the subject that had been touched on.

"You know, Anna, your mother was right to encourage you to use your hand. You do many things well.

"And because of your experiences, you've seen people who have handicaps much worse than yours. You've gotten to the place where you're no longer aware of these defects."

Anna squirmed in her chair as Jennie's gray eyes looked kindly into hers.

"Just let me tell you this, Anna. God had a reason for making you this way and it is up to you to make the best of it. Never feel sorry for yourself," Jennie said. "Don't draw attention to your handicaps, nor expect sympathy from others. You *can* do anything others can do if you want to badly enough. You can't do it in the same way they can, but you can still do it.

"Never use your handicap as an excuse for doing poor work. Do the best you can because you want to, and don't expect others to accept poor work just because your hand and leg aren't normal."

Now Jennie picked up both of Anna's hands in her own and squeezed them gently. "You will go to high school, Anna, and then to college. Education is very important, not just as a means of making money, but rather as a guide for living and enjoying life. There is a real joy in learning, and you should try to get everything you can from your studies and school activities. You can lose possessions so easily, but what you have in your head and your heart will stay with you the rest of your life."

Then, almost embarrassed by her own words that had revealed her life's philosophy, she cleared her throat. In a businesslike tone she said, "Now, young lady, don't you think it's time we set the table for supper?"

19

Lutfisk and Julotta

The evergreen stood resplendent, ablaze with real white candles that transformed the tree into a breathtaking sight. The lights flickered and glowed against its shiny green needles, giving it a halo of radiance like tiny, snowflakes filling the air around it. Homemade cookies and straw figures nestled cozily in its branches, and paper chains encircled the ceiling-high cedar.

Anna snapped off the ceiling light at the button wall switch. Her eyes twinkled, reflecting the glimmering lights in front of her.

"It's magic, isn't it?" she whispered.

"Yes," Ingeborg agreed. "It's the prettiest tree I've ever seen."

"Bet you've never decorated a tree with real candles before, have you, Anna?" Ruth asked.

"No," Anna responded. "We never had real candles at home."

"You did the job just like a pure Swede," Ruth teased her. "You Svenska flicka?"

Anna's eyes crinkled and she laughed. "No, I'm not a Swedish girl, but I'm glad to have a Swedish family."

"Let's bring Aunt Jennie in to see it now," Ingeborg said.

"Come and see!" the three girls called.

Jennie, awaiting the invitation, appeared at the doorway, her sewing glasses in her hand.

"My, my," she chuckled quietly, as she took in the sight, "this house has never had such a tree!" She put her arm across
131

Anna's shoulders. "I hope you have a happy Christmas here," she said. All of them gazed at the tree in silence.

"I think you girls deserve a treat," said Jennie, interrupting their thoughts. "I made *springerle* today. Let's bring the cookies and milk in here so we can enjoy your decorating work."

As they munched on the tasty Swedish butter cookies and sipped milk they chatted about the holiday activities.

"Tomorrow night Anna must come with me to the neighbors," Jennie told her nieces. "We're finishing the costumes for the Sunday school program."

"Yes," Anna exclaimed. "And I get to put the tinsel on the angel wings."

"And try on the costumes so we can mark the hems," Jennie added. "And the next night we'll be filling the sacks of candy so that every child under age fourteen will get a treat at the Christmas program at church."

"Is there anything we can help with?" Ingeborg asked.

"If you want to do something, you can wrap the gifts for my Sunday school class," Jennie suggested.

"What are you giving them this year?" Ingeborg wanted to know. She confided to Anna, "Aunt Jennie always makes Christmas gifts for the children. Such pretty things."

"Bible markers this year," Jennie answered. "Crocheted in the shape of Christmas candles with red ribbons woven through them."

"Let's wrap them," said Ruth. "I feel just like a Christmas elf. What fun!"

Later that night, after Ingeborg had gone home and Ruth was in bed, Anna crept downstairs again. The candles had been put out and there were no lights on anywhere in the house. Only the dim light of a streetlamp and the moonlight that shone in the windows illuminated her way. She sat down at the foot of the darkened tree, pulling her nightgown around her feet.

"My first Christmas in the West," she whispered. She remembered past Christmases, their apartment in New York, going shopping with her dad. Once he'd pulled her over the snow on a sled as she held onto packages for him. They'd tipped over on a hill and a package had come undone — a Santa Claus suit and false whiskers had fallen out. Her father hadn't said a word. He had picked up the articles swiftly, and rewrapped them. On Christmas Eve he'd worn the outfit as he handed out presents to his family.

But the news was out for Anna. She wasted no time in telling Margaret the truth about Santa Claus. But Margaret had refused to believe Anna's report.

Then there were five Christmases at the sanitarium — three of them without her father, because he'd died after two years there. Now here she was, in a strange place, trying to keep Christmas again. She whispered a small, private prayer, then climbed the stairs to bed.

⊱ ✦❀✦ ⊰

Jennie noticed that each day heightened Anna's sense of excitement and anticipation. Getting used to a new home and a new life seemed to be easier when it was accompanied by the joys of the holiday season. Anna had a small part in the Christmas program at church, and she performed well. Now it was the night before Christmas and time for another family gathering.

"Aunt Ida's a wonderful hostess and cook. And you'll meet Ruth's two older brothers, Walter and Carl," Jennie told Anna as they rode in the Swanson's crowded car. "You'll like our Swedish dishes. But if you don't, take a little bit of each anyway," she cautioned Anna. "That would be polite."

The car was packed with eight people, all bundled up and holding packages, so that the old Buick seemed to bulge as it grumbled over the snowy road. Then they arrived, and everyone swarmed inside. The house was bright with decorations, fragrant with cooking chicken, and loud with chatter.

Ruth led Anna up the stairs to put her coat on top of a tall heap of coats on one of the beds. Holly wreaths and bows made the stairway festive and a ceiling-tall tree dominated the living room. All around it lay an array of gifts in all sizes and colors.

Tables had been placed in a row in the dining room and living room so that everyone would be seated together. The women put the finishing touches on the meal while the men went outside to look at the livestock. The youngsters ran in and out, barely containing their excitement.

Then it was time for the meal. Everyone took their places, peering at the handmade placecards to see who was to sit by whom. All the family stood behind their chairs as Uncle Alfred, the host, offered the blessing, then sat down.

The dinner was typically Swedish and included many dishes Anna had never heard of. Jennie quietly explained each dish to Anna, who was seated beside her. There was *lutfisk* (Swedish whitefish), *potatiskorv* (potato sausage), *sill sallat* (herring salad),

133

fruit soup, *bruna boner* (brown beans), *kummin ost* (caraway cheese), head cheese, fresh-butchered roast meat and chicken, *drika* (Swedish root beer), and *ost kaka* (curd pudding) with ling-onberries and whipped cream spread on top. Dutifully Anna began to sample each dish.

"Wait until you taste the lutfisk, Anna," Uncle Joe called down the table to her. All the others looked up expectantly. They knew how Uncle felt about the delicacy.

"Come now, Joe," Jennie answered sweetly. "Don't try to sway Anna's tastes."

"You should learn about lutfisk, Anna, even if you won't eat it," Uncle Joe continued. "Swedes think lutfisk is a wonderful holiday dish. At least some Swedes do. Now me, I never touch it. I have to prepare tanks of it for my customers at the store, and sometimes I think my clothes still smell like fish in the spring-time."

"Now Joe," Jennie put in, as Anna grinned back at him.

"Well, if it doesn't smell, Jennie, then why do you cook your lutfisk on the burner in the washroom on your back porch?"

Jennie chuckled quietly and said nothing.

"I had a German boy who delivered groceries for me," Joe went on. "Said he could tell who the Swedes were just by open-ing the back door during the Christmas season!"

Everyone laughed and picked up their own conversations with their tablemates as serving dishes were passed around the circle. Jennie leaned toward Anna and said, "It's really good, An-na. Dried whitefish, soaked, then cooked slowly, and served in cream sauce. Try it."

Anna speared a piece with her fork and found that it tasted fine.

When the meal was finished, and the tables were cleared and order restored, everyone gathered for the opening of gifts. Anna was surprised to find a pile of presents accumulating at her feet as the packages were passed around the living room by Ruth and Ted. Unwrapping her gifts, Anna found: a book, a new green dress, beautiful rose material for another, and a child's manicure set. In the last box Anna found a large doll with eyes that opened and closed. She lifted it tenderly out of the box, stroked its em-broidered dress, and touched the knitted shoes. "You're beauti-ful," Anna whispered, eyes shining. "I'll call you Mary," and she hugged her close.

If Anna had seen what had happened in the kitchen while

the women were preparing the meal, she would have had no doubt about her place in the family. Discussing the new niece, Jennie told them Anna did not have a doll, her own having been lost somewhere between the orphanage and McPherson, although the valise had come through safely.

"I thought perhaps she was too old for a doll," Jennie tried to say. "Maybe she'd rather have clothes." Jennie looked confused.

Lifting a big wooden spoon for emphasis, Aunt Minnie had stated, "Eleven's not too old for a doll. Maybe she *will* be too old for one next year, so she should have a doll this Christmas! I bought a doll for Elizabeth and sewed some clothes for it — it's under the tree now. But Elizabeth has other dolls. And she's younger. There will be other dolls for her. Let's give this doll to Anna instead."

And so the tag on the package had been stealthily changed. As Anna held the beautiful doll, it seemed to her that the women in the room were watching her closely. The entire family was behind Jennie in helping her to make a home for Anna, but it would be years before Anna was aware of the all-out support.

As they rode back to town that night, Anna sat in the back seat, clutching Mary and singing Christmas carols to herself. Jennie looked up at the winking stars, and it seemed as though she could hear the angels themselves singing.

On Christmas morning, Anna was awakened at five a.m. by Jennie's call. "Get up now, Anna. Time for Julotta services!" Anna had already learned that for Swedish Lutheran families, Christmas morning was not a day for sleeping late. On Christmas morning, they celebrated that most joyous, most holy of services, *Julotta.*

For years, Jennie had never missed a Julotta service. The traditional event took place very early Christmas morning before the first ray of dawn appeared. The service began in the quiet, reverent atmosphere of a darkened church, illuminated by hundreds of candles. Then the music would begin, and gradually the spirit of Christmas would swell until it permeated the hearts and souls of everyone present. The service culminated just as the sun was rising. People came out of the church to find that The Light had come.

It was important to get to church early to find a seat, and Jennie urged Anna to hurry. Anna dressed quickly, made her bed,

135

and dashed downstairs to put on her coat and hat before stepping outside with Jennie into the still night. The stars were out, twinkling serenely in the pure sky. The air was frosty; a little snow had fallen, coating everything with a fresh layer of white. As Anna crunched along on the icy sidewalk, she said quietly to Jennie, "I've never been out of doors this late — or this early, whatever — on a winter night before. Isn't it beautiful?" As they neared the church they were joined by others, walking to church to celebrate the birth of the Savior.

The church was nearly filled. Anna paused at the door to drink in the beauty of the sanctuary. The dark walnut walls glowed with the light of tree lights and candles, the only illumination. Plain white candles stood in each windowsill, surrounded by evergreen wreaths. Two huge Christmas trees flanked the altar. The tall cedars glittered with hundreds of tiny white electric lights, and all but engulfed the minister when he stood up and took his place at the front of the altar. The organ played softly as Jennie and Anna took their seats.

Then the music swelled, and from behind the congregation came the choir, moving in slow and stately procession toward their loft at the front. Their voices rose in the joyous, haunting Swedish carol: "Ho-se-ann-a, Ho-se-ann-a." Goosebumps rose on Anna's arms as she stood up with the others during the processional. The singers marched slowly past her aisle seat, still singing. Anna looked around the church at the many faces, half-seen in the flickering candlelight. They were nearly all strange to her, but in a way, friendly and secure. These plain people — farmers, farm wives, merchants and laborers — were, in a sense, her new family. And this was her home.

❦

It was just after New Year's Day when Jennie realized she had not made any entries in her diary since before Anna arrived in McPherson. That evening, after setting the bread to rise and turning out the lights, she climbed the stairs to Anna's room, looked in to find her sleeping, then went to her own room where she sat down in the old rocker. Lifting the diary from a nearby drawer, she wrote:

Fall and winter, 1924-25. Have for boarders, Miss Hannah Johnson, school nurse, Teddie and Ruth Anderson, and Clarence Benson.

December 1924. Anna Katherine Fuchs came to live with me. She is an orphan girl from New York. She was one of a group of orphan children that Miss Hill brought out here to find homes for. She was the oldest in the group, eleven years old the day she came to me. Her two sisters, Margaret and Helen, also found homes around here.

Their parents are both dead and these girls have no relatives in this country. Poor girls, when our parents are gone, we have lost our best friends. We are sure to find that out. But we have "One Friend" who is always near, and I know Anna has found this Friend.

137

My dear Anna:—

I received your nice letter telling me of your happy Xmas vacation and your good home.

I had intended to see you before I left McPherson but I was so busy I did not have time. Some day when I am again in town I will come around to see you. I saw you one standing outside the Art Shop window with Rosalind Almen and some other girls. I like Rosalind very much, do you?

What grade are you in? and how do you like your teachers?

Just now I am at home on the farm. It is so different from N. Y. City. When we want water we go to the pump; we have no faucets. Instead of steam heat or furnace we burn coal and corn cobs in a big stove. Do you know what corn-cobs are? I didn't when I came out from N. Y. You see I was raised in the center of the city and did not get into the country very much. It was a surprise to me when I found out that pickles grew on a vine and they called them cucumbers. Our big country school here, is one of the biggest in this state but it seemed so small to me. Why our Orphans Home alone in N. Y. City was larger than this ~~city~~ school house and play ground together. And everybody thought I talked so funny. I was afraid of horses ~~city~~ and cows; and when I came out here I expected to see indians and big ~~city~~ buffalo as our history books read. But I got a good home, too and good parents just as you have, so that made it very nice. You must try to

138

good in school and grow up to be a fine, well-mannered and educated lady so that Miss Bengston may be proud of you. That is the biggest way of paying her for her kindness.

I hope you enjoyed all your books and Xmas presents. Have you finished Heidi yet? Do you get to see Julie very often?

Would you like a picture of how I look now — well here it is!

I generally spend most of my evening studying and writing. I read many many books and write to about 40 people all the time. So you see I can keep busy. I like to sit and write or read a book — and drink milk and eat cookies. We have lot of milk on the farm. It comes in bucketfulls not in pint or quart bottles.

We have cows and we also have calves and little pigs and our chickens I guess they are lazy; the old hens just set around all day just sort o' lazy like. And then the rooster crows real loud over nothing. We have white cats also that catch mice and sleep. Write me again.

Uncle Bill

1-12-'35

W.E. Bishop
Route 1
Box 77
Sterling
Kansas

139

20
Inspiration

Anna clattered down the stairs and dashed into the kitchen just as Jennie concluded her grocery order. "And one fifteen-cent soup bone to serve six, please," she said. She hung up the receiver and sat down at the kitchen table where she was going over her accounts. The boarders paid on Friday nights. Saturday mornings, Jennie took care of her finances.

Behind Jennie on the shelf above the cookstove, ten loaves of bread dough were rising. Later, after Anna's chores were done, she would deliver the fat, crusty loaves to Jennie's customers around town. Weekdays were schooldays, but Saturdays were work days for Anna as well as Ingborg and Margaret. The girls were just the right age to help with housecleaning while the women did the extra baking required for Sundays. They also had to shampoo their hair and take baths. It would be a long time before they were freed of their Saturday obligations, and by then they were trying to find paying jobs. Anna performed her work without interest, as did the others. She would have liked more time to play, but she was growing accustomed to Jennie's way of life. Now she slid into a chair beside Jennie and helped herself to the rolls, milk, and juice already set out for her.

"Anna, I think we should go over my budgeting together," Jennie began. "You should be learning how to manage money. I don't suppose you've ever had the chance before."

"No," Anna replied. "I haven't. The first time I ever held a fifty-cent piece was when a man on the train gave me one. But I dropped it behind the seat and we couldn't get it out."

"I'm sure your parents would have taught you to handle money if they'd lived long enough. But I want to show you what I can." She spread the bills and coins on the tablecloth, counted them, and wrote the total on a scrap of paper.

"I take out for the church first. Ten percent. Then I pay all my bills, and set aside some for sickness. If there's anything left, it can be spent for 'extras.' "

Anna looked at the neat stacks. "What are extras?"

"Oh, things like clothing. Furniture. Entertainment."

Anna brightened. "Entertainment! Like tickets to the movies?"

"Now, Anna. We've talked about that before. You know how I feel about you going to the movies. Such things might influence a young girl's mind in the wrong direction." Jennie spoke gently, hoping Anna would understand. "Perhaps if the Swanson children are allowed to go to a special show sometime, then you can go, too." Anna was learning that the Swanson's and the Anderson's privileges were a gauge of what Jennie would allow her to do..

"You said furniture," Anna said, crossing her arms on the table. "What will you buy?"

"Nothing right now. I want to save up enough to pay cash for it first. I don't like to charge anything except groceries, and I pay that bill once a month."

"Yes, I know," Anna grinned. "Uncle Joe gives each customer a little sack of candy when the bill is paid."

"But we need a new ice box. I'll look around to see if I can buy one second-hand. It's cheaper," Jennie went on. "I believe in paying cash and living within my means. Of course, thrift is necessary for a woman like me, making my own way, but it's a trait to be valued and practiced from an early age."

"If you don't have very much money," Anna pondered, sizing up the small stacks of money, "then why do you give so much to the church? I bet there's lots of rich people who can pay for the church." Anna didn't understand Jennie's generosity in the face of her meager income.

"Perhaps, Anna. But I give because the Bible tells us we are to be good stewards and administer our money well, to share our blessings with others. The Lord has blessed me with income, and health, and now you. So I give my time and money back to the Lord. Not because I have to but because I want to thank Him for his blessings. Remember, the Lord loves a cheerful giver."

Anna sat back and thoughtfully chewed her last bit of cinnamon roll.

"There's something else I want to tell you about, Anna. I'm almost fifty years old, older than most mothers of girls your age. And since my father died, I haven't had anyone depending on my income. Well, now you're here and I want to make sure you're provided for. So I've purchased an insurance policy for you. I know you probably don't understand that," she said as she took Anna's hands in hers. "All it means is that when you are grown, you will have a little money for school or whatever you need. Of course you'd have your aunts, uncles, and cousins to care for you if I wasn't here, but you would also have money for your own needs. The insurance man will come every Monday to pick up the thirty-five cents from the hall table. And this is the first payment." She took a quarter and a dime from the coins and went to put them on the table as Anna watched.

Since Jennie would be busy on the back porch with her washing, and wouldn't hear if someone came to the front door, she made arrangements with the insurance man to walk in and pick up the money from the library table.

And each Monday, Anna felt proud of the shiny coins, placed on the table for her future.

And so Anna's life fell into an easy order, fashioned around school, the demands of the boarding house, occasional visits with her sisters, and growing up out West.

Anna liked to watch Jennie cook, and she helped out by setting the table and assisting Jennie. She learned to peel potatoes, carrots, and all kinds of fruit, and to whip cream so it wouldn't turn to butter. And there were always dishes to do, and errands to town to get things Jennie had forgotten to have delivered, or to replace food which had spoiled in Jennie's small icebox.

"I put together meals by color," Jennie explained to her. "If you have something red, white, and green, that makes a balanced meal."

Jennie's boarders were quick to compliment her flaky apple-raisin pie, the light prune whip, and the dependable meat and potato dishes. Oysters and salmon, which were cheap, often appeared on the menu.

It was a challenge to her creativity to serve fine meals on a budget, but Jennie never scrimped. And she felt that good hospitality demanded linen cloths on the dining room table for every meal, even though it made her wash and ironing load heavier.

142

In the evenings, Jennie, Anna, and the boarders often gathered in the parlor to read, as the big base-burner crackled over its coals.

One evening Jennie noticed that Anna had raced down the stairs to the parlor as if she were afraid. "Why do you run on the stairway?"

"I don't like closed stairways," Anna admitted, "they scare me." Then she told how at the sanitarium she'd read the daily newspapers instead of taking naps. One day she'd read about two children who'd been murdered, and their bodies were found stuffed under a stairway.

"Oh," Jennie exclaimed with shock. "From now on, we'll see that the light in the stair is in working order. I don't want my girl afraid of anything around here."

Gradually the two got to know one another. Anna asked about Jennie's father.

"I'm sorry you didn't get to know him," Jennie answered, pleased at Anna's interest. "He was a Swedish immigrant, a farmer, and he came to America about thirty years before your father came from Hungary. So you know something about immigrants, don't you? He settled by New Gottland."

"Out where Ruth and Ted live."

"Yes. First he built a sod house — out of chunks of earth stacked together. I was born in that house, but he built a regular house for us soon after that. He was interested in church work. You see, pastors didn't get a salary. They had to live on donations and gifts of food. Sometimes Dad would hitch up the buggy and take Minnie or me along when he went asking for money for the pastor, or arranging church activites. Some of the large meetings were held in the grove at our homestead. My sisters and I made the coffee and helped at the meetings. Dad was a good farmer, and he trained his sons how to farm. When he got older, we moved to town, Aunt Minnie and Dad and me. Then Minnie got married."

"Was he handsome? His pictures look nice," Anna commented.

"I thought so, Anna. He had white hair and a mustache in later years. And still the ladies set their caps for him. But he was not interested. He liked to garden, and take care of the cow we kept out back, and in the evenings he always read from the Bible, aloud, and then we'd discuss what he'd read."

"Now you do that," Anna observed.

"Yes."

"Why didn't you ever get married?" Anna asked impulsively.

"Well, I had Father to take care of."

"Yes, but I heard a neighbor say you had a boyfriend."

Jennie looked at Anna over the top of her glasses and lightly dismissed the subject. "I am much better off this way."

"But you could have been rich! You wouldn't have had to work so hard."

"Ah, yes, but then I wouldn't have you, would I?"

Anna sat in the backyard swing, the peaceful warmth of spring sunlight on her back, the sweet fragrance of lilacs and a white lace of spirea surrounding her. The backyard, she noticed, already showed signs of growth in the weeks since she and Jennie had planted the garden. The flowering fruit trees, pink and white, and berry bushes, crowded one side. The vegetables were starting to come up, shoving their way in the crowded space. The clothesline poles seemed to raise arms in surrender at being overrun by the advancing vines of honeysuckle and morning glory. And tulips and daffodils nudged their bright and cheery faces along the border of leafing rose bushes. Even the old barn at the back of the lot was put to use to store garden tools, and cucumbers and corn sprang up from its fenced pen, well-fertilized by years of use by Mr. Bengtson's cow.

In a few weeks, the radishes would be bulging out of the earth and before long, potatoes, tomatoes, peas, carrots, cabbage and string beans would require attention. Their first work was done, Jennie had explained, and they would now watch and care for these fruits of their labors till harvest, when they would be picked, canned, pickled, stored, and wrapped away for winter's needs.

"That's how she makes ends meet," Anna thought. "She works so hard, but she never complains. She likes her life."

Although dinner preparations were under way, Anna had been excused. She was still recuperating from her tonsillectomy. It was strange, she thought, how a terrible experience could turn into such a wonderful thing. When she'd become ill, and was taken to the local hospital, she was afraid. Then she was told she'd have to have an operation. She had cried and begged Jennie not to leave her. So Jennie had stayed at her side day and night, until Anna was able to come home again. If ever a bond had been forged between them, it had been in those hours when Anna, terrified and

144

in pain, had opened her eyes to see Jennie sitting in a chair beside her bed, ready to feed her crushed ice, soothe her brow, and murmur comforting words.

Now that she was almost well, Jennie had promised her an extra surprise. She would be going out for "entertainment" this evening. Anna had given up hoping for permission to go to a movie, but she was curious about what entertainment Jennie would consider suitable. She waited patiently.

When dinner was over, Jennie and Anna changed into their best dresses, a new print for Anna which Jennie had made, and a navy blue linen dress with a small dark hat for Jennie. It wasn't long until the Swanson's Buick pulled up alongside the curb in front and honked twice for their passengers.

Anna and Jennie hurried out and climbed in. The Swanson children hadn't come, Aunt Minnie explained, because they'd already heard this performance. As the Buick swept along, Aunt Minnie explained that they were going to Lindsborg and they were going to hear a performance of a special musical event, the annual singing of Handel's famous oratorio, "The Messiah," at Bethany College.

"It's a large choir, Anna, and they will sing a famous composition about Christ's message to us," Jennie added.

Soon a large, white circular-looking building appeared on the horizon. Anna's attention was riveted on this impressive structure which had several flags flapping from the pinnacle and around the circumference. As they neared a large field cleared for parking, Anna could see that it was not round, but had flat sides and two tiers.

"Look at that building! It has so many sides!" she exclaimed. It stood practically in a wheat field at the edge of town.

"That's Ling Auditorium, Anna," Uncle Joe told her. "Yessirree, it's got sixteen sides, all made of wood, and cut from trees right around here."

"Even pioneers had a yearning for a cultural life," Jennie explained. "And this was a start here on the prairie. Many wellknown musical stars have performed right here. Some folks call Ling Auditorium 'the prairie Carnegie,' after Carnegie Hall in New York, Anna."

The doors were jammed with people waiting to get in. Anna put her hand in Jennie's as they joined the crowd entering the double doors. She could see tall, thin windows on various sides and tiny ones around the upper tier.

"You'll like it, I think. It's rather long, so just lean on me and rest when you need to," Jennie told Anna. "I know you're still weak from the surgery."

Anna smiled as she remembered the closeness they shared because of that experience. They sat on backless wooden planks on the main floor. Anna noticed that seats went nearly to the ceiling.

The interior was already darkened, adding to the air of expectation. There was a stage across the round auditorium. Soon it began to fill with men and women wearing dark clothes. Another group of people also came onstage carrying instruments, seating themselves toward the stage's edge nearest the audience. They placed wooden stands before them and started playing, but not together. Each seemed to be playing different music.

Anna watched their movements closely; she was intrigued by them and carefully sorted out the instruments. There were violins, and horns, too, and an organ like the one at church. But she could not identify the other instruments and so she tried to sort their special sounds from the confusion of noise she heard. The lights grew darker; suddenly a tall man dressed in a black suit walked from one side of the stage to the center.

"He's the conductor, Anna," Jennie whispered. "He leads the orchestra and directs the choir so everyone performs together."

Anna nodded and clapped with the audience as he took his place and bowed. As the ovation subsided he turned his back to the audience and raised his arms, holding them high for several seconds, then dropping them to his side. The orchestra and choir burst into powerful music. Anna sat straight — the sounds surprised and delighted her.

She was enchanted with the entire spectacle. The power of the music thrilled her. The organist's fingers were masterfully flying over the keys, creating inspiring runs and trills.

Overcome, Anna felt an urge to become a part of the performance and spontaneously she reached forward, placing her hands on her knees. She began running her hands to the left and right as if she were playing along. Then she realized she might be distracting others so she sat back and folded her hands. Oh, how she'd love to be able to play like that! Looking down at her hands, she realized perhaps she could never play as she'd just pretended. And then Jennie's words came back to her, "You can do anything anyone else can . . . "

The program was long, and Anna was tired, and eventually she dozed off, leaning on Jennie. She awoke to hear a phrase that caught her attention. "All we like sheep have gone astray." The basses boomed the words and the sopranos echoed them back. That verse from Isaiah was a favorite of her mother's. She remembered hearing her mother read it when she was very young. She sat up straight, captured by the beauty of the music.

And then came the Hallelujah Chorus. It was captivating in splendor. Jennie helped Anna to her feet, to stand with the others in respectful silence.

Anna had never heard anything like it before. She thought the music sounded like a coronation, so regal and majestic, so strong yet noble. She listened, she looked, she was too overwhelmed even to speak to Jennie in a whisper until the last notes had died away. Only then did she inquire, and Jennie explained to her the meaning of the oratorio, and the reason the audience had stood. It was said to be a tradition set by the first audience of the Messiah, when the king had been so moved by the music that as the first strains sounded, he had stood in honor of the King even greater than himself; the King of Kings, Lord of Lords. Anna thought she knew how that king must have felt.

On the ride home Anna sat quietly.

"How'd you like it, Anna?" Uncle Joe asked, as he drove.

"It was real nice," Anna responded.

"It's amazing, considering that the chorus is made up of everyday people from this area — not professional singers," Aunt Minnie added.

"Before long, Anna will be old enough to sing in the Messiah," Uncle Joe went on. "They have folks as young as sixteen and as old as eighty."

But Anna was thinking she'd rather be a musician than a singer. She dreamed of the day when she could play music herself. Oh, how she wanted that!

When they arrived home, Anna went straight to the piano and sat down. She couldn't pick out the notes she'd heard, so she spread her fingers over the keys and plunked them loudly. At last, Jennie decided she'd have to end this "entertainment." With summer coming on, the windows were open, and there were three fine musicians in the neighborhood who would hear the awful noise. Next door was the church pianist. Across the street was a teacher at McPherson College, and just down on the corner lived another woman who loved to sing and play. Sometimes, late at night,

Jennie heard their music wafting in her windows. She didn't want to reciprocate with Anna's pounding.

Next morning, Jennie told Anna she had an important announcement. She looked to Ruth, who said, "Anna, I want to teach you how to play the piano."

Anna knew then that prayers are answered.

"We'll start after school tonight," Ruth told her. "When you've learned everything I know, Aunt Jennie will find a real music teacher for you."

Anna Fuchs and her cousin, Ruth Anderson.

And when that time came, although Jennie's phone calls to the town's piano teachers had resulted in refusals to teach Anna, there was one who was willing to try. Anna became her most devoted pupil.

When Anna started junior high, she joined the school orchestra. She was a cellist. Realizing that Anna was not getting sufficient practice on the school's instrument, Jennie resolved to buy a cello for Anna, even though it would sap her savings.

It arrived in a huge crate, and Professor Mark, Anna's cello teacher, was called over to help with the unpacking. Anna's eyes spilled tears as she ran her hand over its shiny surface. "It's beautiful. I'll make you proud of me," she solemnly promised Jennie.

"I have never doubted it," Jennie replied softly.

21

"Where's My Sister?"

"Did you have a good day, Beanie?" Mr. Callahan asked Bernice as she set the steaming bowl of mashed potatoes on the table and took her seat for dinner.

"I was just telling Mom about it," Bernice said. "Today I learned how to kill and dress a chicken. Mrs. Davis showed me how to hold the rooster by his feet, and set his neck on the chopping block, then kill him with a hatchet. I did it, too, then I scalded him and picked the feathers off."

Catching Mrs. Callahan's distateful look, Bernice quickly changed the subject to a topic more suitable for dinner table conversation, "I cleaned out the ice box, too."

"I always said, 'Beanie can do anything!' " Mr. Callahan beamed proudly.

"I do believe Bernice is learning more about keeping a home from Mrs. Davis than I could ever teach her," Mrs. Callahan said.

"At seventeen, the more you know, the better," Mr. Callahan nodded, "though I wish you'd have been able to go on with your schooling."

"I will, Dad. Really. The doctor says I'm all well, but I missed so much school, first with the pneumonia, then blood poisoning, that the principal won't let me start back until next year. And I promise I'll go then."

"Good, Beanie. I don't want you to major in hatchet-wielding, no matter how many talents you learn. You need your education, and I want you to get it."

"She's such a good seamstress, too, Ott," Mrs. Callahan put

149

in. "Besides cleaning and taking care of Mrs. Davis's children, she's been doing a lot of sewing."

"I'm going to make my graduation dress, Dad. And someday," Bernice's eyes took on a faraway look, "I'll even make my own wedding dress."

"After schooling," Mr. Callahan reiterated, and Bernice smiled at his concern.

"Oh, Bernice, I forgot to tell you," Mrs. Callahan said. "A woman was here from the Children's Aid Society looking for you this afternoon. She said she thought you'd be home from school soon and wanted to see you. I told her you weren't in school, you were working out."

"Oh, no. That sounds like trouble."

"I don't think so, Bernice. She said she'd stop in and see you next Saturday. She said the Society sent her out to check on the children and see how they're doing. The ones that aren't adopted."

Bernice suddenly looked down at her plate. She wasn't adopted, and it hurt to be reminded that, although the Callahan's had given her a home, she still carried her own name. Legally, she wasn't theirs, and they weren't hers.

"Grandma Callahan's missed you today, Beanie," Mr. Callahan tried to ease her hurt. "Why don't you go see if she needs anything? She asked to have you come in as soon as you could."

Bernice rose and went through the living room into the tiny downstairs bedroom. An old woman sat up in bed, her tray in her lap. "You're home already," Grandma looked surprised and pleased. Bernice bent to kiss the old woman on the forehead.

"Could I help you with your dinner?" She took the tray and seated herself in a chair. "I missed you today."

⚜

The next Saturday, Bernice stood at the ironing board, pressing her way through a bushel basket of sprinkled chothes at her feet. She sang as she watched the steam rise and the starch shine on the yoke of a shirt. A knock interrupted her thoughts. "I'll get it," she called to Mrs. Callahan and hurried to the door.

"I'm back — and I want to talk to you," the woman began, sternly.

Bernice stood back, taken by surprise, and let the woman enter. Mrs. Callahan came in from the kitchen. "Go get your Dad," she instructed Bernice. "He's in the garden."

150

They all sat down stiffly in the front room. "I've come to take Bernice," the woman announced. "She's not adopted, she's not in school as was agreed to, so it is my duty to take her and put her where she *will* go to school."

"Oh, no you won't!" The words flew from Bernice's mouth in panic and fear.

"Bernice, don't talk that way," her father began. "Let me . . ."

"Dad," she interrupted him, "I know I've never talked back to you before, and I respect my daddy, but just keep still. You let me fight this out."

Callahan looked pained, but knew Bernice must be allowed to fight this battle herself.

"I'm going back to school again next year. I've been sick. I couldn't get started this fall. And I'm working. I clean house for Mrs. Davis, and take care of the children," Bernice began her defense.

"Pack you suitcase, young lady. I have the authority, and I am going to take you with me. I'm taking you away from this place," she announced with finality.

Bernice's tears dropped onto the skirts and blouses as she put them in her suitcase. Mrs. Callahan wrung her hands and stood silently beside Bernice as she prepared to leave. They could hear Mr. Callahan on the phone in the hallway, trying vainly to contact Miss Hill. Surely, Miss Hill could get to the bottom of this problem. Legally, they were helpless, but everyone in Abilene knew that, in spirit, if not on paper, Bernice Switzer was the Callahan's daughter, and a good one, too.

The woman escorted Bernice to her waiting car. The Callahans, unsuccessful in all efforts to reach Miss Hill, had given up and called Callahan's brother-in-law, John Middleton. John had taken an orphan boy from one of the other orphan trains, so Mr. Callahan thought he'd know what to do. "John, come quick," Callahan beseeched him. "They're taking Bernice away! How can they do that?"

The Callahans rushed to their car and followed the woman's as Bernice, confused and weeping, looked back at them. Everyone assumed that she must be taking Bernice back to the orphanage in New York, and there was no hope of getting her back. They were distraught when they found they were at the depot and the woman was rushing Bernice toward an Eastbound passenger train.

Middleton, who'd been following in his car, too, leaped out

and ran after them, going right on to the railroad car. "I demand to know where you're taking this girl!" he shouted.

The woman reluctantly handed over a card printed with the words, *Good Shepherd Home, Kansas City, Missouri.*

Middleton hopped off the train just as it pulled out. Bernice, her eyes streaming tears, waved from the window.

Callahan rushed up to Middleton on the platform. "Look at this," Middleton shook his head. "The Good Shepherd Home. That's an insitution for wayward girls."

"Why are they doing this to our Beanie?" Callahan asked incredulously.

"They can't! Come on, Ott, we're starting proceedings right now to get Bernice back."

That night a family huddle resulted in an unusual decision. Aunt Frances wanted to adopt Bernice. "That way," she explained to the others, "they can't come back and get her." Her normally gentle expression was determined. "We all need her love and laughter. But you know I'll never have any family. I'd be proud to have her as my own."

"Don't you think she should live here with us as she always has?" Mrs. Callahan asked her sister.

"Yes, I suppose so," Aunt Frances agreed. "Grandma and Grandpa are quite old, and Grandpa's a bit cranky. Maybe it would be too much for them if Bernice lived with us — she's such a lively girl. But I want to adopt her and pay her expenses. She can still live here with you. This will never happen again!"

"It wouldn't have happened at all if we'd been able to reach Miss Hill," Callahan put in. "I finally got in touch with the Society. Miss Hill was taken ill and has been recuperating in Chicago. But she is sending a letter recommending that Bernice be sent back to us."

"Then it's all settled," Aunt Frances smiled. Her blue eyes sparkled with pleasure.

Hot dust swirled in threatening coils along the dirt street of the small western Kansas town where Cliff had been helping with the harvest. He stood outside the theater and read its billboards as best he could.

" 'Special Fourth of July Show — Mind Reader. Your questions answered. Problems solved. 7 p.m. Tonight.' "

Worry creased Cliff's sweaty face. He'd heard from Abilene.

152

Bernice was missing. She'd been taken from the Callahans and no one knew where she was.

Maybe the mind-reader could help. Nothing else had worked. After all this time of keeping track of his brothers and sisters, now he'd completely lost contact with Bernice. A teenage girl needs protection. Where could she be? With whom?

He paid his quarter, happily parting with the hard-earned coin in the hope of learning something of his sister's whereabouts. He went in and sat down, joining others in the crowded, already-darkened theater. His promise to his brothers and sisters — that he would always know where and how they were — weighed heavily.

The program began when the Master of Ceremonies threw back the curtain and came dashing out. "Evenin', folks!" he shouted. "Our show tonight begins with local talent."

Cliff sat patiently through the string of singers, joke tellers, and hoofers, whose country brand of entertainment brought forth a few chuckles and light applause. Even though he was anxious to learn where Bernice was, the day's efforts had exhausted him, and his head began to nod. Just then the emcee bounded onstage again. Cliff jerked awake.

"Ladies and gentlemen," he began, "the act you've all been waiting for! He can read minds, foretell future events, find lost people and items. He knows all. Now, direct from an engagement in Chicago, Dr. Perception!"

The theater suddenly went completely dark and a thin light appeared onstage. The audience craned to see. The light illuminated a man's face. He wore a black suit and a cloth turban, its single jewel sparkling in the dimness.

"Good evening," said an ominous, low voice, enunciating each syllable. "I, Doctor Perception, come here tonight to help you with your problems."

He went on, "I ask one thing. Each and every question must be written out. It helps me to relate to the vibrations of the person and creates a closer bond with the unknown."

The audience was hushed and obviously attentive. He continued: "Please write your questions on the cards my assistant will hand out." Immediately another man materialized on the stage and began moving through the audience, passing out pencils and cards.

Cliff's scant schooling made the task difficult. He finally simplified his problem to the single question, "Do you know where my sister is?"

The cards were placed onstage in a large glass bowl. With a great deal of theatrics, Dr. Perception drew the first card from the bowl and read it aloud. "Mrs. G. has lost her diamond ring." He placed the card against his forehead, closed his eyes and appeared to concentrate deeply.

The audience waited breathlessly. "The energy is flowing into me now," he said. "I see . . . a pool of water. Your ring glimmers from the bottom. Do you have a body of water near your home?"

A middle-aged farm woman stood up hesitantly. "No, not even nearby," she said, "The ponds are dry. This drought has dried up everything. Even our cistern is almost empty."

"Cistern?" Dr. Perception alighted on the word, smiling smugly, authoritatively. "Why don't you look there?"

"Oh, yes, thank you, Doctor," the woman said gratefully. The audience burst into applause.

As Dr. Perception proceeded through an assortment of problems, Cliff was suddenly shaken by the realization that the news could be bad. If this fellow really knew what he was doing, he could also know if something terrible had happened to Bernice. Suppose he told him she was dead? Kidnapped?

Cliff was ready to abandon everything and run out. Maybe it was better not to know. Then he heard the familiar question read aloud and the man pressed Cliff's card to his forehead.

Oh, why was he taking so long? Could it be another dear sister was gone . . . like Nellie?

"I have good news for you, sir," Dr. Perception announced with a broad smile. "Your sister is in a large building in a strange city. She will come home soon. She is thinking of you."

<hr/>

It was Friday, the thirteenth of July. Bernice had been at the Home for three weeks. The first day, a doctor had examined her and asked her what she was doing there. When she told him how she'd been taken from her home, the doctor advised her to try to keep to herself.

"Most of the girls here are expecting babies, Bernice," the doctor said kindly. "And others are here because they've done things they shouldn't. If you keep to yourself you'll be better off. I'll tell you which bathroom to use, and when you go in there, be sure and lock the door after you, and wash your hands thoroughly."

All of the girls had been given fictitious names to protect

154

their identities, and all had daily tasks to perform. Bernice was known as "Estelle," and was assigned to sewing collars on shirts. The first day she'd surpassed the quota and had challenged herself to higher production each day.

From the first day, Bernice had begun a practice of praying for deliverance from the Home. When she arrived at the sewing room each morning, and took her place at her machine, she would pretend she'd lost something on the floor. This allowed her to get down on her knees. As she pretended to search for the missing item, she'd pray silently for the Lord to rescue her and return her to her home.

This morning she was still praying when she heard the name called. "Estelle, you're wanted." Mother St. Ukelele, as Bernice called the sour-faced superior, escorted her. They passed through many doors, and at each, the nun produced a key and unlocked it, then turned and locked it behind them.

At last they came to a pleasant drawing room, and there stood Mother St. Jane, Bernice's favorite nun. "There's someone here to see you." Bernice was shocked to see the woman who'd removed her from the Callahans.

"What do you want?" Bernice flared.

"I've come to take you home."

Bernice could only reply, "Well, I'm not leaving here without my suitcase!" Mother St. Jane said, "It's right here. I'll help you dress if you want me to."

"No, thanks. I can do it myself," Bernice replied. She was reeling at this development, but still independent. She went into a small room and took off the hated uniform, donned her own clothes, and came out carrying her case.

Mother St. Jane met her in the hallway and gently whispered, "Please be careful, dear, and never do anything to get put back in here, because," she smiled kindly, "there are much nicer places to be."

Bernice remembered an earlier conversation with this nun who had confided, pathetically, that she would give anything in the world if she could "go out that door and see what the outside world is like." Now Bernice was leaving, and her friend was staying on in this place. "Don't worry," Bernice promised her, "I'll never be back here."

Her escort noticed Bernice's haste to leave and assured her, "There's no hurry. The train won't leave for hours. No hurry at all."

"That's what you think," Bernice retorted. She grabbed her suitcase and literally ran out the door, anxious to leave it all behind. Down the driveway she dashed, a half block to the street. Bernice didn't stop or look back until she stood on the walk beside the busy street. She feared she'd be hauled back there again, and if anyone tried to make her go, she'd shout for help. Someone would hear.

Bernice Switzer at age sixteen.

"Really, Bernice," the woman said sarcastically, as she caught up with the girl, "there's no hurry. Let's take a streetcar ride."

They toured Kansas City from one end to the other, and at mid-afternoon they were making a thorough inspection of the large war monument across the street from Union Station. The woman was pointing out all sorts of facts about the monument. Bernice grew impatient.

"You know," she said, "I'm not a bit interested in any of this. Let's go down to the station and get on a train and go home. I know there must be a train that'll go through Abilene before night." Bernice pleaded in vain; the woman seemed to have a plan.

156

When she finally allowed Bernice to get on a train, it was The Flyer, which left Kansas City so late in the day it arrived in Abilene well after 11 p. m.

As they sat on the train, the woman said to Bernice, as if baiting her, "What are you going to do if there's nobody there to meet you when we get there?"

"I'm not a bit worried about that," Bernice stated flatly, realizing this was probably her escort's idea all along. "And besides, if there isn't, I can always call a taxi."

As they rounded the last turn before the Abilene station, Bernice stood up and peered out into the darkness.

"Look! There's a crowd! I think half of Abilene is there! I bet Dad got word around that I was coming home!" She turned to her escort. "And you thought there wouldn't be anybody to meet me!" There was no reply.

Bernice was so eager to be back that she stood outside the car in the vestibule. When the train slowed, she literally threw herself off into the crowd. She landed in the arms of a man from their church, who staggered backwards and laughed as he caught her. "You're anxious to be back, aren't ya, Bernice!"

The Callahans rushed up to Bernice as her escort got off the train alone and slipped away in the darkness.

"Oh, Beanie. You're so thin!"

"Are you all right?"

"Sure," she laughed. "Now that I'm home."

"We sure had our work cut out for us, getting you out of there," Callahan said.

"How did you do it?"

"Legal work," he explained. "Aunt Frances is adopting you. We're meeting that woman who took you, over at the courthouse tomorrow. It's all arranged. All we have to do is sign some papers. In fact, they wouldn't release you until the papers were ready."

"You'll live with us," Mrs. Callahan said, "just as always, but Aunt Frances wanted to adopt you. That's all right, isn't it?"

Bernice looked at each of them lovingly. "Of course," she said brightly. "Now I'll have two families." And she hugged them again.

Late that night the Callahans heard Bernice screaming and ran into her room. She was down on the floor, fighting with the bedstead. "No, no," she screamed, "you'll never take me back! You can't, 'cause I'm adopted."

22

Time to go Home

Deftly Cliff scraped the spatula across the griddle, his muscular arms directing the puddle of grease toward the drain. He wiped his hands on the white apron that protected his jeans and shirt. Then, rag in hand, he strode toward the booths out front to make certain their linoleum tops were wiped clean. He was "in charge" now — for awhile, anyway. His boss, Mert, allowed him to tend the cafe alone after the women cooks left at 2 p. m. until Mert returned about 3. Then Cliff and Mert would run the cafe until closing time, around midnight. If there was a dance in Abilene, however, they might not get away until 2 or 3; Mert's Cafe had a lively clientele as well as good food.

Cliff was refilling salt shakers when a short, well-dressed woman with a formidable frown suddenly strode into the cafe.

"Where have you been?" she shouted menacingly.

"Why, uh . . . " Cliff stammered, trying to place this woman.

"No matter. We've found you now!" She wagged a finger. "You might as well know that you'll be punished for causing us all this trouble by running away — for causing the Society — and everyone else to lose track of you!"

Cliff didn't know what to say. The woman certainly could take over a conversation, Cliff thought. She evidently represented the Children's Aid Society, but in no way did she resemble the gentle, concerned Miss Hill. She was sore as a boiled owl. After she'd given him a "good hearing" she turned and stomped out, slamming the door behind her.

Cliff watched her bantam hen exit with a sinking heart. The

feeling he had moments before of being a responsible working man and master of his own fate was gone. In its place rose the old fears. But Cliff had little time to sort out his emotions, for just then his old friend, Dr. Jones, dashed into the cafe, breathless.

"I don't like to tell you this, Cliff," Doc said, "but there's a passenger train going through here tomorrow morning, and you're gonna be on it."

"Heck, Doc, I didn't know I was gonna take a trip!"

"Well, you are."

"Where'm I goin'?"

"You're headed for reform school."

Cliff stood stunned, clenching his fists. "Does this have anything to do with the old gal who was just in here?" he asked evenly.

"It does."

Cliff slammed the dishcloth he held onto the counter. "I had a notion to knock her on her rear. She's got the sharpest tongue of any woman I ever talked to — made me so cockeyed mad!" Doc put his hand on Cliff's shoulder. "Calm down, son," he said gently.

"But why would they send me away?"

"Because you've been shunning them for so long. The authorities didn't know where you were. You're not of age, yet, you know," Doc reminded him gently.

"Well, nobody around here ever did me any good. Why should I tell them where I was at?"

Doc paused, searching for words. "I suppose you've got a point, son," was all he could reply.

Finally Cliff ended the conversation, "Thanks, Doc," and the old man left.

Mert, who had come in while Cliff and Doc were talking, motioned Cliff to the back of the cafe. Cliff said, "I guess you heard the news. I got to get out of town before they send me to reform school. So, if it's all right with you, I'll take my seven dollars for my week's pay and I'll be leaving. I got to go."

"What'll you do?"

"Guess I'll catch me a handful of boxcar, Mert."

Mert went to the cash register, withdrew several bills and counted them into Cliff's palm. He added an extra twenty dollars, saying, "Take it, Kid. You've been a lot of help to me. Good luck. Maybe someday you'll come back here. If you do, you know you got a job."

Cliff took off his apron and headed for his dollar-a-week residence. He was living in a small room in the home of a widow and her daughter, across from the west mill. Cliff passed near the Sealy Theater, where he and the other orphans had once stood on a stage hoping for homes. Lately, he'd begun dating, and sometimes he took a girl to a show at the Sealy. At those times he successfully blocked from his memory all recollection of his humiliating start in this town. But now he was reminded again of the degrading experience. It was time to leave Abilene for good.

While working, Cliff had accumulated a few nice clothes and now he quickly gathered them and stuck them into a gunnysack. Then he headed for the railroad yards, and from a concealed area, swung aboard a slow-moving freight.

They'll never catch up with me now. I'll just keep going, he told himself as he huddled in the boxcar. He stuffed the gunnysack under his head for a pillow. By 10 p.m. he was in Texas.

<hr />

A person can run only so long. At last Cliff found himself on a freight headed back to Marion, the only real home he'd ever known. He hopped off as the freight passed through town, and made his way on foot the dusty miles to Ben and Ella's place. But things had changed. The Reents were planning a move to western Nebraska. They were homesteading near Lyman, and the auction bills had already been distributed, announcing a sale of their household goods and machinery. Cliff stayed a while to help Ben with the work, but a thought nagged at him.

Maybe it was time to go home — really home — or whatever you call that place you start out from.

"You're welcome to come with us, Cliff," Ben assured him one evening at dinner. Ella nodded agreement. "We always said there's room for you at our place. And Nebraska has a lot of opportunity."

"I thank you," Cliff replied, "but I guess I'll just be moseying on."

One morning he arose very early, and without saying goodbye, walked to the next town east — Elmdale — where he bought a rail ticket to Chicago. He shipped his one small, fold-up, cardboard suitcase on ahead in care of General Delivery, Corning, New York. Now he had no luggage — he was as barren of worldly goods as when he'd come West on the orphan train.

When he got to Chicago, he went up to a ticket agent in the train station. Dumping a tumble of bills and coins onto the counter, he said, "How close can you put me to Corning, New York, with this?" He and the agent counted it out.

"Not too close," the agent shook his head. "Why don't you go over to the bus depot? It's just a couple blocks from here — I'll give you directions. They ought to be able to get you almost there."

Cliff moved through the throng of Chicago shoppers and businessmen, found the bus depot, and again asked the question. When he learned the bus would carry him as far as Buffalo, he bought a ticket and climbed into a huge, smoke-belching bus.

Once in Buffalo, he made his way to the city limits and started hitchhiking. After several rides, he was picked up by a young man in an old Ford touring car. The top was down and the back seat was jammed with camping gear. The driver was interested in his passenger. "You sure don't travel very heavy," he noted, observing Cliff's stained shirt with rolled-up sleeves, the heavy work boots, and the blue jeans with the extra length turned into a fashionable six-inch cuff.

"Nope," Cliff said. "Had a sweater, but left it in a barbershop someplace," as if that explained his total lack of belongings.

"Where you headed?"

"Corning, New York." Then he added, "That's where I was born. Been gone a long time. Thought maybe it was time to go back."

"I guess folks gravitate back to their old stomping grounds," the driver observed. "Just natural."

He was a good driver and Cliff enjoyed the pleasant drive through New York countryside. They were just passing the city limits of Savona when Cliff suddenly sat up straight. "I didn't know we was going through Savona!" he exclaimed. "I used to have a grandfather lived here."

"Want to stop?"

"Well, sure. Just let me off on a corner somewhere."

They rolled to a stop on Savona's main street. Cliff hopped out, followed by the driver, and went toward a man pumping gas at a service station.

"Do you know where David Moss lives?" Cliff asked.

"Well, Sonny," the man paused to look the youngster up and down. "Dave Moss — he dropped dead right about where you're standin', three months ago. He was a mail carrier. Went to

161

crank his Model T, had a heart atack and died. But I can tell you where Mrs. Moss lives."

Cliff bit his lip. He had looked forward to seeing his grandfather again. When Cliff scrawled a letter to him years ago, at the urging of temporary supervisors at Marion, Grandpa had written him right back.

He turned to the driver. "Say, thanks for the ride. I believe I'll just stay here and look up Grandma Moss."

"I'll just help you look her up, if you don't mind," said the driver, curious and not about to leave before seeing the end of this small drama. "If you don't find her, I'll take you on to Corning."

The man at the pump gave directions, and they sped off in search of Mrs. Moss. But they got mixed up and had to pull into a driveway so Cliff could ask directions at a nearby house.

As he stood on the porch, knocking at the door, he noticed three young men walking up the street toward him. No one answered the door, and he stood awkwardly as they came near.

"Ain't nobody home there!" shouted the youth in the middle.

"There ain't?"

"No!"

"Well, maybe you can tell me where Mrs. Moss lives?"

The one in the middle paused. "What's your name?"

"Clifford."

"What's your last name?"

"Switzer."

"You're *Clifford*?" The boy in the middle began to laugh. "Hey, I'm your gol-darned brother!"

"Howard!" Cliff whooped, running down the steps to embrace his younger brother whom he hadn't seen since leaving home so many years ago. "Imagine finding you this way!" Cliff exclaimed. "I was looking for Grandma Moss."

"Oh, then you heard about Grandpa." Cliff nodded. "Well, Grandma is living with me and Aunt Orrie and Uncle Will across town. I'm working on the railroad with Uncle Will. Bet you could get a job there, too, if you're looking. Are ya back to stay?"

"Guess so," Cliff replied. "Got no better place to be."

Cliff brought Howard over to the car. "Meet my brother," he said. "This here's the guy who helped me find you — gave me a ride into town," Cliff explained. "Guess this is as far as I go. Thanks!" He waved the fellow on his way, and watched as the touring car disappeared down the street.

Howard and Cliff walked to their uncle's, where Howard announced his brother's arrival with ceremony. Grandma wept when she saw him, and Uncle Will talked about getting him a job. Aunt Orrie, his mother's sister, wiped her hands on her apron and gave him a big hug, her eyes brimming with tears.

"Tell us about your adventures out West," Uncle Will asked Cliff as they sat down to supper. Cliff spun out a tale guaranteed to leave the impression that he'd had a full share of adventures. He told about his various jobs, of riding the rods, of helping in the wheat harvest in western Kansas. He left out all the parts about being mistreated and deserted. Aunt Orrie watched him admiringly, and an idea struck her. She went to the phone to call her sister. "Mary? We've got a big surprise for you. Come on over. No, I won't tell you what it is. Just be sure to have Frank bring you to our house tonight."

"Your ma's coming," she told Cliff as she returned to the table. "She's gonna be surprised how you've grown."

"Heck," scowled Cliff. "I ain't sure about this. She may not want to see me — I might remind her of some things she'd rather forget."

"You know she's remarried," Aunt Orrie put in. "She's done a right good job of raising Frank's motherless kids."

"Raised them?" Cliff felt the hair rising on his neck. "Raised somebody else's kids? While her own were scattered over the country?"

"You've done all right for yourself, Cliff. What're you talking about?"

"Nothing." He closed his mouth and got up from the table. He sat down on a daybed in the corner of the front room. "That's what you get for making it sound so good, ole Cliff," he scolded himself. "What're you going to say to her, anyway? She doesn't care a whit about any of her kids."

At last his mother stood in the doorway, gazing around, a bright expression on her face. "What's the surprise, Orrie?" she asked in a voice he'd erased from his memory.

"Don't you know that young fella sitting there?"

The woman surveyed the sober young man. "No," she said finally, "I don't believe I do."

Cliff's bitterness suddenly erupted. "Well, you ought to — I'm your firstborn son!"

"Oh, my God!" she exclaimed, raising her hands to her face. "You poor kid! You've been kicked all over the country!"

163

"Yeah," Cliff accused. "You got three more kids wandering the country, too. Don't ya ever think of them?" His voice rose angrily with a final jab.

Aunt Orrie looked at Cliff in amazement. This surprise wasn't turning out the way she'd hoped at all.

Neither Cliff nor his mother made a move to close the distance between them. Quickly, Frank put his arm around his wife's shoulders. "Come, Mary," he whispered. "Let's go home." Aunt Orrie followed them out the door, apologizing. No one else in the room said anything and Cliff stood up and climbed the stairs to bed.

Next morning, Howard had a proposal. "Let's go visit Grandpa and Grandma Switzer. They ask about you a lot."

Cliff let himself be talked into this. The boys didn't talk much as they trudged the six miles over the mountain to their grandparents' farm near Tyrone.

At last they came to the neat little farmyard, the two-story white house and garden Cliff remembered so well. "Let me go in first," Howard ordered. "You wait up a few minutes." Cliff stood beside the house, watching a flock of geese that were squawking and advancing on him. He heard Howard say: "I brought a friend with me today, Grandpa!" and saw him motioning for Cliff to step out in view. "Friend, heck!" snorted Grandpa. "That there's Clifford!" Rising from his rocker on the porch, the old man called to his wife, "Hey, Loretta, come out here."

"What is it, Ellie? I'm busy frying chicken."

"Come on out — we got company!"

Grandma appeared hesitantly in the doorway, her eyeglasses reflecting the sunlight, and her little flowered sun cap covering the gray braids. "Who's there?"

"You don't know him?"

"Should I, Ellie?"

"Oh, it's Clifford," he said, pleasure mixed with irritation at her lack of perception. "Cliff's back." They quickly embraced their grandson, laughing delightedly.

Again, Cliff recounted his touched-up stories from out West and when asked, made the fate of his siblings considerably brighter than the truth.

"Did you know your dad's married again? He lives pretty close by," Grandpa said. "Let's invite him to come up this weekend. Loretta, write him today. Tell him to come. But don't say why. It's a surprise."

164

"Another surprise," Cliff moaned to Howard when they were alone.

"This one'll be different," Howard promised.

Anticipation. It ground in his stomach like an ache. All day, while he helped Uncle Cecil in the high hay fields, Cliff kept finding excuses to go down to the house so he could see if a car had come. But each time he looked there was no sign of visitors.

In late afternoon Cliff went from the field work to tend to the barn chores. As he milked cows, carried feed, and looked after the calves, he wondered and thought about his father.

Finally, the chores were finished. It was night. As he came from the barn he spotted the shadowy form of a car parked near the porch. Cliff went to the dining room window and looked in. They were all eating supper. "Why, Dad ain't changed a bit," he whispered to himself. "He still parts his hair in the middle and combs it up on the sides."

He lingered at the window a long time watching his father — the man who had abandoned them, yet for whom he still felt affection. He swallowed, rubbed his hands on his overalls, strode to the door and yanked it open.

"It's Cliff!" Howard yelled, making sure his dad wouldn't ruin this reunion. Ivan Switzer sprang up from the table and embraced his eldest son. Cliff, feeling the sturdiness of his father's frame against him, suddenly began to weep, too.

Later that night, when they were alone, Ivan confided to Cliff. "We've had quite a visit, son. But I want to tell you something I've thought about many times."

"What's that?" Cliff asked apprehensively.

"No offense to Hattie, Cliff. She's a good woman, But," Ivan Switzer swallowed, "there never was a woman like your mother, Mary. That night after I left home, I'd have given anything to be back with my family. I knew then I'd made a big mistake, but I was bullheaded, and I wouldn't admit I was wrong. Now that it doesn't make much difference — I can say it."

"Oh, Dad."

"There never was a woman like your mother, Mary."

When Cliff turned down the covers that night, his heart and mind were in turmoil. "How do lives get so mixed up?" he asked Howard. But Howard slept on. "What's right, and what's wrong? How can I forgive one and not the other?"

He fell asleep finally, listening to the steady tick of the hall clock.

23

Riding the Rails

How was it that all of the Switzer boys seemed to know instinctively how to hop a boxcar, David wondered as he crouched in the weeds beside the track, waiting for the evening freight. Heck, he'd never done it, but it couldn't be that hard!

He would just stand up beside the passing train, and as it slowed for the nearby town limits, he'd reach out and grab a handle fastened to the side of a car. He wasn't even scared, he told himself. He'd heard Cliff and Harold tell how they'd done it lots of times. And once you had a hold, you just held on till you got to a place where you could scramble up and into one of the open boxcars. You looked for something to cover you — gunnysacks, maybe a big piece of cardboard — curled up, and you were on your way. By morning you'd be a long ways from where you started. And that's exactly what David Switzer Weber wanted.

He couldn't wait until the "old man" found out that his "slave" had disappeared. Boy, oh, boy! He could just imagine the look on that fat old man's face when he realized that David was gone — long gone.

David squirmed in his uncomfortable crouch and tried not to think about Mom Weber, or the fact that he was leaving with no belongings, or food, or money, dressed only in the overalls and work shoes he'd been wearing when he'd made up his mind about things today. He'd had an argument with Dad Weber while they were out doing field work, and David had suddenly slipped off into a cornfield, his temper flaring. As he made his way across the rows, he decided he would run away. He would go East and look up his brother, Cliff, who was living in New York near the grand-parents. Maybe Harold would be there, too.

David thought of the time Harold had dropped in un-announced at the Webers' a couple of years back. Maybe that visit had helped stir an aching wanderlust in David, an urge for faraway places, the desire for no responsibilities. Now it had burst into action, and all his hostilities were vented on Dad and Mom Weber, his adopted parents.

Sure, they'd taken him in as a little kid and given him a home, and he was their only child. Things had seemed to go well for many years, but now the fever of independence ran high in David's blood. Perhaps it was because there had been so few diffi-culties, but David imagined himself a "put-upon farmhand." David was sure they did not appreciate him; Dad Weber only gave orders and never took his suggestions about how things should be done. And today, after the argument, he was ready to claim his freedom.

He supposed as a little kid he'd been happy with the Web-ers. But lately he'd sensed injustices. Since they'd moved out here to Goodland, in the high plains of western Kansas wheatland, there'd been a lot more work for everyone than when Dad Weber had run the grocery store in Elmo, and commuted from Abilene, fifteen miles away, back when they first took him in. But Mr. Weber's doctor had advised him to get out of the store for health reasons — he was overweight and the doc said he needed more exercise. Weber had bought a different store right there in Abilene. Things had been fine.

David was the only one of the four Switzer kids who'd been legally adopted. He remembered it well. He was nine, and he'd lived with the Webers since age four. Each year, Miss Hill had made a visit to check on him. And when the family had decided to move west to farm near Goodland, they wanted to make the adoption legal. Miss Hill and another agent had come out, and the papers had been drawn up and signed on his ninth birthday.

David huddled down and put his arms around his knees to keep warm; it was a cool night out here on the high prairie. Shivering, he thought of his brother, Harold. How many nights had Harold spent like this — chilled, lonely, waiting just like this for a fast ride from here to there?

He thought back to the day when Harold had turned up at the Weber farm and begged for a place to stay. Poor Harold had been abused every place he'd gone, and he felt absolutely no one had considered him to be a worthwile person. In desperation, he'd come to the Webers. David had been glad to see him. Harold had arrived by train, of course, having been told by Cliff where the Webers had moved. Cliff always knew where everyone was. The Webers had been nice to Harold, David had to admit. They'd offered him a place to stay, and work, until he could get squared away. Harold was with the Webers almost a year. Then the call of the road had overtaken him and he was off again. Meanwhile, he'd given David some ideas to think on — ideas of being free, beholden to no one, able to come and go as he pleased. "No need to work if the railroads would take you where you wanted to go, and your needs were small," Harold had shown him.

Yessirree — today had been the end of it, David mused. What did they think he was? A workhorse to be driven? A darned orphan to be shoved around? Heck, Mom Weber always used to call him her "little mechanic" when the two of them had to stay alone while Mr. Weber ran the grocery at Elmo. David was his mother's helper, a little fix-it man by the age of five. But now it seemed they just wanted to take advantage of him.

When he'd argued with Weber today, he'd talked back, and even called his adopted father a bad name. Then he'd sneaked off into the next field and Weber hadn't known where he was. He'd heard him calling. So what! He could call and call. From now on, there'd be no answer.

The distant whistle of the oncoming train reached David's ears and immediately his stomach tensed. He realized he was about to make a break with all he'd ever known and loved. But he told himself it was worth it to be his own man.

He watched as the train's headlight swung fitfully in the darkness.

He stood up as the freight rumbled past, and choosing his handhold quickly, he swung aboard.

What a thrill it would be to see Cliff again! And he'd have a wonderful reunion with his grandparents, too! Not that Cliff had invited him, though! Nope. Cliff wouldn't like it at first, David was sure, and he'd have plenty to say to him about running away from his adopted home. But then, when David told him about the problems, Cliff would have to agree he'd done the right thing in leaving. Since Cliff had had his share of knocks, he was sure to understand. He'd better, David thought anxiously.

He hung onto the car, pulled himself up, and braced himself between the cars until it would stop and he could climb into an empty boxcar. Fright, exhilaration, and the sense of adventure welled up in him as he was swept along. Only the lights of the distant farmsteads and a few stars lit the night.

❧ ～❦～ ❧

David sat, crosslegged, beside the campfire near the tracks with a bunch of other "bums." Gratefully, he gulped the cup of soup they'd offered from a big pot suspended over the fire. In the past few days he'd learned that boiled-over coffee grounds and a little bread were a meal to be thankful for. Now, by joining up with this hobo group, he was eating better.

"You!" a one-eyed, bearded, scruffily dressed old man growled at David. "You're so shy, I think you'd starve to death if you wasn't relying on us to feed ya. Yup, you're pretty wet behind the ears yet."

David blushed and looked down at his cup. He was afraid of this man, who sometimes took out his artificial eye and cleaned it, then popped it back into the empty socket. David had never seen anything like that before. Summoning a courage he didn't know he had, he answered at last, "Aw, Willie, you don't mind helping me out, do ya? Bet somebody helped you when you first started bumming." David's heart thudded so loud he was sure the whole crowd could hear it.

Willie looked him over, and finally answered. "Guess you're

right, kid. We're all young sometime. How old are ya? And where ya going?"

"Almost fourteen," David replied, eager now to engage in civilized conversation. "I figured on going back East to find my oldest brother, Clifford. He's around Ithaca, New York."

"You just keep riding the rails — you'll get there," Willie advised. "Watch it in the city railyards though. The guards there are kinda tough on free-riders."

"Oh, I sure will." David lifted the cup to his lips. He hadn't counted on railroad guards!

Soon, David was on his way again. But it wasn't a direct route East, for David was filled with conflicting emotions. On the one hand, he wanted to be on his own and find his "real family." Yet he was afraid — afraid that Cliff would beat him up for leaving home. Soon, he found himself like a yoyo attached to the tracks. He would travel East awhile, then lose his nerve, turn around and head West again. But once he was nearly back to western Kansas, he'd again decide to risk it, and hop an Eastbound. Altogether, he spent nearly a month traveling between Kansas and Illinois. He was in Quincy when he turned back one more time. He arrived at the Kansas City railyards to learn that Hobo Willie was right about the railroad guards.

David and another youth-on-the-run were hanging around the yards waiting for the train they wanted to hitch, when they were surprised by two guards.

"Stop, or we'll shoot!" one of the guards yelled, as the boys darted off. They escaped into a field of tall, thick-growing sunflowers beside the yard as shots whizzed over their heads.

David dashed headlong through the unyielding, heavy stalks with their stinging leaves. Ordinarily, he would have thought it impossible to walk through such a thicket, but sheer terror clawed at him as savagely as the stinging, prickly sunflowers. Scrambling, tumbling, thrashing, he propelled himself on and on. Breathless, horrified, he faced the reality that he could be killed without ever finding his way home — wherever that was.

At last David felt he was safe. The shots and the shouting had stopped. Hidden from the guards by the field, the boys laid low, hardly daring to breathe, yet gasping like two sunperch on a crick bank. They waited until it was dark, then started walking, too afraid to try hitching another ride. They stopped along the way and put some mud on the stings and burns they received during their flight through the sunflower patch. In all, the two walked over forty miles, to Lawrence, Kansas.

It was at Lawrence that David arrived at a sudden decision. His stomach was empty, his shoes were worn out, and he'd been on the run for more than a month. And through his mind had been flashing pictures from the past. There was Dad Weber, a beaming, heavy-set man, coming up to the stage of the Sealy Theater, pointing him out and saying, "We'd like to have that cute little boy." He remembered how they'd taken him shopping right away, and outfitted him, head to toe, in new clothes, the first he'd ever had. His stomach yearned for the delicious rolls Mom Weber baked just for him every week, and he recalled with a terrible pang how sweet she'd always been to him.

David remembered how the Webers had taken Harold into their home without a complaint, when Harold had limped in like a lost pup. Maybe he'd been wrong to leave. Maybe home wasn't such a bad place after all. At last he swung aboard a westbound train and was on his way back to Goodland. But his heart was heavy. He had cussed Dad Weber, run off, embarrassed them, and hadn't written even one letter in all those weeks. Would they forgive him?

It was not yet dawn when David struggled the last weary mile from the rail line to the farm. There he saw a light burning in the front-room window. Why, that must be his mom's good kerosene lamp that sat on the pedestal table. But no one left kerosene lamps burn all night. Why was it burning now? Then he realized she must have kept it burning every night since he'd been gone. It was a signal, David realized. A signal that if he came close enough to home to see it, he'd know he was welcome, and all was forgiven. Encouraged, excited, and so relieved, he ran up, pounded on the door, and was welcomed back home.

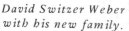

David Switzer Weber with his new family.

171

24

Never Alone Again

A cageful of butterflies seemed to have escaped in Cliff's stomach as he drove the old brown Chevy coupe toward PennYan. He had a blind date, arranged for him by an old friend. Herb's wife, Marie, had a girlfriend who'd helped them move from Fredonia and was staying with them awhile. Marie had written to Cliff to "come over Saturday after work — we have a nice girlfriend for you to meet."

His hands gripped the steering wheel. It wasn't that he hadn't dated girls before. He was twenty-six, and had gotten around some. But this time, he was nervous. He remembered what his brother had once said about these things. "Cliff, don't get in over your head; you could be sorry." He laughed out loud at that thought. He hadn't yet met a girl he wanted to marry.

He turned into the drive of Herb's neat two-story house.

"Seven o'clock on the button, that's Clifford," Herb grinned, opening the door.

Cliff stepped inside, smiling broadly. "Well, I couldn't miss this date!" he said with a twinkle in his eye. And then he saw her, rising to meet him with a pleasant smile. She had dark hair, and her simple green dress accented her willowy figure. Herb made the introductions. "This is Hazel Washburn, Clifford Switzer."

"Hello, Cliff," she said in a low, pleasing voice.

Cliff rubbed his sweaty palms on his good gray suit and shook her hand. "Hi, Hazel."

"Well, we can't stand here talking," Marie broke in. "We better get going, or we won't find seats at the theater."

It was a warm May evening and they all piled into Cliff's car, Herb and Marie riding in the rumble seat. Cliff had the window down and all the way to the theater the air was filled with birds singing and the sweet smell of flowers.

The foursome got along fine, talking and laughing until late. When they returned home, Herb and Marie hurried inside so that Cliff and Hazel could have some moments alone.

"Okay if I come again next week?"

"Fine." Hazel's laughing eyes crinkled her response.

"I'd come over in the middle of the week, but it's too long a drive."

"That's all right. I'll be waiting," she said softly.

Cliff Switzer

Each weekend Cliff sped off to Penn Yan. He and Hazel went for drives in the country, and out to pick wild strawberries in the rolling woodlands. One evening they decided to go roller-skating.

The crowd was slowly circling the rink as the loudspeaker

oozed popular songs, "Isle of Capri," "Deep Purple," and the up-beat "Continental."

On wobbly legs, bending to keep balance, Cliff and Hazel started out, holding on to one another. As Cliff teetered this way and that, Hazel teased him, "I thought you said you could skate."

"Well, maybe we're not skaters, but I'm trying," Cliff laughed. He stood up straight and stopped watching his wavering feet. He even began humming "Blue Moon," and then started singing along with the loudspeaker. Suddenly he lost his balance and with the clatter of shuffling skates, he went down, taking Hazel with him. They sat, laughing helplessly while the herd of skaters veered out and around them. Then they gamely scrambled up, attempting again to make a complete round.

With arms linked, they'd start out, but one or the other would falter and again and again they landed flat on the floor. But rather than venture it alone, they preferred falling together, laughing harder with each spill.

"We've spent more time looking at the ceiling than we have skating," Cliff admitted at last. "Let's take these skates off and go get a soft drink."

They sat and talked at length, especially about their commond bond — they were both from broken homes. Over the past weeks they had talked briefly of this, and Cliff had openly shared the most embarrassing, humiliating scenes from his past. Hazel began to realize that nothing would ever wipe out the terrible scars of his childhood and adolescent years.

He had made a success of himself in spite of limited schooling, and he had a steady job at the electric company, and he was fun to be with. While his experiences could have made him bitter, he did not express a bitterness at life — although he seemed to hold a grudge against his mother. Instead he tried to comfort Hazel in the unsettled situation she found herself. She was twenty years old, and her parents had recently separated. Cliff knew there must be hurts under the surface of her charm.

"You're kind of like an orphan Annie yourself," Cliff said. "Guess that kind of makes us birds of a feather."

Hazel found herself captivated by the quiet strength of the handsome young man.

By late June, Cliff discovered he'd been thinking of something he'd never had in his life. A home of his own. A vision of love, security, and a peaceful sanctuary claimed his thoughts. He resolved when he saw Hazel that weekend, he would offer her everything he had . . . his name . . . his income . . . himself.

Heart pounding, he knocked at her door. When Hazel answered it, she seemed to sense his urgency. "Sit down," she invited, a bit worried at his distracted state.

"Look, Hazel, I want to ask you something."

"Yes, Cliff."

His fear of rejection suddenly welled up. Maybe this wasn't the time. Maybe he was wrong about how Hazel felt. Maybe she didn't want a poor orphan kid for a mate. But he couldn't forget Hazel's warmth and his conviction that they belonged together.

"Honey, I want you to be my one-and-only. I think you're the one for me. Fact is, I fell in love with you the moment I saw you. And I bet you'd make a decent home for us." He gulped, watching her face. "Well, how about it? Will you marry me?"

"Oh, Cliff," she answered, "I love you, too. I'd be proud to be your wife. You're a dependable man; I admire you. And I promise you I'll make a good home for us." She wept as he gathered her in his arms. Her quick answer had surprised and delighted him. For the first time in his life, he felt that he belonged to someone, and that someone belonged to him. There was mutual understanding, trust, and deep love between them. Surely that could surmount anything the future might bring. His heart was bursting with joy. He could not remember feeling such happiness. As he cradled her tender form close to him, he couldn't imagine ever parting from her . . . not now, not ever.

"What's the sense of waiting," he suddenly decided. "Let's go out and tie the knot right now."

"Now?"

"Sure. We can spring it on the families later. But I gotta buy you a ring."

"Why not go down to the five-and-dime? They've got rings."

"If that suits you?"

"It does."

"Then let's go!"

Hazel paused. When she'd awakened this morning, she'd had no idea this would be her wedding day. She had no proper gown, and there would be no flowers. It would be the simplest of weddings. But she wanted to look her best.

"I don't expect to have another wedding day," she said, eyes sparkling. "Let me put on a good dress. I'll hurry."

She rushed to the closet, and chose a steel blue princess style dress with tiny buttons all down the back and a perky bow at the neckline. She slipped into it quickly and brushed her hair. "Ready," she announced, beaming, in the doorway. "It's my sister's, but it's the best I got. Since the Depression, we've shared our clothes." She looked up at him, smiling, seeking his approval.

Cliff held her at arm's length, then embraced her. "Honey, you're my dream come true."

They hurried to the nearest dime store and picked out Hazel's wedding band. It cost ten cents. Then they started in search of a justice of the peace.

Three hours later, they were still single. No one would perform the ceremony without proof of Hazel's age and she had no driver's license or other proof. The several justices they'd approached had turned them down.

"Maybe we better go find Herb and Marie," Hazel suggested, snuggling close to Cliff and trying to console him. "We need someone to stand up with us anyway."

They found their friends at home. Marie abandoned her bread-baking, leaving the dough to rise as she whipped off her apron. "Let's go to Dundee. It's a small town. Ought to be able to get you hitched there."

"Yeah," Herb added, "maybe the justice there ain't so particular."

As they rolled along, Cliff's joy bubbled over. He waved one arm out the window, hooting and hollering with happy abandon, and pounded on the car roof for emphasis.

When they entered the justice's office at Dundee, and announced their intentions, the justice began trying to talk them out of it. "Marriage is a pretty big step," he said.

At last it was clear to everyone that this justice had never performed a wedding ceremony. Finally seeing that they would not be swayed, he excused himself to go study up a bit. "Wait here while I read the book, then I'll perform the ceremony."

They watched as he hurried into the next room and flipped through a book. When he came out again, Herb and Marie jumped to their feet to stand beside their friends, as Cliff and Hazel held hands. The justice stumbled through the ceremony, then Cliff placed the ring on Hazel's finger.

As he took her in his arms, all the hurts and defeats of the past seemed behind him — a fragile, distant memory — as he held this dear person. He would never be alone again. They would be together. They were one.

"Let's go back to our house," Marie broke in. "You have to take us home anyway."

When Marie came into her kitchen she discovered that the dough had run over the pans and down into the stove burners, making a sticky mess. "Oh, well," she said cheerily, as she kissed the newlyweds goodby, "I know your marriage will be better than my bread."

Cliff decided to take his bride honeymooning at Owascow Lake, a nearby resort. They set out as a gentle rain began falling. Hazel leaned close to Cliff and he kept his right arm around her, steering wih his left.

"Why are all the cars honking at us?" she asked, dreamily.

"Oh, gee. Do you suppose this old car's got trouble again," Cliff was dismayed. "Better stop and check."

As they walked around the car, looking at the tires, they discovered a hastily scrawled JUST MARRIED sign on the back. "That rascal Herb!" Cliff exclaimed.

That evening they went to a public park where a bingo game was in progress. They played, and Hazel won a stainless steel singing teakettle.

"Guess that's your hope chest," Cliff laughed as she blushingly accepted her prize.

When the weekend was over, they realized they had no place to live. Cliff hadn't known Hazel would say yes, or he'd have made arrangements before leaving Ithaca. He had to return to his job with the electric company. Since he was boarding at a rooming house for linemen, he had no choice but to leave Hazel in the care of his brother, Howard, and wife, Claudia. "But I'll find us a place real quick," he promised.

Searching after work each night, he found it — the perfect love nest, cozy and neat. It was just a big room with a kitchenette, but when he carried Hazel over the threshold the next weekend, it became their castle.

25
Rejection

As Anna stepped quickly along, she could hear the voices of her admiring school friends resounding in her ears. During lunch hour she had confided she would be applying today for the fall class of nurses' training, and they had responded with every encouragement.

"Oh, Anna, you're so lucky to have such an important career! Just think of the help you'll give people who really need it!"

"Yes, and you're sure to be accepted. You've been working at the hospital for two and a half years. They know what good help you are!"

"That's right, you've had lots of experience there. I can hardly believe you loaded that huge old dishwasher all by yourself, especially last summer in that heat!"

"And I've scrubbed floors every Saturday, till they lowered the pay from a dollar to seventy-five cents a day," Anna had told her friends. "And I still scrub bathrooms and work in the kitchen after school."

She was enveloped in her thoughts, smiling at her friends' reactions and the prospects that lay before her. She didn't notice that the April sky had grown suddenly dark, and ominous steel-gray clouds billowed rapidly from the southwest. It was warm and humid, and the monstrous dark thunderheads indicated a storm was imminent; they stood tall above the land, puffy with wind and power.

Anna bounded up the tall steps of the hospital feeling very important as her navy pleated skirt swung neatly with her quick steps. She felt on top of the world as she entered the building and hurried along the corridor. All of her studies, and her part-time work at the hospital, doing back-breaking menial tasks, had been in preparation for this day. Now she was about to embark on her chosen career. She turned in at the nursing supervisor's office and took a seat and waited.

All her life, Anna had dreamed of becoming a nurse, someone who would be of help and comfort to others.

"Hello, ma'am," Anna said, standing as the woman came into the room. "I came to pick up my application for nurses' training. I'll be entering the class this fall," she said brightly. Anna sensed something was wrong. This was not the same woman she'd talked to earlier. "The other supervisor told me to be sure and come in at this time to fill out my written application."

A frown creased the older woman's face, making her tight features even more stern. "I'm in charge now. The woman you spoke to has taken a job in the city."

"But I can still apply . . . " Anna began.

"I cannot give you an application. I've been watching you work in the kitchen and with the cleaning crew on Saturdays. I'm afraid it would be a mistake to let you enter training. Nursing is a very taxing profession. Your hand and hip are against you. You would never be able to do the hard work required, or much walking."

Anna stared in utter disbelief. "Oh, no! You don't mean it! I *can* do the work. I know I can! Dr. Heaston has encouraged me; he said he saw no reason why I can't become a very good nurse and help others."

But the woman only shook her head, looking down at a stack of papers. Already completed applications, Anna noticed. She struggled on.

"I've contacted all the instructors connected with the training program and they all said there was no reason why I couldn't become a nurse."

"I'm sorry," came the words, totally devoid of emotion. "The decision is final. You cannot enter nurses training. You are handicapped."

Anna jerked back, turned on her heel and fled the hospital. The tears she tried to conceal flowed freely down her face. She dashed down the stairs she had just climbed so happily and ran out into the rain. She started for home, crying, running, sobbing.

Wild lightning flashed and thunder rolled in the heavens as

Anna hurried home in the cloudburst. At last she was safely onto the painted gray porch. She flung open the door and raced up the stairs. She took off her soaked clothes, slipped into her robe and threw herself on her bed, sobbing deeply.

Jennie was working in the kitchen and heard the door slam and quick footsteps on the stairs. She wiped the flour from her hands, took off her apron, and hurried through the house. She opened the door to the stairs. Anna's sobs wafted down the stairwell. Jennie climbed the steps as quickly as she could.

She found Anna in her room, flopped across her quilt-covered bed, weeping into a pillow. "What is it, Anna?" she asked in alarm. "Are you hurt? What has happened?"

Anna suddenly sat up, her feet curled under her, the pillow clutched in front of her like a giant handkerchief. Her face bore a look of deep hurt and her swollen eyes mirrored her despair.

"Everything is ruined! I'll never be anything worthwhile now! Oh, it's so awful, I wish I could die!"

"Anna, please tell me what's happened."

"The supervisor at the hospital. She won't let me apply for nurses training. Says I'm too crippled. I hate her! I hate her! Why did I have to be born this way?" Anna gave vent to every dark feeling. "She's so mean! Why can't she give me a chance?"

Her lifetime dream torn away, Anna lamented her desperation. "I've just got to be a nurse! I planned on it all my life! I know I could do the work, but she won't even give me a chance. I wish I'd never been born!"

With that, the girl sank back onto the bed and buried her face in the pillow, her sobs rising again.

Jennie realized that this was a crisis like none other they'd faced together since Anna came to live with her seven years ago. She approached the bed, praying for guidance. Finally she sat down on the edge of the bed and put out her hand to touch Anna's hair.

"I'm sorry, dear," she said. "I know you would be a good nurse. You're smart, and compassionate, and you have such high ideals. But there are other opportunities open to a girl with such qualifications."

Anna's despair seemed bone deep, soul deep. If she was listening, there was no indication of it. She sobbed on.

Jennie continued, "We haven't come this far to be beaten back now, have we? First, you must realize that you are discouraged, and all discouragement is from the devil. We must find a way to overcome this discouragement so you can look forward to other bright and happy things. I have some stock in a utility company, and that will help pay your tuition to college. Would you like to go to college? We can see about it tomorrow."

But the tempest in Anna's heart went on and on. Jennie continued to sit by her side, stroking her hair, offering comfort, listening to the girl as she gave vent to frustrations never before mentioned. And outside, the dreary rain continued to pour down on the young grass, the tulip buds, the streets. It seemed like hours as Jennie waited for the storm to pass. Patiently she waited it out.

Finally, Anna became quiet, and lifted her head. "I think I'll go wash my face," she said. With Jennie on her side, surely something would turn out right.

But even though Jennie's plans were unshakable, and though Anna eventually became encouraged by the prospect of a college education, it was to be a time of crisis, frustration and disappointments. As always, Jennie stood by Anna, even though she wondered if Anna would ever be able to get her temper and rebellious spirit under control. Jennie worried about the bitterness and hatred Anna was developing toward life, but did her best to comfort her in this deepest disappointment.

With no other opportunities open to her, Anna continued to work at the hospital after graduation from high school. But it was a difficult task, now that the building itself and the staff represented only discouragement and a closed door to all her carefully laid and hoped-for plans. But she stayed on. She needed the forty-dollars-a-month salary.

Whenever she had a chance, she tried to find another job. Even though she wanted to go to college, the money situation was critical. It was the Depression. She felt if she could obtain a full-time job and work for a year or two, then maybe she would go on to school.

One bright summer day, she went downtown to a small business where she'd heard they needed help. The woman who greeted her seemed very kind and then asked what sort of typing and shorthand training Anna had. It seemed that everywhere she went, those two requirements cropped up — both skills she'd never learned.

Anna looked down at her hands, folded in her lap, knowing that it was the end of this interview, as it had been with every other. As she trudged home, she remembered the day during her senior year last fall when the principal had suggested she take a typing class as her elective. But when Jennie went to see the typing teacher, she refused to have Anna in the class. "I wouldn't be able to teach that girl how to type," she snapped, "and she'd hold everyone else back, too." Even though Jennie pointed out that Anna was an accomplished musician, skilled at piano and cello, the teacher had remained firm.

When Anna got home she told Jennie about this new disappointment. Jennie responded by encouraging Anna to decide on a college and make plans. Somehow they'd find the needed funds.

"Where would you like to go to school, Anna? How about Bethany? It's a fine arts school, and you're a musician."

"If I went there, I'd need to be rich, or an outstanding music student, and I'm neither. I'd have to belong to a sorority, and that requires money for good clothes and a fur coat. Otherwise, I wouldn't fit in," Anna summed up dejectedly.

"If you don't want to pursue music, how about home economics," Jennie persisted hopefully. "You love to sew, you're good at it. You make all your own clothes now and you don't even use a pattern."

At last it was decided — Anna would major in home ec. And she would go to McPherson College.

"You can live at home and save the cost of room and board," Jennie replied. "Getting your education is the important thing. I'll contact the officials."

When Jennie dropped in to discuss the fine points of Anna's college education — such as whether the college officials would allow Anna to take business courses — she was surprised that they agreed she could take typing, shorthand, and accounting. And even though the value of stocks was depleted, they agreed that the stock Jennie held in the utility company could be applied toward the tuition cost.

Jennie then set about scraping up the rest of the tuition. Her only assets were a small savings account which she'd put aside for her old age. Tears gleamed in her eyes as she gently pressed the money on Anna, explaining: "This way it'll be an investment in the future."

Anna was overcome. She knew from the years of observing Jennie scrimping along and watching every nickel, that this was a gift of rare value. Jennie feared old age, but she wanted "her girl" to have what she needed — an education. If it came down to a choice between the two, Anna's needs came first.

On the first day of classes, Anna walked through the drifting autumn leaves. She'd first seen this college when Bill Bishop had brought her here on her eleventh birthday. Who'd have dreamed then that someday she'd enter this same college?

The day was summer-warm, yet the tang of changing seasons was in the air. "Just like every other year in Kansas when school starts," Anna mused to herself. She turned and cut across the large park, creating a path she would follow for many months.

She recalled with amusement the family's frantic efforts to prepare a wardrobe for her. She was glad that Aunt Minnie and Ingeborg were generous in sharing their used clothes and their sewing capabilities. Since Anna was petite, she had the advantage of being able to wear things Ingeborg had outgrown. Jennie and Minnie devised outfits for Anna by taking worn dresses and making jumpers of them. Or they combined two dresses, putting in sleeves and yokes of contrasting colors.

Anna knew that many freshmen were going to school for the main purpose of getting a job in the spring. As she neared the school and saw other students, she noticed that her made-over clothes and hand-me-downs were right in style.

Then she stood at the foot of the stone steps which rose to the impressive administration building. As she looked up to the open doors she remembered Jennie's words the night before, while she was sewing a pretty print outfit from an old dress. "It's surprising what you can do when you really have to!" Anna smiled to herself and started up the steps.

Anna and Jennie

26
Two are One

Bernice hovered near Mrs. Callahan's shoulder as she bent over her old Domestic machine. She watched as two pieces of fabric were melded into one by the flying needle which was powered by Mrs. Callahan's foot upon the treadle.

"I bet I could do that," Bernice whispered, her brown eyes eager. "Could I try?"

"Every time I sew anything, you're right here wanting to sew, too. But you're hardly ten years old! It takes coodination to pedal the treadle while guiding the stitching," Mrs. Callahan answered.

"I bet I could do it," Bernice said again.

Mrs. Callahan stopped sewing and looked at the girl. "All right. If you can find a piece of material in the scrap box, I'll let you try to sew."

Bernice flew down the cellar steps and poked through the big box of remnants and scraps. She held up a piece of blue and white calico, and measured it to her short figure. It was long enough.

"For a dress? All right. Lay it out on the table, and I'll make a pattern for a dress. Then we'll cut it out together."

Bernice was dancing up and down as Mrs. Callahan pinned the pattern, cut from newspaper, to the fabric, then handed Bernice the shears. "This Mother Hubbard style with butterfly sleeves will be easy to sew, and it'll look nice with a belt," Mrs. Callahan said.

Then she sat down at the machine and showed Bernice how to start the needle going with a flick of her hand on the wheel. An hour later, Bernice snipped the threads and held up her creation. She slipped it on and stood, smiling.

"I never thought you'd be able to sew like that. You've got a natural gift for sewing, Bernice," Mrs. Callahan observed.

⚜

"Next, she'll be wanting to embroider," Mrs. Callahan told her sister as they sat visiting that weekend. Bernice had modeled her dress.

"Then let her, Cora," Aunt Frances said. "Clerking at Pinkhams, I see so many young women coming in for fabric and thread, and they don't know beans about sewing."

Mrs. Callahan was embroidering a bedspread as she spoke. She paused and looked at Bernice. "Well?"

"I could make a bedspread for my dolly — the one you got me my first Christmas here," Bernice grinned. "I'll put bluebirds on it!"

Mrs. Callahan and Aunt Frances burst out laughing.

Later, after Bernice had told how she had played at knitting in the orphanage, using sticks and thread, Grandma Stowitz took Bernice under her wing as a knitting protege, and bought her needles and yarn. And Bernice decided to make a sweater for herself in American Beauty rose. She was on her way as a seamstress.

⚜

Despite interruptions caused by illness, Bernice finished high school and graduated with the class of 1932. Then she started work as a housekeeper. During school she had done babysitting and housework, Saturdays and after school. After a year and a half doing housework for the elite of Abilene, she became a live-in housekeeper for a family who operated a cafe. She took care of their two sons and kept house for a year, until the family sold the cafe and moved away.

When the family was moving, Callahan dropped by to see Bernice. "What are your plans now, Bernice?" he asked.

"I think I should do what I'm best suited for, Dad, and that's sewing," Bernice replied. "I want to set up my own dressmaking shop. With the Depression, women are trying to save money, and they can dress cheaper by having their clothes made."

"Your room is still waiting for you, and we could make a dressmaking shop for you in the basement," Callahan offered.

"Why not move back home?"

"Thanks, Dad."

Callahan bought a large screen as a room divider, put a rug over the cement floor and moved her sewing machine to the basement. Together they went downtown and picked out a large electric fan, a necessity in Kansas summer heat. Bernice was set up in business.

Her prices were reasonable. She received a dollar-fifty for making one good dress. She also had an apron business, sewing work aprons for sale by the C. H. Pinkham dry goods store in Abilene, where Aunt Frances worked.

Aunt Frances bought print remnants, and bias tape for trim, and Bernice sewed the aprons for a dollar apiece. At Christmastime she made organdy aprons with lots of ruffles and lace, and these brought two dollars and fifty cents. In addition to operating her own business, she sewed for the family and helped with the cleaning, in return for her board and room.

Since high school days, Bernice had made it a practice to accompany Aunt Frances to their church camp at Forest Park, Topeka. They took various Bible courses, sang in the large choir, and attended evening worship services in the huge tabernacle on campus.

One evening at camp — it was August, 1937 — when Bernice came out of their cabin to go to the tabernacle, she noticed a young man was waiting nearby. He stepped up to her and said, "May I walk to church with you?"

Bernice laughingly answered, "I guess there's room."

And off they went.

They sat down at the service, and the hymn number was announced. The young man picked up the book and held it for Bernice. She looked at it, and then reached over and turned the book right side up. Earl Enyeart, the young pastor from Alden, Kansas, was dazzled by the brown eyes and bubbly personality of Bernice Switzer Callahan.

Before the ten-day church camp had ended, Earl had asked Bernice to marry him.

"I want you to share my pastorate with me," he'd said later that week.

Bernice answered, "Let me think about it, Earl. Let's write to each other, and we'll see each other again in the fall."

In October, Bernice received her engagement ring, and the

wedding date was set for June 26, 1938. Bernice was twenty-five years old.

Bernice found that some of her loved ones were not as enthusiastic as others about the wedding. Perhaps they realized how much would be required of a minister's wife. But Bernice had given a lot of thought to the matter. She had had doubts, and had consulted a superintendent in the church. He told her, "Ever since I've known you, I've pictured you as mistress of a parsonage. You've got the energy, the ability, and the faith. I think that's the place for you. You've chosen wisely."

Then she spoke to the minister who was to perform the ceremony, and he too insisted she'd chosen well.

Aunt Frances encouraged Bernice, too, during the many little chats they shared. Aunt Frances recalled her own loss of love through an unexpected accident, and she wanted very much for Bernice to find fulfillment in marriage.

As Bernice herself explained to Aunt Frances, "I've been around ministers' families so much — cooking for them, doing housework, and helping out at church in many ways, that I think I know what it's all about. A minister's wife must always hold open house. Anyone is welcome who wants or needs to come to the parsonage for any reason. And I'll be expected to teach a Sunday school class whenever I'm asked, and to help out in lots of ways. I know it's not an easy life, but I love Earl and I want to be his helpmate in serving the Lord."

Aunt Frances took her hands and said, "Then the decision is made!"

Bernice nodded. "I guess it is!"

Bernice, assisted by her best friend, Leota Thurber, picked out the Simplicity pattern for her wedding gown. Of course she would sew it herself. Aunt Frances paid for the beautiful white silk and lace for the dress. Bernice bought her veil on a visit to Leota who was in college at Emporia, and smuggled it into the house. When the dress was ready, Leota took the hem length for her, so that no one would see her in the dress and veil until she came down the aisle.

As the wedding date neared, Callahan expressed his interest in the ceremony. Mrs. Callahan said, "What do you want to know for? You're not a part of it."

"Well, I guess I am!" he had responded. "I'm gonna give my daughter away!"

Bernice, listening, immediately changed her plans to walk down the aisle alone.

At last it was the day before, and a telegram from Cliff and Hazel had put a fine glow on Bernice's preparations. They wished her every happiness.

On the day of the wedding, Earl awoke with the flu, but he called Bernice to insist that the wedding go on as scheduled.

The wedding was to take place at the close of the morning worship service, at high noon. There would be a dinner at the Callahan's afterward, then Earl would take his bride to their home. There was no money for a honeymoon.

As Bernice paused at the back of the church, she looked at Earl up front, pale but handsome in his navy blue suit, with a white carnation in his lapel. She glanced at Mrs. Callahan and Aunt Frances and the grandparents, then at Dad Callahan, who shook with nerves and pleasure at his duty. The organist was playing "Ah, Sweet Mystery of Life," and the choir, still seated up front, watched from their perfect seats.

Bernice, in her lovely white dress, with a corsage of white roses and blue delphiniums, and a happy smile on her face, went forward on the arm of Mr. Callahan. She had a fleeting thought of a long ago loved one. "I bet my Mom — my real mom — would like to see me now."

Bernice and Earl on their wedding day. Her brother Harold Switzer was only relative attending.

188

27

New York Roots

Through the years, Ida and Bill had kept up efforts to learn more about their real parents. The desire to know their own background kept them seeking facts about their family — details they could not remember because they had been too young when the orphan train swept them away from their past. Theirs was a compulsion shared by virtually all of the western orphans — caused by this void of heritage, this rootlessness.

When Ida and her husband planned a trip to the New York World's Fair, Bill urged Ida to check out all available information about their family. Although she had just one name and address, that of her father's cousin, a Mrs. Cummings, who'd notified the Bishops when Bill and Ida's father died, Ida promised to do her best. When she returned to Wichita, she wrote her brother about the results of her search.

August 17, 1939

Dear Kid and Arlene,

I wouldn't take a world for my trip to New York City. I don't know why I hadn't done it sooner. I only wish you and Arlene could have been along. The trip was inexpensive, the fuel requirement for a Ford is very moderate and we had no trouble at all. We ate hamburgers and hot dogs mostly on the road as we could eat them as we rode along. We went by way of Buffalo and Niagara Falls, then through the Catskills on down to the city. It was a beautiful drive, and everything was so green and fresh compared to what it is here in Kansas now.

To enter the city we came down the western side of Manhattan on a highway that finally becomes an elevated speedway down the entire side of the island to Canal Street. You will recall that N.Y.C., that is, the business area, is in itself an island, Manhattan Island, about 25 square miles in area, then there are what are called boroughs, nine in all, I belive. Brooklyn, Flushing (where the World's Fair is), Corona, Queens, Long Island. I can't think of the rest of them, anyhow those are the ones we were in. We cut across the tip of Manhattan Island on Canal Street and took the Williamsburg Bridge across the East River into Brooklyn, where Mrs. Cummings owns a rooming house. We found the place easily, but did not find her at home. We went on up to Queens and then Flushing and the fair grounds. We found a room there in a private home and a garage for the car, all for a dollar per head and the car free. Went down on Broadway by way of subway that same night, and Broadway is just as bright as they say it is. I have read they wear dark glasses at night on Broadway and it is true, I saw lots of them that night.

I can't begin to describe the beauty or grandeur of the colored lights. We got off at Times Square, the brightest point at night. The Times Building had a flashing electric band (it is the shape of the original Flatiron Building) around the top part of the building which flashes continuously the news in lights, at least twenty-five feet tall. One can stand at any point from the building and read the news almost as it happens. Of course there is lots of neon, and lots of colored flashing bulbs, advertising dancing girls, swimming fish, flashing names, etc., all in colors. We wandered up and down Broadway, 5th and 7th Streets until 3 a.m., and when we left things were still going strong, just like in daylight. Shops and stores open, shows, shooting galleries, game places, taxi dances (where patrons pay to dance with a partner), night clubs, picture shows, and I guess the hotel signs flash all night, too.

We spent Thursday and Thursday night at the fair. Of course it is tremendous, and much imporvement over the Chicago Fair only because of the passing of time. However business is poor at the fair. The admission was $1.50 but down to 75 cents at the time we were there and 40 cents on Saturday. The fair ground was laid on an old dumping ground. They plan to make a permanent park. The trylon and phersphere are mammoth in size, made of good cement to remain as permanent in the park after the fair is over. A story is told that an Italian employed by the city, in clearing away the dump, found an old satchel with $20,000 in it. He took the next boat to Italy. Makes a good story, anyhow.

I wanted to see those things I recalled from childhood so we decided that one day and night of the fair was enough. We wandered around downtown, past the big stores, peeked in old Trinity Church, walked down Maiden Lane where more diamonds are sold than any other street in the world. Arlene, that is where that little chip diamond came from that you are wearing. You recall Fred Cummings sent that to me in a breast pin when I graduated from grade school. We saw the Exchange building, largest board of trade center in the world. We walked by the Chase National Bank, more international banking and exchange done there than any other place in the world. In this vicinity, lower Manhattan, was the Woolworth building. At the time of our stay in the orphanage it was the world's tallest building. It looked very short indeed in comparison to those new tall ones in upper Manhattan, such as the Empire State and Chrysler buildings.

We called cousin Fred Cummings midafternoon. I kept putting that off until I saw as much of the city as possible. We were allowing ourselves two weeks away from Wichita and I didn't want to go out there and accept their hospitality then expect them to go with us to see the sights. We decided we couldn't see it all if we stayed a month, so we picked certain things to see quickly. We took a ferry ride to Staten Island, which is a little city in itself, and quite a thriving place at that. We returned about 9 p.m. and decided if we were going to see Coney Island there was no time like the present so away we went by subway. Coney Island is really much larger than I expected. I did expect something perhaps twice as large as our state fair at Hutchinson but it was even greater than that. Not one roller coaster but several, and lots and lots of ferris wheels to say nothing of all the other fun rides. Then there was an endless boardwalk along the shore, and of course concessions everywhere you turned. There were also picture shows, groceries, and shops.

We picked Fred up the next day about noon at his office on Wall Street. He insisted we go out to their house for dinner and even on the new overhead speedway it was about a two-hour drive. He has a very nice wife and two boys about 11 and 7 years of age. Fred himself is forty years of age, very blond with milky skin. I consider him of a very good mentality and on the brainy order. He said he intended to be a millionaire by the time he was forty but Roosevelt called in the gold. It seems he had a lot of gold stowed away under the floor of their home. He says the calling in of gold here even ruined the foreign marketing. He has a beautiful home in the country but they may rent it and move to an apartment in town until things take an upward trend. Fred has two brothers, Malcolm and Donald. They talk in that New York accent, "foist," "thoity," "Joisey," "toin," etc.

Fred did not know a great deal about our family only that Dad Elder was always reading religion and philosophy, was of a very serious turn of mind. It seems that Dad wanted to marry their mother, this Mrs. Cummings, and the two together try to bring up her three boys and you and me. But her former husband, a drinking man, was continually in the background. That's why Dad finally sent us West.

The next day, after seeing the Statue of Liberty and Grant's Tomb, we went around to the Orphan's Home at 110 Manhattan Avenue East. I believe I'd have known the front of that building without looking for numbers. We went up and rang the bell and discovered a penciled note on the door that it was closed for the summer and the children were in the Catskills. I went around to the side to see if I could peek in at the iron gate into the play yard. You might recall there was a wrought-iron double gate, and the sheet iron door inside the gate. I could see in. The outside walls were of brick like the building and as high as the tall gate. I climbed a fire escape and peered over and sure enough, there it was just as I remembered it, only no board fence between.

Remember how you used to come to the fence and holler through the hole that you wanted to talk to me? Now the boys and girls play together. I took some pictures I will send later. I saw a janitor and called to him and told him what I wanted and he came down and let us in. I went all through the place. They now have a swimming pool in the basement, otherwise it is much the same. I went out to the play yard and peered in at the window where we girls used to look into the basement dining room to see what we were going to have for supper. I also looked up at that third-story window where that old caretaker used to lean out and clap her hands to quell us whenever we got a big fight worked up.

The steps are the same inside, a slate substance. I remember we used to see who could scrape her fingers the longest without getting the shivers. You will also remember there was some sort of wrought iron under the bannister to keep the kids from falling through. Used to be painted and is still painted green.

The washrooms are the same. Four and five faucets to a lavatory or wash bowl. A row of hooks with metal numbers beside them for each child's toothbrush and wash cloth. Then behind a sort of swing affair swung from the ceiling where there were also metal numbers for towels.

Nearly every room has some sort of radio now. They also have a gym and the youngsters are given speech work and dancing. The janitor told me they had one boy last year that won a scholarship to Harvard. Now the children go out to city schools and are not made to leave until they at least have a high school education. There are only 135 children here now. The home is called "Stewart House."

I got into the office but the old files were all securely

locked or else I would have maybe learned something more about us. The janitor helped me hunt for a key to fit the files but we could not find it.

There were trees at one side of the girls' yard, I recall. The janitor remembered when they dug them out and cemented the dirt spots in, so the complete surface is now cement. In the play rooms there are only a few of the old wooden wall trunks built in, with latches and padlocks where we kept our toys. They are being replaced with tall steel lockers like we see in school buildings here in the west. I also got some outside views of the building which I will forward to you as soon as I get them all finished.

We went over to Battery Park, then drove around in Chinatown and the Bowery. The Bowery, you may recall, is where all the old time saloons used to be, over which all the derelicts and forgotten people used to live. It is not quite as it used to be although we did see several drunken souls wandering aimlessly down the center of the street or just anywhere. At six each evening certain short blocks all over these lower residential districts are blocked off for a playground for the kiddies. They have a whole block in which to play ball, pitch horse shoes, play hopscotch, or marbles. We also drove down around the wharf and saw a lot of forgotten souls numbly watching the kids play catch in the evening. The next day we got over to the Statue of Liberty alright and were able to go up this time. Well I remember those winding stairs. The arm was not open. The winding stair starts at the hem of her skirt and winds up and up until you reach her crown, from where you can look down or over at Manhattan. There is now a WPA project going to build an elevator to the top of her head. The arm is a little decrepit and therefore unsafe for much traffic.

We went back to Fred's for a two-day visit, then Monday went over to see Marion Cummings. Marion Cummings is a woman about the size of Mom Bishop, very gray, nervous and worn looking. She inherited this rooming house from her sister and is trying to make a living. I took notes all along and it is a good thing I did, because I saw and learned so many things.

It seems no one can recall that we spent any time in Pennsylvania. Shortly after Mother's death, Dad Elder put us or rather lived with us at a Mrs. Ferris' house on Third Street and she took care of us while he was at work. It seemed the family didn't keep much contact with one another. Maybe relatives are like that in the city.

Mrs. Cummings told me that Dad Elder died in Lincoln Hospital, the result of live burns. She was then working at Chase National Bank and had more or less lost contact with him. He insisted no one be told of his plight as he seemed to know he was going to die. A Mrs. Michaels, who worked beside her at the bank, told her of her cousin's death. On hearing of it, Mrs. Cummings went to the hospital and took charge. Dad had died alone in his room. She made funeral arrangements, and the only people there were Mrs. Cummings, her sister, and a preacher. The burial place is over the 99th ferry, in the St. Joseph Cemetery. I only wish I had had more time to hunt all things up. Mrs. Cummings does not know whether there was a marker.

She speaks very highly of Dad and says he was a very well read man and very brainy. Elizabeth Pratt, our mother, was his third wife. It is not known what became of the other two, whether it was divorce or death or separation. The second wife was a schoolteacher.

Now for the relationship. I didn't get it clearly from Mrs. Cummings. Dad Elder was named for his father, and his middle name, Clark, comes from Hugh Clark, an uncle to both Marion Cummings and our father. This uncle Hugh Clark was a very enterprising fellow and owned a small wine place down near the Bowery and as times got better, owned more and more, and built buildings down there and became wealthy in the wine business. This is perhaps what I had thought of as the restaurant business of which Mom Bishop spoke on the Elder side. Somehow that wealth was dissipated and neither Dad nor Mrs. Cummings ever realized any value from it.

There were three Elder children: William Clark Elder (our father), Ida Elder, and Anna Elder. After their parents died, our dad was never really adopted by anyone; however, he lived for a time with a doctor and became interested enough in surgery that he bought a body and dissected it. Ida and Anna were adoped by millionaires of New York and Philadelphia.

Ida Elder tried to get hold of us at the time our father died, so she could bring suit against the railroad. Marion Cummings takes credit for keeping her from getting us.

William Elder, our father, and our mother played in public. She played the piano, he the violin, and she also sang quite well, and was very versatile and apt in every way, according to Mrs. Cummings. She said Dad never seemed to find himself. He was a painter and stripper on wagons and buggies for quite some time and worked in railroading off and on for some years until the railroad accident that killed him.

There were five children in our family. An older girl, Bessie, a boy whose name no one seems to recall, you, me, and one a little younger than I that died before Mother died. Mrs. Cummings recalls an incident when I came to the door and met her and took her by the hand and told her that Mother

194

had told me the baby had gone to Heaven.

At this point Mrs. Cummings cried, and told of circumstances of living that were not conducive to the rearing of children or the health of the mother. She was not present at the time of death or at the funeral of our mother. She said there was no getting any of the books or the trunk, as the landlady at that time was dead and gone by now. However, she did get a glass fruit bowl that our father had won in a contest in his work and brought home to her. She had kept it all through these years to give to you or me. I thought I would keep it awhile and then send it on to you to keep as I know you remember Father Elder much better than I do. It's just an inexpensive thing, but all we have of him.

From Mrs. Cummings' house we proceded to Uncle Harry's. There were two Harry Pratts in the phone book, but the first one I called turned out to be he. He and his wife, Aunt Lucy, are gray-haired but they look like their pictures. Their daughter is to be married this fall. Uncle Harry is still carrying mail, as he was years ago. He said I was the image of my mother and he would have known me anywhere. Uncle Harry says his mother died early and our mother "mothered" him and he thought a great deal of her. (Uncle Harry and our mother are only half brother and sister — the same father but different mothers.) He does not seem to know much of mother's mother, nor of the Spanish strain we supposedly have in our bloodline. There were four children: Harry, Mother, Aunt Minnie Bailey, and Uncle Edwin, who has died. Uncle Harry says our mother was quite a dancer, and so was father; in fact, they met at a dance. She played and sang in public, and at one time gave piano lessons to help keep her children. Uncle Harry says Dad played a clarinet or a horn of some kind. He worked for the New York, New Haven, and Hartford lines at the time of his accident. Mother is buried in Bayview in Bayonne, N.J., near a florist's shop. Both Father and Mother were Protestants, Mother Episcopalian. Uncle Harry Pratt and Dad Elder had a disagreement before Mother's death, and were not on speaking terms.

Now about the birth certificates. I got them both and tried to trace the other children but there was no record of a Bessie Elder. I also tried to contact the two doctors mentioned on our birth certificates but they were not in any of the directories I checked. Notice we were both born in Jersey City but on different streets. I hunted up the streets and numbers, they are and always have been the slum districts. At the time of your birth, Father was 42 and Mother 35. There is a discrepancy in my age, because my certificate says at the time of my birth Father was 44 and Mother 37, making me only two years younger than you, instead of three, as we thought. Also, my birth was recorded in March of the same year I was born, and yours was not recorded until 6 years after your birth. I have Father Elder's letter saying you were born in Feb., 1900 and I was born in Feb., 1903. Uncle Harry insists there is only two years difference in our ages. You can readily see there is a mistake somewhere in regard to me. It could have been that my birth certificate or registration was confused (by some relative) with that of the baby that died, for no one seems to know her name and according to the certificate this female child was not named. All of which doesn't matter in regard to my age. From here on out I'll choose the age I please and dare any one to dispute me.

I was very disappointed not to find a trace of Bessie or the little boy in our family, but Bessie could have been born on the Manhattan side or elsewhere, and not knowing the boy's name there was no way of tracing him. It is possible that somewhere we have a brother and/or a sister we will never meet.

I showed the pictures of your three daughters to all the relatives and everyone seemed to think Joy looked like an Elder.

Must close. Just wanted to add that we saw the Queen Mary dock and we toured it for 25 cents. The crew alone before passengers is a little over 1100 in number. Every bar and grill and dining room had orchestra pits and pianos, and there were swimming pools and tennis courts, just like a young city.

I will send the pictures soon, and after keeping the fruit bowl awhile, I will send it on to you, as a reminder of our Dad.

Love to you all,
Ida

28

Forgiveness At Last

After Cliff and Hazel were married, Cliff began to feel closer to all his family, including his mother. There had been a time in his late teens, after he'd returned to New York, when Cliff would deliberately cross the street to avoid meeting his mother. But through the years the hate he'd nourished so long gradually began to dissolve.

This was partly due to the security he found in his own marriage and Hazel's compassionate understanding of those early painful years he'd endured. Hazel tried to be a bridge for their relationship. She voiced her affection for Mother Mary, and praised her for her good qualities, always stressing the positive aspects. She suggested they invite Mother Mary and Frank over to dinner. Hazel considered Cliff's mother one of the finest cooks she'd ever known, and treasured any compliments Mother Mary gave on her own cooking.

When Hazel became pregnant with their first child, Cliff's joy was boundless. "Darling," he rejoiced with her, "I couldn't be happier, with a lovely wife, and a baby on the way."

They'd lie awake for hours, talking about their family-to-be. Cliff took his responsibilities seriously.

"Hazel," he promised her, "I'd do anything to raise our children right, and take good care of you all. You and our babies and our home mean everything to me."

When little David was born, Cliff began his career as a devoted daddy. He was so proud of the baby that he wanted to show him off to Mother Mary. Little by little, the gulf between Cliff and his mother was narrowing.

But then Cliff brought home sad news. "Ma's gonna die," he said tonelessly.

"What do you mean?" Hazel asked in alarm.

"She's got cancer."

"Oh, Cliff . . . "

"And she's gonna die. The doctor told her there's nothing they can do for her."

"I'm so sorry. She's a good woman in lots of ways."

"The way I see it, her and that husband was a big reason for me and the others being kicked all over the country," Cliff began an old, old refrain.

"But you understand her better now. Now that you're grown, you can see that a lot of the mistakes she made were because she was so young, and had no resources, no faith."

"Yes, I know. I was born when she was fifteen . . . "

"And she had three children by the time she was seventeen, and a husband who drank, too. You can imagine how hard life was for her," Hazel said. "I'm sure she'd have kept you if there was any way for her to do it."

"I suppose so, Hazel. What do you think we can do for her? Something that will comfort her."

"I'll stay with her as much as I can."

"And I'm gonna write Bernice. She's a preacher's wife. Maybe she can say something . . . "

"I'm glad you're going to try to help."

"Well," Cliff answered, taking Hazel in his arms, "blood's thicker than water."

Dear Bernice, Cliff wrote. *Our mother has cancer and she is on her deathbed. If you can find it in your heart to write to her, I think it would do her a lot of good. She's lonely, and she asks about you often. Cliff.*

"What do you think, Earl?" Bernice asked her husband at supper. "Should I write? What can I say? I haven't seen her since I was six."

"I think you should write," Earl replied, "if you can. It would be the kind thing to do."

So Bernice sat down and began a weekly correspondence with her mother, the woman she had not seen in over twenty years. The first letter concerned Bernice's marriage to Earl a year ago, and the recent death of their first child, a little boy, at birth.

Immediately a letter came back. Bernice's mother was obviously grateful for her daughter's concern during this time of suffering. She asked for a photograph of Bernice's wedding party. Bernice sent it.

But Bernice now faced an even greater challenge; she decided she would try to be the instrument by which her mother might become a Christian. *Mother,* she wrote, *it would mean so much more to you, and your pain would be so much easier to bear, if you would turn your life over to Christ.* Bernice went on to explain the message of the gospel.

Revival meetings were being held at Earl's church at Industry, Kansas, at the time, and Bernice's friend, the visiting minister, asked her, "It's nearly Christmas. What do you want this year?"

"There wouldn't be anything in the world that would please me more than to hear that my mother has finally given her heart to Christ," Bernice answered.

Two days after Christmas, the letter came.

You sure have put a new life in me. I don't know now as if I would have ever been a Christian if it had not been for your letters. Bernice's mother had called on a Methodist minister and he had "prayed her through." It was a day Bernice would never forget.

The letters between Bernice and her mother continued for several weeks. Then she received a letter from Claudia, the wife of Bernice's brother, Howard.

Reading Center
Tuesday, May 7, 1940

Dear Bernice and Earl,

Well, I believe it's your turn to write but as you know, Mother passed away. I thought I'd write you the particulars. She died ten minutes after midnight May 4. When I get a paper with the obituary I will send you one.

We were down to see her just a week before she died and she seemed to be quite good that day. She talked to us every minute for about two hours. Frieda and Alvin, and Cliff and Hazel were to see her the next day. She had several hemorhages the next few days and on Saturday she had three. That was too much. No one realized that she was so bad until about two hours before she went. She waited on herself till the very end and was conscious up the last fifteen minutes. I guess she realized she couldn't stay here much longer and she certainly bore her pain bravely and patiently. No one knows what she has gone through these past few months. And as for Frank, he sure did all that could be done for her. He said that she was the best woman a man ever had or could want and that he had had her and lost her. He was so afraid that he wouldn't have things as her children would like but I guess all of us back here were perfectly satisfied.

He had her put in the lot with his first wife and left a place in between them for him. We all feel very sorry for him. He had a beautiful casket for her. It was mahogany, lined with peach satin. She wore the dress and beads that we had her picture taken in, when we got her out of bed last February for a photograph to keep. She was awfully thin but one could not help but be thankful that the Dear Lord took her to rest and as she lay there she looked so peaceful, so much out of distress.

We all took it very hard, but Bernice, you know that if she had to be in so much pain this is a lot better for her. The minister talked about you writing letters to her and how you helped lead her to God through your letters. I think Frank would appreciate it if you sent a card or letter of sympathy. He would have liked it if you could have come. Frank had a beautiful heart of flowers for her and it had WIFE in gold letters in the center. Howard got a pretty spray of red roses, Cliff's spray was of orchids. Frieda and Harold put in together and got a spray of snapdragons and lilies. There were also flowers from the office where Frank works, and beautiful baskets from her neighbors, the Sunday school, the rural school, the company where Cliff works, and others. She did love her flowers so.

With loads of love to you both,

Howard, Claudia and Kiddies

When Bernice and Cliff were able to talk about their mother, they agreed on one thing. Whatever she had been as a young woman, she had died a changed person. And, Bernice insisted, "Our mother loved us, Cliff. I know she did. She couldn't have helped but love us. Kids belong with their mothers, but once in a while there's an exception. I often wonder what would have happened to us if we'd been left in New York to eat other people's garbage."

Cliff nodded. "It was better, in the long run, I guess, that she let us go. It was a tough life to live, but I guess I can understand how hard it was for her."

The bitterness had finally crumbled and vanished.

29
Faithfulness Rewarded

The pastor drew Anna aside as she shook hands with him at the church door after Sunday services. "I wonder if I could speak with you a moment, Anna?" he asked.

Jennie assumed the pastor wanted to discuss plans for an upcoming musical event in which Anna was taking part. She went on out the door, calling to Anna, "I'll wait outside."

But the minister had something else in mind. "Anna," he began, and Anna smiled. (Everyone called her Anna. Many people never even knew her last name.) "The church has been wanting to honor Jennie for her many years of faithful services to the Sunday school. What do you think of a little surprise party for her after next Sunday's service? Nothing elaborate. We'd like to acknowledge her work, give her a little gift — just pay tribute where it's due. She's taught Sunday school longer than anyone else here. What do you think?" He looked hopefully at Anna.

Anna knew Jennie wouldn't want all this fuss made over her, and if it had to be done, she was sure Jennie would have preferred it be done at Sunday school or at the teachers' meeting, rather than in front of all the people at church. As far as Anna knew, this was the first time something like this was being done.

"Well, I don't know . . . "

"Our only concern is to make sure you think it's all right, and that she'll be here. Even though she hardly ever makes plans to go out of town, we wanted to be sure . . . "

Anna suppressed a smile. "She'll be there. But I wouldn't advise making a fuss over her. You know how modest she is."

"That's why we're asking you. I know she doesn't want attention called to her efforts, but we really do want to do something for her. A lot of our members got their first Bible training in her class."

"Well," Anna said finally, "you can try it, but I won't take responsibility for the results." She laughed.

"Sit by her," the pastor replied. "When the announcement is made, just take her arm and lead her toward the pulpit. I'll handle it from there."

Anna smiled. "I'll do all I can to help."

Next Sunday, Jennie and Anna taught their respective Sunday school classes as usual, then took their places in a pew for the worship service. At the end of the sermon, Jennie found that the pastor was deviating from his normal closing. Then she heard her name being called. She felt Anna's firm support at her side, and she stood up shyly. She smiled tolerantly as the secret was disclosed. She stood up front, listening as the pastor told of her good works, the faithful attendance over a period of many years, the dedication to teaching children. He even mentioned how she had taken in an orphan girl who had herself become a pillar of their church. And then she was presented with an orchid, and a new white Bible to replace her old, worn one. As she slipped back into her seat, she glanced around at the faces in the audience. Some she had taught as children, many others she'd known for years. There were friendly smiles as Jennie sat down, humbled.

"You knew, didn't you?" Jennie reproached Anna with a good-natured grin, afterwards. They were sharing dinner at home.

"I did," Anna admitted. "But I couldn't say no, and deprive your former students of the joy of telling you how much they appreciate you."

"Well, it was kind of nice, even if I was embarrassed," Jennie finally admitted.

"How many of your former students congratulated you afterwards?"

"Oh, there must have been thirty or forty of them there," Jennie answered. "One of them reminded me how strict I had been about making them learn their Bible verses. He said he didn't realize until later that if you loved a child you disciplined him."

"Yes, you always believed in the verse, 'Train up a child in the way he should go, and when he is grown he will not depart from it.' Tell me, Jennie, did I give you a lot of trouble when I first came to you?" Anna still wanted to know about her growing up — here and back in New York.

"No, you really didn't," Jennie responded. "You'd had good training. And your mother must have instilled in you the idea that you should not sit idly by and let society take care of you, that each should learn to take care of himself, because you already had that idea of life when you came to me."

"When I came to Kansas, I remember that I didn't want people to know I'd been at a sanitarium. I was ashamed of having been on welfare, and I'd made up my mind I wasn't going to live on welfare. I wanted to earn my own living."

"And you certainly have! Now you take care of me, too! Of course I never planned on that, way back then, I just wanted to give you a home."

"But I like taking care of you," Anna insisted. "I do my work at the insurance company, and we're together all the rest of the time. That's just the way I like it." She put out her hand and covered Jennie's.

Anna laughed suddenly. "Remember how I'd always beg to go to shows, even though I knew you knew best?"

Jennie chuckled.

"I bet you never knew that Margaret tried to get me to run away back to New York!"

"I didn't," Jennie admitted. "When? Why?"

"It was a few years after we'd come here. She was so frustrated here that she decided we should go back to the orphanage. I went over there one night to stay, and she tried to talk me into running away with her — back to New York. I said I wouldn't leave unless there was no other way. After awhile she gave up on her big idea. It did please her though, that she and her husband were able to visit New York recently. She found our parents' burial places, and looked up the old neighborhoods and landmarks. I think it satisfied her to know some of the answers to questions she'd had for so many years. Strange, isn't it, she's the only one of us who made it to California. She says she likes living out there." Anna thought back to her dreams of California so long ago.

"Anna. I want you to promise me something. After I'm gone . . . "

"Please," Anna said forcefully, "Don't even talk about that.
204

Why, you're going to live a long time yet. Look, I've got more gray in my hair than you have in yours . . . "

"No. Listen to me. When I'm gone, I want you to travel. You've always had such an itchy foot — you should get out and see the world. Go to Europe! Go visit Margaret in California. You've been so tied down taking care of me."

"Nonsense," Anna stated firmly. "I wouldn't want to be any place but here with you. You know I didn't like teaching school out West. After one year in western Kansas I was ready to come back here and be with you."

"But someday, Anna."

Anna looked at her directly. How precious she was, Anna thought again. "Someday," she whispered. Someday she would have to face Jennie's going. But not yet. She remembered the old letter she'd found that Jennie had written shortly after her father died. Until the moment she read that letter, Anna had not realized the immensity of Jennie's struggle for independence.

When Jennie went to take a nap that afternoon, Anna found herself looking at the old letter again. *I miss my father so much,* Jennie's handwriting had confessed. *It is so lonely without him, and I must go ahead and take care of all the things he used to do. All the folks are good to me, and help me in so many ways, but they have their own families and homes to keep up. I depend on them so much; this is not right. I must learn to do things for myself, for though it would be so easy to depend on them for everything, I must learn to take care of myself so I do not become a burden. The nieces and nephews are so good to me, they are all such darlings.*

Again, Anna felt a wave of deep sympathy and love for her foster mother. Now it was as if their roles were being reversed, and she was becoming the caretaker of Jennie. She wondered how she could provide for their futures. And then a thought occured to her. The business manager at the insurance company had asked her if she had been legally adopted. No, she hadn't. "Too bad," he had said. "You could claim Miss Bengtson on your income tax as a dependent." Maybe it was time to settle some old business — something left undone because it seemed unneeded for so many years.

When Jennie awakened, Anna said, "I just had an idea. Why don't we go down to the courthouse and legally adopt each other? You're the only mother I've had, and we do belong to each other. Why not make it official?"

From the delighted expression in Jennie's eyes, Anna could

tell she'd hit on a brilliant idea. Jennie hadn't wanted to mention it, because it would emphasize her dependency on Anna. But nothing would please her more, she was sure.

And so, within a few weeks, the papers were ready, and one day they went down and signed the papers. Anna had bought a little present for Jennie, and Jennie gave Anna a beautiful ring, her birthstone.

Jennie tried to appear calm and collected, but Anna heard her telling her neighbor, Mrs. Wyborg, "Oh, Myrtle, the most wonderful thing has happened! Years ago, I adopted Anna. Now she's adopted me. Now Anna really is my daughter."

Anna and Jennie

30

And Where We Love . . .

And where we love is home,
Home that our feet may leave,
But not our hearts.
The chain may lengthen, but it never parts.

Oliver Wendell Holmes

Coming home! The prairie panorama from Earl and Bernice Enyeart's pastorate at St. John, in west central Kansas, to Abilene, 150 miles northeast, reflected distinctive autumn beauty. It was nearly Thanksgiving, and Indian summer. Mild, warm, hazy weather had followed the first frosts of late autumn. Browned cornstalks marched in rows to the horizon and there met the bright azure sky. The Enyeart's old sedan stirred up pheasants beside backroads shortcuts, and the birds lifted from their nests of thistles and weeds. But they would find their way back.

Fragrances of harvest lingered in the sunlit haze — alfalfa hay, plowed earth, dust. Fat pumpkins and squash stacked in fields echoed the orange and yellow hues of drifting cottonwood and oak leaves, and melted into a cornucopia of color. Occasional fields of pale green — the tender young blades of winter wheat coming up — were the only suggestion that this was not the end of a season.

In thirteen years of marriage there had been little time or money for Bernice to make visits home, so occasional trips were a special thrill.   It was always the same.   As they neared their destination it seemed as though she'd drawn a breath and not let it out. Closer, closer, but not yet there, she felt the excitement of expectation, as the quiet pleasures of home welled inside made her as eager as a child at Christmas.

The first distant sight of Abilene was its water tower, a silvery sentinel shining above the valley in the brilliant autumn sun.

Everything along the way was radiant and alive to Bernice's heightened senses. A meadowlark perched on a gnarled and worn fencepost caroled sweetly. Holsteins, a black and white crowd against a pasture fence, lowed and stared as the car passed. Another mile, she thought, as they crossed a section line. Her heart leaped at familiar sights — the Riley Farm, neat and trim as a picture; the creamery station run by Harve Oat. She caught a glimpse of him bending at his work. And there was the old concrete bridge spanning the Smoky Hill river, its tree-lined path etched in the distance. A warm, familiar glow grew inside her with each passing landmark.

She glanced at her three children, perched on the back seat and mesmerized by the sun's warmth filtering through the car windows. She smiled. They were anxious to see their grandparents, but they could not share her feelings at coming home. What a rush of memories and emotions! Some were as bittersweet as the orange berries growing wild along the roadside. Yet this was home and always would be.

"Here's the street, children," Earl announced as they rounded the corner.

They clapped and shouted, "Faster, faster!" The street was gravel and dust kicked up behind them.

The last block. Would it look the same? Was everyone all right? Earl sped up a little more. "There it is," he said, smiling, and wheeled into the drive. Bernice sprang out and hurried up the sidewalk. Her son Kent skipped to keep pace with her up the walk and concrete steps to the old stucco bungalow. "Tell us what Grandpa did the time you jumped off the porch swing," he urged. Bernice laughed. "There will be plenty of time for stories later. It's hard to believe that your Mama was once a little girl, isn't it? That swing was my favorite play-spot when I was a kid."

They knocked at the door and were quickly enveloped in hugs, kisses, and welcomes from Mr. and Mrs. Callahan and Aunt Frances. In no time the children were entertaining their elders with long, involved tales of their school and activities.

Bernice noted that Mom Callahan looked well; her brown eyes were clear, though her hair had turned whiter. Aunt Frances, too, seemed fit. But even at first glance she sensed that her father was ill. Beneath the jovial exterior, as he lifted baby Cynthia, "the apple of his eye," she noticed a weakness. She was concerned but she couldn't speak to him about it in front of everyone, knowing he would want his illness kept private. Perhaps laughter would do some good. She joined in the conversation, adding details to the children's accounts, and filling in on Earl's reports about his congregation. Finally, after supper, she saw the opportunity to talk. She sat down beside his old brown chair.

"Dad," she said in her direct way, "I think you need to go to a doctor."

"Now, Bernice," came the familiar reply, "there's just no money to spare." He did not deny that he felt ill, she noted.

"Well, you've got to go anyhow," she concluded. "I'm calling Dr. Heinz in the morning." Callahan didn't argue; he knew her determination.

Before breakfast she rang up "central" and asked for Dr. Heinz, an old friend. Years ago she'd been his patient when he treated her for blood poisoning after she'd scratched her hand on a school locker.

"Your father needs to have x-rays taken in Salina," Dr. Heinz told Bernice.

"All right, we'll get him there," she assured him.

That day Bernice and Earl drove Callahan into Salina, twenty-five miles west, where tests were made. When the results came back, Dr. Heinz called at the house. His patient was resting in bed, Bernice seated nearby.

"Otto," he said frankly, "you've got a tumor. We don't know if it's malignant, but we have to go in there and find out."

Callahan was reluctant to undergo surgery; he just didn't know where the money would come from.

"Dad," Bernice said, "I don't have any money, either. And I've got three little kids. But I tell you what I'll do — I'll start taking sewing again to help you pay the bill, if you'll go into the hospital and have the operation."

Callahan looked up, and his brown eyes met hers. "Beanie," he said, using his old term of endearment, "if you think it's that important, I'll go. But under one condition — that you'll go with me and stay with me." He placed his hand on hers.

"Well, Dad, Lucrecia and Kent have to get back to St. John

209

to go to school. But I could send them with Earl, and keep Cynthia here with me. Yes, I believe that would work. If Earl will take care of them, I'll stay until you're through with the surgery."

"If you'll do that, I'll go."

"All right." She leaned over and hugged him encouragingly.

Callahan went into the Abilene hospital, and his operation took place four days after Thanksgiving. Then came the news: the tumor was malignant. His condition was serious. For ten days Bernice kept vigil at his side from 7 a. m. till 7 p. m., when a night nurse came on duty. The room was small and sterile. There was a table beside the narrow bed, a dresser, and a rocker for Bernice and the nurse. Bernice placed the rocker at the foot of his bed so she could see him at all times. While Callahan slept, she crocheted doll dresses to sell and help with expenses.

One day Bernice said, "Dad, I need to run home and see Cynthia for a little while, and clean up. I'm beginning to feel like yesterday's flowers. I'll get someone to come and sit with you."

She rushed home, took a bath, changed dresses — she had only two — and spent some time playing with four-year-old Cynthia. When she returned to the hospital, she learned that Callahan had taken a turn for the worse. He was vomiting and very ill. He'd apparently overheard a thoughtless remark made by a relative to the effect of "getting him out of here before the bill gets any higher." Bernice called the nurse, who summoned the doctor. Dr. Heinz was able to bring Callahan out of the attack.

As Callahan began feeling better, he and Bernice shared confidences they'd kept all their lives. One day she looked up from her crocheting to find him watching her. "Beanie," he said, "I wish if I had a dozen daughters, every one of them would be like you!"

"Oh, Dad!" Bernice glowed, and tears brimmed her eyes. "That's worth a million dollars to me. But why do you say that?"

"I always knew where I stood with you, Beanie. If you were mad, you slammed the door. Do you remember how many times you had to come back downstairs and shut that door quietly?" He chuckled. "And if you had something to say, you said it. I just want you to know what you mean to me."

Then he told her how they'd decided to take her into their home permanently. "Think back to when you and David were staying with us, right after the orphan train brought you to town. Do you remember the day the Webers came to get your little brother, and I took you for a walk?"

"Yes. I had been David's 'mama' up till then, and I didn't want to see him go. You took me out and we walked in a field on the edge of town. We walked and walked."

"You looked up at me with those sad, brown eyes, and you said, 'I wish I could call you Daddy.' Then I knew I just couldn't give you up."

He reached out and held her hand until he fell asleep again.

Sometimes he'd ask her to sing to him old favorite hymns she'd learned when she'd joined the senior choir he directed. Her clear voice and the songs, "In the Garden," "The Old Rugged Cross," and "Shall We Gather at the River?" meant a great deal to him.

"Dad," she said, "when you were in St. John last time and we sang a duet for the service, I was so proud of you. And the next week a woman came up to me and said, 'Mrs. Enyeart, now we know where you get your singing ability. You inherited it from your dad!' " He smiled.

Next day Callahan was sitting up in bed. "I'm feeling stronger every day," he announced. "But, these whiskers," he murmured, stroking the stubble. "If I could only have a shave . . ." Rising to the challenge, Bernice said, "I'll do it, Pop!"

"Bernice, you've never shaved me before!"

"No, but I can do it."

She went to town and bought razor blades and soap and came back and announced, "Now I'm going to do it."

She steamed his face with hot cloths wrung from a washbasin, and built up a good lather, then bent over his bed and started in. He found it amusing.

Just as she finished the job, the town barber happened to walk down the hallway and peek in the door. Bernice, who had worked for the Harlow Davis' doing housework many years before, saw him and called, "Come on in and inspect my job, Harlow. I just got through shaving my dad."

"You did a darned good job," laughed the barber. "I should hire you."

Callahan delighted in telling Mr. Davis and others that "Beanie shaved me — she can do anything! If she makes up her mind she's going to do something, she'll do it!"

On his twelfth day after surgery, Callahan was told he could go home the next day. So Bernice brought up the subject of her family. "Dad, if you're going home tomorrow, would it be all right if I leave today? My two little kids back in St. John are probably

211

looking like orphans themselves by now. Earl doesn't use an iron and he's not much at combing Lucrecia's hair. Besides, Dad, it's not long till Christmas. I should try to get a tree up and make a few presents for the kids."

Callahan nodded, understanding. "Sure you can go. But I'm going to miss you."

"Now, Pop," Bernice teased him, "you don't need me to sit here in a chair and watch you sleep, and that's about all you've been doing."

He grinned. "Well, I don't blame you a bit. I've been kind of unthoughtful."

"No," Bernice answered. "I promised to stay so I did."

Bernice returned to her family, and for the next five months Callahan got along fairly well. But in April, Bernice received a phone call. "Dad wants to see you."

"Oh, I really can't come. I don't have the money. I just don't have the money!"

Suddenly a third voice was heard on the party-line. "Hey, Mrs. Enyeart," said the listener, "if that's your dad and he wants you, you better go. I'll buy your ticket for you."

Bernice recognized that the voice belonged to the man they bought milk from. "All right — thank you! I'll pay you back some way," she responded, touched by the unexpected offer.

The milk man drove to town and paid twelve dollars for the round-trip ticket, then drove out in his truck, picked up Bernice, and took her to the train.

When she arrived at Callahan's beside, Bernice bent over the white-haired man. "What's the matter, Dad?"

"I just can't breathe," he gasped. She tried to help him, but he was nearly strangling. Finally she dashed to the phone and called Dr. Heinz. "This is Bernice, and Dad's having an awful time breathing," she reported. "I've been fanning him for half an hour. What could be the matter?"

Dr. Heinz said, "It's his nerves. Make him some strong coffee — real hot — and have him drink that. Wait five minutes, and if his breathing doesn't get easier, I'll come out."

Bernice made the coffee and spooned it into his mouth. After he began breathing easier again, he said, "I knew if you got here, I'd feel better."

Bernice went home two days later. On the fourth of July, she told her family, "Let's drive to Abilene and see Grandpa today." It was hot and dry, and the temperature was near 100 degrees.

They spent the day visiting. When she went to leave Callahan that night, she explained, "Now, Dad, we have to get up at five in the morning to drive home and we don't want to disturb you. So, we'll go down to Aunt Frances' house for the night, and we'll tell you goodbye now."

Lucrecia, Kent, and Cynthia kissed their grandpa, and Earl shook his hand. Then Bernice bent toward him, and he gently pulled her close. He kissed her on the forehead and said, "Beanie, this is the last time I'll see you."

"Oh, no, Dad!" Bernice shook her head. "You just feel bad now because it's so hot. When it gets cooler, you're going to feel better. This heat is hard on everyone."

"No," he answered, breathing heavily. "But Beanie — " he looked into her eyes with deep love, "I'm going to be up there. And I'm going to be looking for you."

Bernice clutched his hand, and put her face beside his to hide the tears. "I'll see you, Dad," she whispered. "We'll all see you."

On July 7th, the phone rang at 6:30 a. m. Bernice heard, "Your Dad is gone."

On Father's Day, a month earlier, Bernice had taken time to write her dad a letter. "I've always said it's no disgrace to be poor, but it sure is unhandy at times. I can't send you a gift for Father's Day," she wrote, "because there's no money for a gift, but I want to tell you what you've meant to me in my life . . . " And she did. She told him how she'd gotten strength from his love, his guidance, and his confidence in her. He had kept the letter, and when the undertaker returned his personl effects, the letter had been found in his shirt pocket.

The Epilogue
August, 1963

Anna wheeled into her driveway, parked the car in the garage to protect it from the afternoon sun, and hurried toward the house, her stylish short graying hair lifting on the hot breath of wind. She plucked the mail from the box beside the house and hurried in out of the heat. It was so hot — as hot as those first weeks of school, that year she'd taught school out in western Kansas. That was during the Dust Bowl times, and she couldn't forget the stifling, oppressive air with the dust that covered everything and made every action a supreme effort of will. No, that had not been her calling. She had not enjoyed teaching, and she'd missed Jennie so much she had returned after the year was up to care for her. With her excellent business skills, Anna had had no trouble finding a good job at the large insurance company in town. Anna settled there, content to be with Jennie.

Now she stepped inside the empty house, cool and darkened, and sat down to look through her mail. A postcard from a cousin vacationing in California. Two bills. And a letter from New Jersey.

She held it up and murmured to herself, "I don't know anyone in New Jersey." She put the other mail aside.

She opened the letter and read:

Miss Fuchs,

As a regular correspondent of Miss Hill, I'm sure you will want to know that she passed away earlier this month. She was bright, right up to the end. A copy of her obituary is enclosed. She always took such pleasure in the letters from "her children." Please excuse the brevity of this letter. I have many more persons to contact.

Sincerely,
John Hill,
(nephew of Anna Laura Hill)

214

Anna took a deep breath. It had always seemed to her that Miss Hill was immortal — she was so strong, so courageous, so loving and concerned. Now she was gone. The obituary made little mention of her work, dismissing it with one sentence. Perhaps the world would never know what good Miss Hill had done. But there were many who would never forget her.

Anna fixed herself a sandwich, then hurried out to the car again, taking the letter with her. Jennie would want to know. She turned the car toward Lindsborg, where Jennie had been a patient at the nursing home for more than a year now. What a struggle it had been to make that decision, Anna reflected. She'd had to ask the help of their minister to break the news to Jennie that Anna couldn't continue to care for her properly, while holding down the full-time job to cover their living expenses. Anna visited her every day.

Jennie beamed with joy when she saw Anna, and Anna sat down to help Jennie with her supper tray. She was nearly eighty-nine now. When her old friend, Lyda Swanson, had visited her not long ago, Jennie had told her, "Oh, Lyda, who would have thought we'd live to be so old." But Anna was grateful for every day of Jennie's life. She'd built her own around it, and their love was mutually supportive.

She told Jennie about Miss Hill.

"She was a saint of a woman," Jennie answered. "And she brought you to me." She reached for Anna's hand and squeezed it. "What wonderful work she did, helping so many children to find homes."

"That's right," Anna agreed. "Some of them had a really hard time of it, though, in spite of Miss Hill's diligence. Some of the orphan kids were treated badly or rejected by relatives. I never had that trouble. Your family welcomed me with arms opened wide. There was never any bickering like in some families. Some of my best friends are my cousins. And you were always the best kind of mother and friend, patient through all my growing up, putting up with my moods, and the swarms of kids that made our house headquarters." She laughed at pleasant memories.

"I wouldn't have had it any other way," Jennie replied. "And you already had good training when you came to me, Anna. Even though we had many misunderstandings, we learned to accept them, and not let them separate us, or destroy the feelings we had for each other."

"I'm sure you often wondered if I'd ever get control of my

215

Hungarian temperament," Anna observed.

"Don't take all the blame," Jennie put in. "I know I was plenty headstrong about carrying through on my ideas, even though folks always thought I was a mild person."

They laughed together. Anna picked up the hairbrush from the bedstand and gently unpinned Jennie's hair and began carefully brushing it. She couldn't help but recall the times when Jennie had brushed her hair on Saturday nights while drilling her on her Sunday school lesson. It was a tradition from the time when she first came to Jennie. Now the roles were reversed. Anna comforted and cared for Jennie. "You know," she said wistfully, starting to braid it again, "I was very close to my father. It was probably a good thing that I didn't have to adjust to a new dad when I got you."

"It just seemed that God wanted the two of us to be together, didn't He?"

"Yes."

"I guess if I had one big fault in raising you, it was that I didn't kick you out of the nest sooner, and let you be on your own."

"Oh, come on! I didn't want to go anywhere. Why would I want to leave the love and security I'd finally found?" Anna finished pinning the braids into a crown on Jennie's head, then bent and kissed her cheek. "I know that nobody else would have helped me get to college, or become a musician. Anyone else would have given up, considering my handicaps, but you never did!"

"It was your determination that did it, Anna," Jennie responded affectionately.

"Well, I don't know about that. But I know we make quite a team, don't we?" Anna summarized in her amiable midwestern drawl. "I'd better be getting along, Jennie. I'll see you tomorrow."

As Anna left the home, she felt a wave of loneliness for Jennie. She thought of the times when Jennie could sense that she was lonely, and she would comfort Anna, assuring her it was not wrong to miss her parents, for Jennie told her that she too still felt lonely at times, and missed her own mother, and her mother had been gone a lot longer time than Anna's.

Anna was thankful that Jennie had not once turned against her or spoken in anger to her about placing her in the home. And every time she visited her, she would comment on how good and kind all the workers were to her, and how they had noticed that her nieces and nephews were good about visiting her.

Anna impulsively turned down a side street and circled the Bethany College campus. She stopped near Presser Hall and was alone with her thoughts. In 1927 this building had replaced Ling Auditorium, and for years, Anna had participated in the Messiah Oratorio Society, either singing soprano in the chorus, or as cellist with the orchestra. In over thirty years she'd missed very few performances of the annual Easter week Messiah events.

Anna remembered the many times Jennie had ridden with her when she drove to Lindsborg for the practices. Sometimes Jennie would visit friends in Lindsborg while Anna was practicing, but more often she would sit in the auditorium and listen to the music. How many times had Anna looked up to see the solitary figure sitting loyally in the almost empty auditorium?

Anna was glad she'd had the opportunity to be a part of the Society as a member of the 500-voice chorus, and also having a chance to play in the orchestra during the difficult war years. In those days it was hard to keep orchestras going, and even after the war, schools had problems getting back in full swing again. She knew she owed a lot to Jennie for encouraging her.

As Anna started the car and headed toward home, she pondered the depth of Jennie's devotion. When Anna had finished high school, Jennie had completed her part of the bargain — she had given Anna a Christian home and sent her through school and now she was to be on her own. But Jennie never considered her job over. When Anna could not enter nurses training, it was a period of extreme frustration and bitterness. Anna remembered those painful days. She must have been at her worst! Why hadn't Jennie given up then? Anyone else would have told her to get out and take care of herself, but Jennie had stood by, urging Anna to try to get a new interest in life, giving her moral support all the way, and hoping for the day when Anna would accept things the way they were, and make the best of it. Jennie's love must have been greater then than at any other time.

Anna was grateful that Jennie was always ready to listen when Anna felt like talking about her parents. She didn't resent it, and often remarked that it would be nice if Anna and her sisters would be able to find out more about their folks. And when Margaret visited New York and located their parents' graves, Jennie told Anna that she was sure Anna's mother, who was buried in a Lutheran cemetery, would have approved of Anna being brought up a Lutheran.

Looking back, Anna could see that there had to be a lot of

217

love along the way to conquer the differences in their back-
grounds and attitudes. The bond which united them kept them together even through the squabbles they had, and seemed to grow
even stronger every day now.

Anna realized that she had really and truly had "the love of
two mothers."

❧❀❧

Cliff loved going fishing with his boys. Their frequent camping trips gave them a chance for fellowship. Cliff adored his fine,
handsome sons — David, Pete, and Daniel. Dave was married and
living in Greeley, Colorado, not far from Cliff and Hazel's. Pete
had just gotten out of the service, married and settled in a little
town outside Greeley. Dan was still in high school.

This time they were headed out for a good trout stream, in
the Rockies west of Greeley. They would camp two nights. Cliff
had helped Hazel pack up everything they would need. The four
men were in high spirits as they sped toward their campground.
But, setting up camp, it was discovered that they were without
cooking utensils.

"Oh, boy! Am I ever gonna rib Hazel about this," Cliff
chuckled.

"Maybe, Pop," Pete answered, "but we'll sure be mighty
hungry in two days if we don't find something to cook in."

"I'll drive down and try to borrow a few things from that
camp store we saw," Cliff offered. He hopped in the pickup and
went down the mountain to the store.

"Ma'am, we're short on pans," Cliff explained to the owner.
"Could we borrow an old frying pan, and maybe a coffee pot and
some silverware?"

"Sure. I keep things like that just for campers like you. Just
bring them back when you leave."

"Would you mind if I used your phone for a collect call?"

"Help yourself. Phone's right behind the counter there,"
The proprietress went to the back room to dig out the old pans.

"Honey," Cliff teased Hazel when she came on the line,
"you sure done a great job of fixing us up. To starve, that is!"

"What do you mean?" Hazel sounded puzzled.

"You sent us off without any pots and pans and utensils!"

"Oh, no! I thought that looked like a pretty tidy little box
of stuff," she laughed. "What are you gonna do?"

"Done it already. Borrowed what we need. We'll be okay. I
just wanted to give you a hard time."

218

"Well, I'm sorry, Cliff. I hope you have a good time with the boys. By the way, you got some mail today I might as well tell you about."

"What's that?"

"Well, we got a letter from Miss Hill's nephew in New Jersey. He wanted us to know Miss Hill had passed away."

"Oh, I'm so sorry to hear that. She sure was a nice person. Did a lot for me."

"I knew you'd want to know."

"Yeah, well, thanks. We'll see you in a few days, Honey!"

Back in camp, Cliff set about making bacon and eggs in the old iron skillet, cooking over a fire the boys had already built. Cliff was proud of his sons. They were hard workers, excellent companions, and all of them were his good friends as well as his sons. He'd worked hard to be a good father to them. This was going to be a fine weekend, like many they'd had before, and more they would share.

The sun was dropping behind the pine-fringed moutains, and the tang of pine in the air mingled with the pleasant fragrance of their little fire. There was a soft swish of water from the trout stream, rushing headlong on its way. Such peace! Cliff sat back, thinking.

Cliff told the boys about Miss Hill. Although they'd never known her, they had all heard the stories. As Cliff stirred the coals, Pete asked him a tough question.

"Dad, I want to know how you really felt about the Dutchman and his wife? They treated you so mean — why, you might have died if Miss Hill hadn't rescued you."

"Well, to tell the truth, for a long, long time, I hated their guts," Cliff answered bluntly. "I was always gonna go back someday and even the score. But as time went on, I could sort of understand why they did what they did."

"What do you mean?"

"One of their sons visited us out here not too long ago. Made a special effort to look us up. He said he wanted to know how his folks had treated me. See, he wasn't even born yet when I was there. I told him the truth. Told him all about it. Know what he said? He said he thought so. I asked him why and he said, because they treated their own kids the same way. They all left home as quick as they could. It was just the Dutchman's way to be harsh and cruel, I guess. It was just the way they were."

"Man," Pete exclaimed.

"So I decided I wanted to see them again. It had been so many years. We made a little trip back that way to visit your Aunt Bernice and Uncle Earl. By the way, they're all fine. Kent's still in the Air Force in England. Lucrecia's in nurses training, and Cynthia is a junior at Haven High. And Earl and Bernice are busy with their church work. Well, once we was there, it wasn't that far from Pleasant Grove on over to Schmidt, so I told Mom we ought to go over to the Dutchman's place. I kinda wanted her to see them, too."

"Well, what happened?"

"Oh, it was something! It was really something!"

"You mean you had it out with them, finally?"

"No," Cliff grinned and shook his head. "Not at all. I come driving up, and it looked just the same as it always did. Not very well cared for, and dogs all over the yard."

"How did you feel?"

"I was kinda wondering what they were gonna look like, but I couldn't find nobody home at first. I hollered, and pretty soon here comes the Missus from the barn. She was wearin' an old pair of overalls with patches and holes. She looked terrible. I told her who I was and she said, 'Cleefie, you sure growed up big!' I asked her where her husband was, and she said he was in the house. She called and he came out, slow-like, and crippled. He'd been kicked by a horse and broken something in his neck. He couldn't work no more."

"How did you feel about them then?"

"Pity. I just pitied them. They was old, and they was beat, and life hadn't done 'em very well. And if they treated their own kids just as bad as me — heck, what could you feel for 'em but pity?"

"No hate?" Pete asked.

"No hate." Cliff sighed, and stirred the coals again, so that they glowed warmly in the clear night. Stars were coming out overhead.

☙ ⟋⟋⟋ ❧

"Hello, Kid?"

"Hi, Bill! How are you doing?"

"Fine. My work is fine. Family too. And you? I worry about you, now that you're alone."

"I'm feeling good. Can't complain. I like living in Wichita."

"Say, I called to give you some news. It's about Miss Hill. Remember her?"

"You mean Anna Laura Hill? Of course!"

"Yes, I do. I still kept in touch with her, you know. Heard from her family she passed away recently."

"I'm sorry to hear that, Bill. But she must have been up in years. We're not so young ourselves anymore. Why, I'll be retiring soon."

"Right. The obituary says she was eighty-four."

"What else does it say?"

"Listen, I'll read it to you. It's short. Headline says, 'Anna Hill, Retired NYC Aide, Dies.'"

He read: "Miss Anna Laura Hill, age 84, of 1525 W. Water Street, Elmira, a retired placement officer of the Children's Aid Society, died early Saturday morning, August 17.

"Miss Hill worked for the Society in the western states for thirty years, placing children in foster homes and maintaining contact with them until they grew up. She had resided in Elmira since her retirement thirty-three years ago. Born in Burlington, Pennsylvania, Miss Hill moved to Elmira as a young girl. She was a graduate of the former Mansfield Normal School, a member of the Hedding Methodist Church in Elmira, the Chemung County Historical Society, the DAR, and the Good Cheer Sunshine Circle."

"Well," Ida observed, "she certainly helped change our lives. I don't know what we'd have become without her help. Sometimes I think, with our brains, independence, and lack of guidance, you'd have been a gangster and I a gun moll back in New York if it hadn't been for her."

"Sis, that might be an exaggeration. But you never know. And a lot of orphan kids owe a lot to her."

Bill then went on to report on his work as an inspector for the federal government, and the latest news on his three daughters and his wife Arlene. At last he said goodbye.

Ida hung up the phone and went straight to her bedroom. She paused before the dresser and ran her hand around the rim of the cut-glass fruit bowl that she and Bill still shared as a remembrance of Dad Elder. Then she opened a drawer and rummaged through an assortment of keepsakes until she came to a faded pink fabric that still held the shape of a rosette.

THE END

Titus Studio, Lyons, KS., captured the energetic young agent's idealism.

Miss Hill on vacation.

Bailey's Normal School Gallery photo shows student Anna Hill in 1898.

A fur coat and hat protected Miss Hill from winter storms out West.

Retired, Miss Hill, at right, is shown with her sister and aunt, Betsy Peterson, left, and Mary A. Pratt, center.

Ida and Bill Bishop, at about 17 and 20 years of age.

Mr. and Mrs. Ward Bishop, adoptive parents of Ida and Bill.

Bill and Arlene Bishop, retirees in Peoria, AZ, 1976.

Ida Bishop Walton, with the fruitbowl, Wichita, KS, 1977.

Bill Bishop—1976.

Bernice and Earl Enyeart after moving to Kansas City with daughter Lucretia Smith and granddaughter Kristi.

Bernice Enyeart addressing the graduating class of Rio Hondo Prep School, Arcadia, California, in June, 1985.

"Goin' Somewhere," a live musical show with professional lighting, staging, and original music, carried the Switzers' story to over 8,000 people during Rio Hondo Prep School's summer tour across the U.S. in 1984.

The Enyeart family celebrates parents' 40th wedding anniversary. From left: Aaron, Brenda, Kent, and Casey Enyeart, Cynthia, O.B., Daccari, and Doug Johnston, Bernice and Earl Enyeart, and Lucrecia, Kristi, and John Smith. Bernice sewed all the dresses.

Dan and Mary Switzer and children Toni Jo and Nicholas.

Hazel and Cliff's 25th wedding anniversary.

Hazel Switzer, center, makes her home in Mankato, KS with son, Dan and his wife Mary. Photo 1995.

Cliff Switzer

Cliff and Hazel Switzer with son Pete and granddaughter Heather, Kanorado, KS, 1978. Pete died in an accident later that year.

Cliff Switzer and David Weber share a brotherly chat on vacation in Texas.

Anna (left), Helen and Margaret Fuchs during high school days. Helen's family moved frequently, Margaret had many household duties, so the sisters seldom got together.

Anna Fuchs, 1924, in front of Children's Aid Society in New York City taken just before leaving on the train to Kansas.

Margaret and Anna are very close and visit one another regularly.

Anna and Jennie at home. Note Anna's cello.

Anna and Margaret Fuchs' story was carried on a national television program, "CBS Sunday Morning News," in 1979 and again in 1986.

Authors Pat Vogt (left) and Chris Vogt (right) watching the re-broadcast on CBS

In the Years Since . . .

The authors feel fortunate to have shared in the lives of these individuals who so willingly related their experiences so that history could be recorded before it was lost. Thus, others may know what it was like to have been on an orphan train, to have made a new life in the "west", and to have learned what "home" truly means.

Bill and Arlene Bishop retired to Peoria, AZ in 1973. Bill kept in close touch with Ida, who remained in Wichita. Bill passed away in May, 1976 at age 76. Ida died the following June, 1977, at age 74. Arlene Bishop has entrusted the fruitbowl, the precious memento of Bill and Ida's early life in New York, to the second of their three daughters who lives in South Dakota.

Cliff Switzer continued to lovingly shepherd his family until his death in July, 1979, while tending his garden in Kanorado, KS. Hazel, Dan, their only surviving son, and his family remained in Kanorado, where Dan took over the family business, later closing it to move to Mankato where he directs EMT services.

David Weber and his wife Maxine also lived in Kanorado but have passed away. Howard Switzer is deceased. Harold died in March, 1986. Freda lives in New York state.

After serving Methodist and EUB pastorates in KS for forty years, Bernice and the Rev. Earl Enyeart retired to Red Oak, OK. Bernice maintained a thriving sewing business and kept busy with her five grandchildren. In 1984, Rio Hondo Preparatory School of Arcadia, CA became fascinated with Bernice and Cliff's story and chose it as the theme for their summer tour musical play. The cast and crew of 70 students presented their show, "Goin' Somewhere," to over 8,000 persons in some 70 performances all across the USA that summer. After meeting Bernice (in Abilene, KS) the school children voted to invite her as their commencement speaker, which she was in June, 1985. In 1990, the Enyearts moved to live with daughter, Lucretia Smith in Kansas City.

Jennie Bengston passed away in 1964 at age 89. Anna remained in McPherson, surrounded by many adoptive cousins and other relatives. Helen died in 1966 but Margaret, who lives in CA, and Anna have maintained the closest of sisterly ties. After Margaret located their parents' graves in New York, she and Anna saw that headstones were placed for the elder Fuchs.

Anna and Margaret's story was featured on the television program "CBS Sunday Morning News with Charles Kurault" in December, 1979 and rebroadcast in January, 1986. Anna retired from her firm in 1978, allowing her more time for her interests in travel, china painting, and music.

1995 Update

Hazel Switzer, Cliff's widow, now makes her home with her son, Dan and his wife, Mary, in Mankato, KS where the Enyearts' son, Kent and family also reside.

Anna and her sister Margaret remain the only living orphan train riders from this story. Anna retired to Lindsborg, KS and Margaret to Santa Rosa, CA; they are still close and visit frequently. In 1992 Anna was honored by her alma mater, presented with the Alumni Citation of Merit Award from McPherson (KS) College, for Outstanding Service to Profession, Community, Church and College.

The passing of Bernice Switzer Enyeart in April, 1995 leaves a void in the lives of all who knew her. Earl had preceded her in death in 1992. Their funeral services at Abilene's United Methodist Church were just 5 blocks away from the train depot where Bernice had come with her brothers in 1920. At her passing, Bernice had roused from pain and confusion, not knowing where she was; she reached up, hugged an unseen figure, and said to him, "I love you, too, Jesus. Now I know I'm home."

P.S.

Writing to her mother in New York, Anna Laura Hill tells of her trip West with a group of children through floods in Ohio. Although none of the orphans in this book had such an eventful train trip West, and the trip itself is unrelated to their lives, this account reveals the dangers Miss Hill faced, and her courage during a lifetime spent escorting orphans to new homes.

Decorah, Iowa   April 2, 1913

Dear Mama,

...We certainly had a very strenuous trip. All went well until we reached Cleveland and found that city about flooded. From there on to Fort Wayne we had an awful experience. We went from Cleveland to Bellevue on the Nickel Plate... There they pulled the train on a side track and said we would wait for orders.

We waited until two other trains came in from the East, then we took on the passengers from these trains and proceeded westward.

While at Bellevue we could see the men and boys going about town on rafts, many houses entirely surrounded by water. We were in constant danger for twenty-four hours. Such awful places that we went over—submerged tracks, water on both sides and two terrible rivers. We crossed a river at midnight. They sent a work train and 200 men ahead of us. They worked about two hours making the bridge a little more secure. They put in 8 carloads of rock and many sandbags, then took two engines across; and then we went over. It was an anxious time for everyone on that train. Not a berth was occupied that night. I shall never forget the awful roar of that mighty torrent. Just as we were in the center, there was a sudden jar. I closed my eyes, I couldn't look, for I thought it was all over and we were going down. But God continued to look after his helpless little ones as he has in all the years of the past history of the Children's Aid Society.

There was many a prayer offered on that train that night, and by men who had not mentioned God's name before in many a day. There were nine houses washed down next to the bridge, that we could see distinctly through the storm, for to add to the horror the ground was covered with a heavy snow, and a terrible sleet storm was falling, accompanied by a biting wind. In these houses were people whom the life-savers were working desperately to rescue. There was a light in one house. Think what could have been the feelings of those people, held prisoners in those awful places. I hope I shall be spared witnessing such a scene again.

The train crew were with us 26 hours with no relief. In all my experience I have never seen trainmen that would talk about any trouble or accidents but these men were under such tension for so long they had to relieve themselves, by talking with us.

I shall be here over Sunday and then go to Kansas. We have taken a three-week-old baby born here, and I don't know yet what we will do with her. Will have to wait and help Miss Comstock out with it. Don't forget that I now have a P.O. Box #26, Topeka, Kan. and will have mail forwarded from there.

Love to all and write soon,   Anna Laura